Language Shock

OTHER WORKS BY MICHAEL AGAR

Angel Dust (coeditor)

Anthropological Studies of Drug Use (editor)

Cognition and Ethnography

*The Professional Stranger: An Informal
Introduction to Ethnography*

*Ripping and Running: A Formal Ethnographic
Study of Urban Heroin Addicts*

Speaking of Ethnography

*Independents Declared: The Dilemmas
of Independent Trucking*

LANGUAGE
SHOCK / *Understanding*

the Culture of Conversation

MICHAEL AGAR

WILLIAM MORROW

An Imprint of HarperCollins*Publishers*

HarperCollins books may be purchased for educational, business, or sales promotional use. For information, please e-mail the Special Markets Department at SPsales@harpercollins.com.

First Quill edition published 1996.

Reprinted in Perennial 2002.

Designed by Dorothy Baker

Library of Congress Cataloging-in-Publication Data

Agar, Michael.
  Language shock / Michael Agar.
  p. cm.
ISBN 0-688-14949-9
1. Language and culture. I. Title.
P35.A37   1993   92-21470
306.4'4—dc20   CIP

     16 RRD 30 29 28 27 26 25 24 23

Contents

PREFACE / 7

CULTURE BLENDS / 13

Language carries more meanings than you ever dreamed, and culture is where you find them

THE CIRCLE / 31

A circle around language isolates grammar and dictionary, but it leaves culture out

THE CIRCLE AND THE FIELD / 49

The story of how language and culture came unglued

CULTURAL SIGNIFIEDS / 61

How a fire-prevention engineer argued that you couldn't pull language and culture apart

SIMILARITIES AND DIFFERENCES / 73

The way that language and culture—"languaculture"—differences turn transparent when laid against our common human background

CONTENTS

SITUATIONS / 89

Language comes to life in the real world and changes from words and sentences into discourse

CULTURE / 108

The story of an important and confusing concept, and how the confusion clears up when you attach culture to language

SPEECH ACTS / 140

How people do things with words, and why the lie you thought you were telling turns out to be the truth

SPEECH ACT LUMBER AND PAINT / 164

How to recognize a speech act when you meet one, and how to hear the culture that gives it color

COHERENCE / 192

The pieces fall together when you figure out a different languaculture, and the blend takes you somewhere new

VARIATIONS ON A FRAME / 211

Just when you think you've got it straight, some new bit of languaculture always springs up

SAILORS AND IMMIGRANTS / 242

Why people who know where they're from but live someplace else are guides into the next century

NOTES / 259

INDEX / 273

Preface

BACK in the eighties I went off to live for the summer on the island of Skyros in Greece. I went for all the obvious reasons, but I also had two projects in mind. I wanted to try my hand at demotic Greek, a language with a fascinating history and strong current political passions behind it, with the idea of writing something about what it was really like to learn a second language in a new place. My second project involved fiction. I'd been a professional ethnographer for many years, but I wanted to experiment and see if I couldn't build a book using scenes from life on the island to create a novelistic portrayal rather than an academic one.

Neither project quite worked out. I kept some notes on learning Greek, but I didn't have a way to think about what I was going through. The experience started me wondering about what way of thinking would have made sense. I did write a novel, though as I've learned more over the years I can see what a mediocre effort it was. But it did start me thinking about using scenes, human stories, to bring ideas to life.

In retrospect I see how these two threads eventually led to this book. What I've tried to do here is organize some stories to show the many ways an encounter with language and culture is one of the most challenging, interesting, and enriching experiences available, to anyone, not just professional linguists and anthropologists. I'm doing this for motives both noble and base: noble because I'd like to pitch in and help make a multicultural world work in a time when language and culture conflict threatens to tear that same world apart; base because with increasing contact among different cultures, the time is right to find a market for such a book.

The book attempts to present clearly ideas that have been around in anthropology and linguistics and several other fields for quite some time. People I've spoken with over the years have found them interesting and useful, and usually they had no idea that such views of language were available. I've blazed one trail through the work of hundreds of others, living and dead, to try and give the reader a general view of some fascinating territory. Those hundreds of others don't always get the credit they deserve, nor do their detailed arguments always surface in what is to come, but I'll obsess about that later in the reference notes.

The Neumann family in Austria first led me, with tender loving care, into a new language and continue to do so today. Vickie Ferguson, Diane Johnson, and Dana Holland read a first draft of this book and gave generously of their time to help me write a better second version. Dana read subsequent drafts and talked things over too many times to figure out all the different ways she helped shape this book. Three colleagues at the University of Maryland—Bill Stuart in anthropology, Linda Coleman in the linguistics program in the English department, and Marty Gannon in the School of Business and Management—gave me thorough reviews to help keep me honest. I presented different parts of the book to academic colleagues and practitioners in different conferences and workshops, and their questions and reactions helped me out a great deal as well. Finally, I used a draft in a course I teach, a graduate seminar in cultural analysis, and the students reacted with good and helpful critiques as well. As the saying goes, none of them is responsible for the final product—that's my problem—but their good advice, some of which I didn't follow, made the book a better piece of work. Maria Guarnaschelli, my editor at Morrow, crawled inside this book and made it in part her own, and a much better book for it.

I want to dedicate this book, for reasons that are spelled out in Chapter 10, to the memory of Bruce Spivey. When we first met,

Bruce was a former Green Beret in Vietnam who'd gone into anthropology, and I was an anthropologist who'd protested against that war. Until his death we'd meet and talk about what was then the forbidden topic, about Vietnam, about the missing connection between two halves of our generation. When I finished this preface it was Memorial Day, 1993, and I went downtown to visit the Vietnam Memorial. I wish I could have chiseled his name onto that wall.

Language Shock

Culture Blends

A FEW years ago I was talking to a Black colleague at the University of Maryland, a faculty member from another department. I was trying to jump-start a program, but to do so I had to tangle with the university bureaucracy, and universities are just as bad as governments and corporations. I complained because the various offices that were supposed to help start programs actually made it more difficult to do so.

My colleague looked at me, shook his head, and started talking: "The system is *not* your friend." He talked some more, with the "*not* your friend" chant repeated every so often. The irony is that his life was the mythic American success story. He'd worked his way up from poverty to a Ph.D., but, as far as he was concerned, he'd done it *in spite of* the walls American institutions had built rather than with their help.

His journey out of an Afro-American urban neighborhood had convinced him that institutions—the "system"—took care of themselves and nobody else. My journey out of a White small town had led me to expect institutions to do their job and help you out; if they didn't, you had a right to complain.

These different ways of looking at things had come to life in our common language, and they tied in with who we were, with our different social identities. The differences happened *inside the same language,* just as differences do between languages as distinct as Japanese and English.

One Friday afternoon, not long afterward, I went to a faculty reception. I met a colleague whom I'd corresponded and talked on the phone with but never met in person. She'd helped me out, a lot, by sending me some bibliographies and course outlines from her field. She'd handed me a shortcut into the way things of mutual interest looked from a different discipline's point of view.

When I finally met her, I thanked her and said something like "The least I can do is buy you a drink."

She snapped to attention and said, rather sharply, "I can pay for my *own* drink."

I explained that I'd have made the same offer to any colleague who'd helped me out, male or female or any other variation on the theme. I guess you could say that she just didn't understand. But, in this case, we both did. She'd read my invitation as a come-on, converting her from colleague to pickup; I'd meant it as thanks.

Something happened, in our common language, something that had to do with who we were. Something came up, jolted us with a difference, made us aware that the "natural" way of doing things wasn't "natural" at all. And, once again, it happened *inside the same language,* not between two different ones.

Differences like these—the sort of misunderstandings that we usually associate with a *foreign* language—happen inside a language all the time. It happens when a traveler stops in a small southern town during his drive from New York City to Atlanta and realizes that his impatience with slow service in a store is deeply rooted in how New Yorkers expect a customer to be treated.

It happens when a doctor sees that what a patient is trying to tell her won't fit the tried and true diagnostic categories, so if she wants to figure out the patient's illness, she's going to have to learn more about the patient's world.

It happens when a graduate of a Black university lands his first job in an all-White office, finds that some of his humor doesn't work, and sets out to learn what it is that people in the office think is funny.

Differences happen *within* languages as well as *across* them. The way of seeing I'm trying to bring to life in this book works *inside* your own language as well as when you learn a second language. In the course of the book, stories about American English will come up frequently. By the end of the book, the moral of these stories will have been brought into focus more sharply—learning a second language and learning more about your own language are, in principle, *the same thing.*

///

Usually when the subject of language differences comes up in the United States, images of ethnic groups come to mind. And usually the subject carries a message that the differences are a *problem.*

A while ago *The Washington Post* reported a riot in the Mount Pleasant neighborhood downtown. A police officer had shot a Hispanic man. Some said the latter had pulled a knife. Others said he was already in handcuffs.

At several points in the story the *Post* mentioned that communication had been a problem, that the officers didn't speak Spanish and many of the neighborhood residents didn't speak English. Suspicions of bad intentions, with no chance of communicating to the contrary, fueled both sides until the situation exploded like lighter fluid poured over smoldering wood.

The *Post* pointed out that Spanish-speaking officers are conspicuous by their absence on the D.C. police force. The *Post* mentioned the obvious solution—hire more Hispanic officers and teach the others Spanish. Another solution, not mentioned in the paper—provide free English instruction for all new immigrants.

The *Post,* and most everybody else, assumes that language instruction would solve the problem. The *Post,* and most everybody else, is wrong. The majority think that language is mostly grammar. Teach people the grammar, give them a dictionary, and they'll communicate. But anyone who's studied a second language in the classroom and then tried to use it in the real world knows better than that. A friend's main memory of his Spanish course was the sentence *El oso ni baila ni canta*—"The bear neither dances nor sings." The main use for this timeless passage was to show his Hispanic colleagues how little he'd learned.

Popular ideas about "language" squeeze the concept much too

tightly. The tendency is to draw a *circle* around language, to herd neat sentences into the corral and wrangle out the parts of speech. But most problems with language, the problems that come up when you try to *use* it to *communicate,* aren't about sentences and parts of speech. They have to do with wild herds of sentences, out on the open range.

Don't get me wrong. Had there been a shared grammar and dictionary in the midst of that passionate confrontation between Hispanics and police in Mount Pleasant, it couldn't have hurt. But, as the meetings and arguments and newspaper articles since the riot make clear, the confrontation in Mount Pleasant was an encounter between different worlds of *meaning,* meaning that travels well beyond the dictionary, meaning that tells you who you are, whom you're dealing with, the kind of situation you're in, how life works and what's important in it—meaning that ties language *inside* the circle, grammar and the dictionary, to the world *outside.*

If you want to use language, if you want to communicate, language inside the circle isn't enough. The circle is a lie. It's like saying that if you can put rings on a piston, you can drive in traffic.

To understand language, you have to understand that *differences in language go well beyond what you find in the grammar and the dictionary.* Otherwise, why would my Black and female colleagues and I have had trouble, even though we all spoke the "same" language?

///

In fact, the world outside the circle may be even *more* important than the grammar and dictionary. Consider immigrant workers in Germany—mostly Turks and Slavs and Greeks. It turns out that many never master all the fine points of German grammar. But then who could?

Not Mark Twain. An Austrian once told me a story. During Twain's visit to Heidelberg, he attended a play with a friend. During the intermission the bored friend said he was leaving and asked if Twain wanted to leave with him.

"No," said Twain, "I think I'll stick around and wait for the verb."

In many constructions in German, the main verb doesn't appear until the end of the sentence. Immigrant German speakers break rules like that one all the time. But breaking the grammatical rule doesn't mean they can't communicate. The immigrant workers can communicate, even without a fine-tuned grammar and vocabulary, because they've put together a theory of how Germans think and what their world is like. They fit what they *do* know how to say into those assumptions.

Knowing who the Germans are, knowing what the situation they're involved in is all about, packs more power than the grammar, as far as real communication goes. Such facts offend grammar teachers, and an impoverished grammar holds the new immigrants back in their social aspirations. On the other hand, some *communicate* better than grammar mavens fresh out of the university, because they know more about their boss and their workplace than a recently minted Ph.D. would.

///

Recently an Austrian friend of mine came to Washington to teach and study at Georgetown University. She could tack through English grammar with the best of them and had a better vocabulary than most of the native-born undergraduates in my lecture class.

After a couple of months I met her for dinner and asked her how everything was going. "Fine," she said, and then, after a moment's hesitation, "But what is a 'date'?"

She knew how to use the word in a sentence—"I'm going on a date"; "How about a date?" She wasn't confused because the word also means a number on a calendar or a sweet piece of fruit. But none of that explained what a "date" was.

I started to answer, and the more I talked the more lost I became in how Americans see men and women, how they see relationships, intimacy—a host of connected assumptions that I'd never put into words before. And I was only trying to handle straight dates. It was quite different from her Austrian understanding of men and women and what they are to each other. For a while she looked at me as if I'd just stepped out of a flying saucer, until she finally decided I was serious.

I gave up trying to explain *date*. I told her I'd just try to do one. But what with wisecracks and shifts between Austrian German and

American English, the scene turned into a Marx Brothers movie. She never did learn what a date was all about, at least not from me. But we found out that whatever *date* meant, it went far beyond what the grammar and the dictionary could handle.

///

It hadn't been easy moving in the other direction, either. I've lived in Austria several times, and even after all these years I'm still puzzled by *Du* and *Sie*.

Du is "you," the informal second person singular pronoun, and *Sie* is "you," only it's the formal version. English hasn't made the distinction since we lost *thou,* but many of the world's languages do—*tu* and *vous* in French, *tú* and *usted* in Spanish, to mention a couple of other European examples.

The grammar books are clear as freshly washed crystal. *Du,* the informal version, is for relatives, friends, and kids. *Sie* is for everybody else. However, the rule doesn't carry you very far.

I was at a professional meeting in Vienna. A female colleague, about my age, talked with me in the hall between sessions. We called each other *Sie*. At midday I was walking down the street, alone, and she passed me, alone. As she passed, she chatted for a second and used *Du*. That's nice, I thought, she's promoted me to a friend.

Later in the afternoon, back in the hall, she called me *Sie*. I turned to a male friend, with whom I was already *per Du,* as they say in Austria, and asked him just what was going on. He stared back, amazed at how stupid the human species could be when it tried.

"She's flirting with you. Obviously."

More embarrassing still—at a party a few months later, an Austrian man, about my age, one of the few other people informally dressed, walked up and started a conversation. I used *Sie,* and so did he. After a while, his girlfriend walked up, said hello, turned to me, and said, "What do you do in Vienna?" using the *Du* form.

I smiled and asked her what it was that made her choose *Du* instead of *Sie*. I meant it as a pure research question.

She stiffened, looked annoyed, and said, "*Entschuldigen* Sie"— "*You* excuse," using the formal pronoun. You'd have to translate that as "Excuse *me*" to get the right effect in English.

After some social acrobatics on the part of everybody, we straightened out the misunderstanding. Since her boyfriend and I were talking in a friendly way, she assumed we were already friends, and a friend of her boyfriend got an automatic *Du*. The rule was hers, not a general one you could rely on.

I turned to the amused boyfriend and asked how he figured out what to call people. He shrugged his shoulders and said the Austrian equivalent of "Hell if I know, I just listen to the other person and fake it from there."

I still can't spell out the rules. And I've barely touched all the generational, political, and lifestyle issues that move *Du* and *Sie* around. Pronouns, something you'd think would be classic grammar-book material, turned out to be one of the worst problems I had.

There's no escape, either. Every time you talk you have to use pronouns, though I learned that some tortured German is produced just to avoid the issue. Little wonder that people try to avoid it. Every time you use the pronouns you have to look at who you are, whom you're talking with, and the circumstances, and then make a choice, a rapid choice that won't disrupt the flow of talk. And you have to do it using rules that not everyone will agree are correct.

A couple of years ago, my friend and colleague Ruth Wodak and I taught a seminar in Vienna. We decided to take on *Du* and *Sie*. The first day we asked the students to tell one or two stories that showed how the rules weren't clear. These, remember, were Austrian German speakers talking *about* their native language *in* their native language.

Each of the students had several stories. They told them with passion. It turned into a linguistic therapy group. I imagined—it never happened, but it wasn't difficult to picture—that at any moment they were going to fall from their chairs, crying and pounding the floor with their fists, and scream, "God, please free us from this pronominal system that causes so many traumas and crises in our lives!"

///

On the one hand, you might be speaking the *same* language—like my American colleagues and me, or the Germans and the foreign workers. On the other hand, you might be learning a *different* language—like Spanish or German. Grammar and the dictionary, *language inside the circle,* are important, no doubt about it. But grammar isn't enough to communicate, and communication can occur without all the grammar.

Language has to include more than just language *inside* the circle. To *use* a language, to *live* in it, all those meanings that go beyond grammar and the dictionary have to fit in somewhere. The circle that people—and *some* linguists—draw around language has to be erased.

Culture is the eraser.

Usually people think of "culture" as something that a particular group of people *have.* Cultures roll around the planet like so many billiard balls, self-contained objects that might collide or bounce off the cushion but still retain their perfect round shape.

People use "culture" this way all the time. I just gave an example of Austrian culture using *Du* and *Sie.* Before that, the example had to do with American culture surrounding the word *date.* The newspaper story dealt with Hispanic culture, and the two anecdotes the book opened with were about Black culture and women's culture. The labels are way too general, because a lot of variations on the theme live under those names, but that's a problem that will fill a later chapter.

Culture is something those people "have," but it's more than that. It's also something that happens to *you* when you encounter them. As long as they're just out there, just a different group of folks, you won't have to deal with them. When you deal with them, culture turns *personal.* Culture is no longer just what some group has; it's what *happens to you* when you encounter differences, become aware of something in yourself, and work to figure out why the differences appeared. Culture is an awareness, a consciousness, one that reveals the hidden self and opens paths to other ways of being.

Culture happens when you learn to *use* a second language. It happened to my Austrian friend when she tried to figure out what a date was, and it happened to me when I stumbled over *Du* and *Sie* in Austrian German. But it also happens inside your *own* language, as it did with my colleagues and me.

Culture starts when you realize that you've got a problem with language, and the problem has to do with who you are. Culture happens *in* language, but the consciousness it inspires goes well beyond it.

Meanings usually float at the edge of awareness. Even when meanings make a selective appearance in the mind's eye, they're somehow "natural" or "right." They're not only the water in which you swim; they're the water in which you first *learned* to swim at all.

Culture changes all that. The "natural" or "right" meanings, the ones that tell you *who you are and how the world works,* turn arbitrary, one of a number of possibilities. Your "natural" language shines under the light of a new awareness; it blossoms into a fascinating complexity; you see possibilities you never imagined existed. Culture changes you into a person who can navigate the modern multi*cultural* world.

Culture is an elusive beast. Different cultures color the landscape of modern life. But as long as they stay out there, objects of contemplation, problems won't get solved and minds will chug along as they did when we all lived in isolated villages. In this book, culture is about to change from a distant object into a personal experience. Culture may be something *they* have, all well and good, but personal contact makes culture *your own.* Until it's your own, culture won't make a damn bit of difference.

///

Americans carry an unfortunate stereotype. They're known worldwide for holding culture at bay. Several years ago, I went to live on a Greek island for the summer. A friend of mine, a Swiss architect who owned a home there, invited me up for dinner. After dinner I chatted with him and his wife, in English. He hated to speak High German, he explained, because of its associations with Nazi Germany. He was old enough to remember the war.

Culture has to do with who you are.

We got around to the image of Americans as the world's worst second-language learners. There's an old linguistics joke: What do you call a person who speaks three languages? A trilingual. Two languages? A bilingual. One language? You guessed it, an American.

My friend wasn't an America-hater. Far from it. But he was genuinely puzzled. It's not, he said, that Americans aren't capable of learning grammar as well as anyone else. Maybe even better. The problem, he thought, is that they have trouble understanding a different mentality.

I thought about how America had never understood Vietnam, how it was shocked when the Ayatollah Khomeini took over Iran. I thought about Mexican friends and acquaintances who told stories of how Americans hadn't shown them any "respect." I recalled a party in Austria, where two Americans who knew German grammar much better than I did spoke in American ways that the Austrians found abrasive.

Americans have trouble understanding another mentality, suggested my Swiss friend. They have trouble entering into another world that goes with another language, another point of view, another way of doing things. Americans have trouble with culture. That's a stereotype I've heard all over the world.

I don't know how true the stereotype is, and God knows I've met plenty of people from *other* lands who showed little awareness that anything other than their way of seeing things ever existed, or even deserved to. But the fact remains: You can't *use* a new language unless you change the consciousness that is tied to the old one, unless you stretch beyond the circle of grammar and dictionary, out of the old world and into a new one. And Americans are famous for thinking they've got the best consciousness around.

Americans are the best, number one, free and rich and capable of doing anything. Where did such a stereotype come from? It's easy to think of reasons. A nation of immigrants who broke with tradition and improved their economic situation. A melting-pot ideology that cried out, "Hurry and become one of *us*." The insecurity of a colony vis-à-vis the former masters. An exploitable frontier that called out that the sky was the limit. The anti-immigrant mentality that grew up at the turn of the century. A global savior role in two world wars, followed by a righteous stance against the Stalinist state.

Do all Americans run around with the number-one mentality, looking at other languages *only* through their own? No, of course not. Don't people from other places besides America live locked into a one-dimensional consciousness? Of course they do.

But, for a while anyway, I'm going to let the stereotype stand. Americans without the experience of culture are number-one Americans. I've met plenty of them. Some of them run the most important institutions in the country. They hold America back from sailing in the new winds of history. The mentality that the number-one types represent—in America or anywhere else—must change.

///

There are two ways of looking at differences between you and somebody else. One way is to figure out that the differences are the tip of the iceberg, the signal that two different *systems* are at work. Another way is to notice all the things that the other person *lacks* when compared to you, the so-called *deficit theory* approach.

Number-one types—American or any other—use the deficit theory. They're the best, anything else is less than the best, and anyone who would call into question who they are when they're already the best is a fool or a masochist or even, as they used to say in America before *perestroika,* a Communist. Ronald Reagan was elected, in part, on a wave of number-one sentiment.

The deficit theory does have its advantages. But it's a prison. It locks you into a closed room in an old building with no windows. It inoculates you against culture. You might tinker with the grammar and dictionary of a language, but you never communicate—except in terms of the world that shaped your attitudes, the language designed to fit your assumptions about what the world is and how it works, the native language you learned when you first stumbled around the house in diapers.

The situation has to change. It's a cliché of the nineties to observe that we live in a multicultural world, whether we want to or not. Revolutions in information and transportation have pulled us all together. Wars and the economy move us physically all over the globe. It's hard to think of many jobs in which contact with "different people" isn't normal. Entertainment—film, food, and fiction—often involves the products of "foreigners."

Communication in today's world *requires* culture. Problems in communication are rooted in *who you are,* in encounters with a *different mentality, different meanings,* a *different tie* between language and consciousness. Solving the problems inspired by such encounters inspires culture.

For number-one types, it means changing from "best" to "different." If they take culture seriously, they embark on a lifelong process of transformation that only ends when they do. It opens up new possibilities and stokes the fires of creativity. It subverts the amiable naïveté that Americans are famous for the world over.

Those wedded to the number-one identity, the identity that holds them captive in the monolingual prison, see culture as a threat. They are right. Personally, I think the real threat is the way the number-one identity holds culture at bay. Without it, such a person stands banished from the growing global conversation.

///

When people learn culture, when they burst out of their former unconscious ways and gaze at the new landscape of possibilities, they change in positive ways. I've seen it happen more times than I can remember.

Just after I'd returned from a year in Austria, I talked with a businessman in that great purgatory that brings us together, an airport waiting lounge. He was an "America is number one" man who complained about how "foreigners" did business.

I told him a story. I told him how Austrian businessmen I'd met who worked with Americans knew our language, watched our TV shows and movies, read our novels, looked at the *Herald Tribune* and our weekly newsmagazines. They had come up with theories of what we were like. They knew about us, about our ties between language and consciousness, but we knew nothing about them.

In a business negotiation where X knows a great deal about Y, and Y knows almost nothing about X, who has the advantage? I asked. The businessman bought me a beer.

In an interview with Felipe González, the socialist prime minister of Spain, a reporter asked what it was like dealing with the Americans. At first, he said, he'd had the usual stereotype—who do these world colonizers think they are, anyway? But after a few meetings, he changed his mind. It's kind of touching, he said. In walk the representatives of this world power, and the main thing they care about is whether you like them or not.

In the corridor of a train, a German woman and I struck up a conversation while we stared out the window at the passing farmland. She'd just returned from a month-long trip around the United States. I asked her how she liked Americans. She launched into an enthusiastic story about how she'd learned from them, how they looked at themselves and the situations they faced as something you could change, something you could transform in a favorable direction.

In her world, she'd learned that you are what you are, you do what you have to, and that's it. No more. Now her world was full of new possibilities that, she said, sometimes shocked her family and friends.

The stories of the businessman in the airport, the prime minister of Spain, and the German woman on the train show what happens when you "catch" culture. They all noticed a difference in language tied to who they were, realized other ties were possible, set out to figure them out, and then changed themselves as a result.

Culture lights the darkened countryside into a landscape of new choices. It changes the way you look at things.

///

Culture has its downside as well. It can wash you away into a sea of anomie. Some lose the certainty of the world that tied them to their original language and never recover.

In Vienna, an older Kurdish student attending one of my classes had trouble with the final paper. Toward the end of the semester, he came in to talk with me. His German was confused and confusing. I'd attributed it to what was probably his recent immigration to Austria. I was wrong.

He spoke of a childhood with one Kurdish parent and one Iraqi, of migration to Vienna years ago when he was still a child, of his study of English, since he really wanted to go to the United States or Canada and thought and read about little else. He'd taken my course, he explained, because he thought I'd be teaching about American language in English.

He didn't know who he was anymore, he said. He couldn't speak any of his four languages well enough to give voice to what was inside of him, and what was inside of him was a contradictory mess anyway. He had culture, but for him it was a cancer that consumed his coherence.

His story was a sad one, and it's not the only time I've heard it. Stories like his are sometimes used by proponents of the number-one theory to explain the dangers of going outside the circle, of venturing into culture. From their point of view, it's dangerous, no matter what, because it always knocks you out of the "our way is the only way" mentality, which the number-one types fight to preserve.

Cases like the Kurd's show that culture is powerful, and power unrecognized and uncontrolled can destroy rather than create. The answer isn't to fight it, to banish it, to legislate it away. The answer is to understand it, to keep an eye on it, to learn how to use it to shift into gear for lifelong travel into the contemporary multicultural world.

///

Culture has come out of the American closet. America was built— so goes the old story, which conveniently ignores Indians, slaves, and the Chinese—on waves of European immigration, waves made up of people committed to melting into the pot. Nowadays, the waves of immigration are neither Anglo nor European, and a lot of them don't want to melt. They want to be *Americans,* but they don't want to be *Anglo-Europeans.*

"Multiculturalism" is the new cliché of our times, a call to recognize a new American phenomenon on the part of our institutions—education, health care, the workplace, law enforcement, and the rest. But no one quite knows what to make of it or what to do about it. The results are tragic. Rich differences are converted into threatening deficits. The old myth is dead, but the new reality still baffles, confuses, and sometimes explodes into violence.

America has an opportunity, a chance to change a breaking point into a turning point, a chance to make a global contribution, a chance to make multiculturalism work. One traditional strength of America is the ability to innovate, to look at a problem and figure out a solution without holding hands with centuries of tradition. Remember the story of the German woman on the train, the one who learned during her American travels that she could change? Even Abbie Hoffman, former sixties radical and cultural critic until his death, said he couldn't imagine working anywhere else because of America's "can do" attitude.

Culture and language aren't just issues here, either. Recent events in the former Yugoslavia and Czechoslovakia and the old Soviet Union, in Iraq and Ethiopia, in Kenya and South Africa, in Mexico and Nicaragua, in India and Indonesia, to name just a few examples, testify to the global concern with multiculturalism, the feeling that it's a situation to be feared rather than a historic possibility to be celebrated.

Besides, the world economy, the speed of information and transportation, tourism and war, the internationalization of business and politics and academics, not to mention music, have taught growing numbers of people that multiculturalism isn't just a feature of *home;* it's a feature of anyone's life, anywhere, when that life expands beyond national boundaries. And the number of lives so expanded increases each year.

There are alternatives to circling the wagons, alternatives to forebodings of fear or aggressive threats to bring those "different" people into line. But to figure out alternatives, we've got to figure out what those differences are all about and how to handle them. Conversations and newspapers often hang the problems on "culture" and "language," but the concepts are more complicated, more interesting, than what those conversations and newspapers would lead you to believe.

"Language," goes the first mistake, lies inside the circle. People don't speak the same language; if they'd only learn the other one everything would be fine. But the stories I've told show that grammar and the dictionary—what we usually think of as "learning a language"—aren't enough. People who speak the *same* language don't always communicate, and people who learn a *second* language and stay inside the circle don't either. The concept of "language" has to change.

"Culture," goes the second mistake, is something "those people" have. Cultures, those different-colored billiard balls, roll around, collide with each other, and wreak havoc with what used to be a straightforward game. But the stories I've told show that culture is more than just something a group has. It's something that happens to people when they realize that their way of doing things isn't natural law, that other ways are possible. Something they've just heard, something that jolted their sense of who they are, invites them into a different way of seeing. The concept of "culture," like the concept of "language," has to change.

The two concepts have to change *together*. Language, in all its varieties, in all the ways it appears in everyday life, builds a world of meanings. When you run into different meanings, when you become aware of your own and work to build a bridge to the others, "culture" is what you're up to. Language fills the spaces between us with sound; culture forges the human connection through them. Culture is in language, and language is loaded with culture.

If you do start to see things this way, you change. The old "self," the one in your heart and mind and soul, mutates as it comes into relationships with others. The self stretches to comprehend them all. A life of Being turns into a life of Becoming. You turn into a sailor and an immigrant for as long as you live—a theme I'll return to later.

This way of seeing, a way that grew out of several fields, mostly linguistics and anthropology, is one I've been talking about for years, to undergrads and grads, to community groups, to organizations, and I thought the time was right to write it down. I thought the time was right because the world in general, and America in particular, is waking from its long, number-one slumber. It has to. The way the world works now, the only alternative is isolation, and the way the world works now, isolation is no longer an option.

Mostly, this is a book of stories that bring to life this way of seeing, personal stories and some others that I've borrowed. Many of them are classic second-language adventures—I'll talk a lot about Austria and Mexico. "Second" languages, "different" cultures, they stand out because the differences are so grand, so fundamental. A first encounter reduces the articulate and self-possessed into a babbling child. Different worlds call for the kind of courage that lets you handle mistakes.

But lessons learned in encounters with radically different worlds apply at home as well. At home those other kinds of people, those other ways of using the "same" language, aren't as distant. You and *they,* whoever the "they" of the moment happens to be, already share some common grammar and some common experience. Differences close to home are less different, more immediately accessible, but fascinating and complex all the same.

What I want to do is show you how interesting and important language and cultural differences really are, how encounters with them disrupt buried routines and open up possibilities previously unimagined. Differences aren't a *threat;* they're an *opportunity.*

When you finish the book, what you will have, if I've done my job, is a way of seeing, one you'll never lose, one that will change the way you move through daily life. I *want* to try to reveal language and culture in a new way, because I want to help make a multicultural world work. This book is aimed at people, not institutions or countries, because the secret—the one that Tom Paine knew—is that if enough people change the way they see things, institutions and countries have to follow suit.

It's a vision through rose-colored glasses, I know, to think a piece of writing could have such an effect. With all the conflict around us based on language and cultural differences, why even try? When an independent trucker I once interviewed talked about his second marriage, he called it "the triumph of hope over experience." I'd like to twist that a little and try to show that experience, some of it anyway, might turn out to be a source of hope.

Hope, of course, isn't enough. While I was writing this book, I presented some of the ideas in it to a conference on intercultural communication in Germany. Afterward, a colleague from Bulgaria came up to talk. Interesting, he said, and optimistic, thereby attributing to me one common stereotype of Americans. But what do you do, he asked, with hatred of the Moslem minority in Christian Bulgaria, a hatred grounded in the occupation of Bulgaria by the Ottomans centuries ago?

Language and culture savvy won't wave a magic wand over deep-seated historical hatreds and make them disappear. It won't dissolve the gross social inequities that often drive conflicts attributed to language and culture. What it will do is open lines of communication based on what people *are* rather than on what they are *not.* When the time comes for talking instead of shooting, such lines of communication can only help. With any luck, a little talking before the shooting might melt the bullets. That's where the hope part comes in.

///

Culture erases the circle around language that people usually draw. You can master grammar and the dictionary, but *without* culture you won't communicate. With culture, you can communicate *with* rocky grammar and a limited vocabulary. This statement seems paradoxical because of the circle around language, the circle that exists in most people's imagination. Without the circle, the paradox disappears.

The circle has to go.

For the next few chapters, I'll present some history to help erase the circle. The history won't range across all the great ideas about language. Instead, I'll lift out one theme that runs through it, a theme aimed at understanding how fragile the narrow circle really is. Contained in the story of the circle are the ways to eliminate it.

The story of the founding father of modern linguistics is a fine place to start. Though he did set up one version of a circle around language himself, the ideas he developed have traveled well beyond it. Once the fundamentals he established are under control, erasing that circle won't seem like such a radical move after all.

The Circle

THE creation myth for modern linguistics usually begins with Ferdinand de Saussure, a Swiss linguist who taught at the University of Geneva around the turn of the century. It's not hard to imagine why a Swiss would be fascinated with language, since the country has three official languages, a fourth national language, and countless dialects tucked away in the mountains.

There's an old linguistics joke: What's the difference between a *language* and a *dialect*? The "language" speakers are the ones with an army.

Saussure created a way of looking at language, a way that guides you to the right questions to recognize problems when you communicate with others. He didn't quite make it to culture, though his ideas aim in that direction. But what he did do was magnificent.

He grew up in the tradition of *historical* linguistics, the mainstream of the late nineteenth century. To understand what he did, to understand the genius that he was, the historical approach has to be sketched first. In the English-speaking world, historical linguistics started in the eighteenth century with Sir William Jones, a friend of Benjamin Franklin who tried to help convince King George III that trouble was brewing in the American colonies.

Sir William had worked in India and dabbled in Sanskrit. He noticed—to his amazement—that some Sanskrit words resembled words in classical Greek and Latin. He built up comparative vocabulary lists from the three languages until he became convinced that the ties were no accident, that somewhere back in history the three had a common ancestor.

He summarized what he'd learned in one of his more famous statements:

> The Sanskrit language, whatever may be its antiquity, is of a wonderful structure; more perfect than the Greek, more copious than the Latin, and more exquisitely refined than either, yet bearing to both of them a stronger affinity, both in the roots of verbs and in the forms of grammar, than could possibly have been produced by accident; so strong indeed, that no philologer could examine all three, without believing them to have sprung from some common source, which, perhaps, no longer exists. There is a similar reason, thought not quite so forcible, for supposing that both the Gothic and the Celtic had the same origin with the Sanskrit.

One has to think back into the eighteenth century to imagine what a startling claim he'd made. Greek and Latin were the perfect languages, the languages of the educated, the sources of the flourishing European civilization that Sir William Jones and his contemporaries celebrated.

That attitude was still around when I was in high school in the early 1960s. I was told to take Latin because it was a perfect language, one that would improve my mind, and was the sign of an educated person. I did, but mostly because I'd been an altar boy and wondered what we'd been saying all those years. I'm not sure what it did for me, except I can sing the first few lines of "Gaudeamus Igitur," and I still think of *illegitimi non carborundum*—"don't let the bastards grind you down"—as a useful motto to help me make it through the day.

Sir William complicated the image of Latin and Greek considerably. The linguistic evidence showed that the line from Greece and Rome to modern Europe wasn't quite so neat, that people in a distant land had to be fit into the picture as well, that the story of

European language had to be rewritten as the story of *Indo-European* language.

Jones's work founded a line of thinking that continues into the present. Language, in this view, is a source of items to compare with similar items from other languages. The point of the comparison is to reconstruct language's family tree, to show how the siblings and cousins are related, and to figure out what the ancestors might have looked like.

Here's a quick example:

ENGLISH	GERMAN	FRENCH	SPANISH
father	*Vater*	*père*	*padre*
mother	*Mutter*	*mère*	*madre*
red	*rot*	*rouge*	*rojo*
hand	*Hand*	*main*	*mano*

This is classic raw material for the historical linguist, lists of vocabulary items from universal human domains—kinship, color, and body parts. The sample list makes us suspect what we all know, that the four languages are related, and that German and English look like one branch and French and Spanish look like another.

Historical linguistics is of course much more complicated. The lists are longer, grammar is taken into account, and general patterns in the sound shift from one language to another are examined. And modern historical linguists have gone well beyond words into matters of genre and style as well. Hypothetical models of the ancestor languages are built, all the way back to the so-called proto-world, the great-granddaddy of them all. (In fact, the question of whether there was one proto-world or more is a burning issue right now. If you meet a linguist sometime, tell him or her that you're a native speaker of proto-world.)

But for historical linguistics, or at least for the part I've described here, a particular language is a warehouse of vocabulary items, a source of words to pull out and set on a list alongside words with similar meanings from other languages. The list, once you've built it, is what's interesting, not the language that the individual items came from.

///

Saussure studied historical linguistics, but he thought his way into a different view. What bothered him was that, from the point of view of the speakers of a particular language, the truths that historical linguistics uncovered didn't really matter. Speakers don't know or care that when they throw a word out in public it signals a relationship with an ancient language of India.

What do speakers care about? They care about *communicating* with each other. And they don't do that by chanting a list of kinship terms and body parts; they do it by choosing among streams of sounds that carry tons of meanings and arranging them in some systematic way. From the point of view of the speakers, language is a *symbolic system* that they use to communicate.

Saussure was fond of comparing language to a chessboard, and since then countless philosophers and linguists have been doing the same. A player makes sense out of a chess game at a particular point in time. He knows that there are a certain number of pieces of different types, that the rules of the game tell you which pieces you can move in which way, and that the point of the game is to checkmate the king.

What the game looked like half an hour before is interesting but irrelevant. How the carved wood knight compares with the ivory knight from another chess set is interesting but irrelevant. The game, at that moment, is a symbolic system, an arrangement of objects that mean something in terms of what they represent and what they can do.

Saussure never published his ideas. He never would have earned tenure at an American university. It's said he had Darwin's disease, that is, he was anxious about going public with ideas so radically different from the conventional wisdom. But his students pooled their notes after his death and put together the famous *Course in General Linguistics.*

Personally, I get an attack of Darwin's disease just thinking that students who have heard my lectures would publish something. I've seen their notes. But even if the students got it wrong in Saussure's case, they at least made it interesting.

Saussure thought in distinctions, in oppositions. He set up categories to show that what he wanted to do was different from what
the historical linguists were up to. Genius is like that—a mind that
introduces a new way of seeing things, a way that simply didn't exist
before. His distinctions signal the difference between the new way
of seeing and the old. But when he tagged his distinctions with
words, he did add some cumbersome jargon to the dictionary.

Most jargon, in academics or any other line of work, puts an
outsider off. With good reason. Most of it is a twisted substitute for
just plain English (or whatever other language) that sets off the
expert and allows him or her to charge exorbitant fees for translation. But I think Saussure's new terminology was justified, because
he needed it to signal that something different was going on, something that the old ways of talking didn't let you see.

///

First of all, said Saussure, historical linguistics is *diachronic,*
"through-time," the study of how languages change and shift and
branch off from each other throughout the history of the human
species. Fine as far as it goes, but he had something else in mind.

What he had in mind was *synchronic* linguistics, "with-time,"
the study of a particular language as it existed at a particular point
in time. Where it came from, what it had looked like a thousand
years before, what other languages it was related to—interesting
questions all, just not what he was after.

Why did he want to do synchronic linguistics? He didn't want
to write grammar books for secondary schools. He didn't want to
determine the "correct" form of a language. He didn't want linguistics to tell people how they *should* speak, something he called
prescriptive linguistics. He didn't want to prescribe language as doctors prescribe medicine. Instead, he wanted to *describe* it.

With this distinction Saussure wasn't struggling against the historical linguists so much; instead, he was after the official—or self-
appointed—arbiters of the "right" way to speak.

Linguists have a shorthand term for the right way to speak. They
call it the *standard.* The standard is what they teach you in school,
the way you're *supposed* to talk in formal or official settings—the

correct way to speak, usually on the model of the upper reaches of
the social stratosphere, since the wealthy and powerful are the ones
who pay the prescriptivists.

Some countries, like France and Spain and India, have government committees that meet and decide what proper French, Spanish,
or Hindi in fact "is." Every so often there's an article in the American press about a French Academy member having a fit because too
many people are saying "bluejeans." Other countries, like Kenya or
Canada or India, boil up on a regular basis around the issue of
which of their country's several languages should, in fact, be the
standard.

Countries like the United States don't have official committees;
they have pundits who write columns and books about proper English, or people like Noah Webster, who wrote a dictionary to prove
that American English was different from the language of the former
colonial power, or individual states that pass amendments declaring
English to be the official language.

Saussure didn't want to be held captive by someone's idea of
how a group *should* speak. He didn't care whether the language of
some group measured up to the standard as dictated by the linguistic
powers that be. If the members of the group communicated with
each other, they used a symbolic system. Whatever that system was,
however it worked, he wanted linguistics to be able to figure it out.
He called his kind of linguistics *descriptive* rather than prescriptive.

The difference isn't trivial. Consider the simple case of the double
negative: "I ain't got no money." Negative with the "ain't" and
negative with the "no." Double negatives are found in several dialects of American English, including one that I grew up with as an
adolescent. In fact, the example sentence is one we uttered every
day, even more frequently on the weekends.

Linguists call such dialects *nonstandard,* since they don't follow
the same rules as the standard. One can argue that such dialects put
the speaker at a social disadvantage, lead to unfortunate stereotypes,
block him or her from entry into the higher-status arenas where the
pay is better and where such speech is not tolerated. One can argue
about the *social consequences* of nonstandard speech.

But many prescriptivists go beyond that reasonable discussion.
They argue that a double negative, like "ain't got no," is the sign
of a confused mind. Everyone knows that two negatives make a

positive. Speakers who use double negatives actually affirm something, and they don't even know it. Double negatives indicate irrational minds.

A while ago I mentioned the *deficit theory*, the view that differences between self and other are signs of the other's deficiencies. Someone who isn't like me *lacks* something. I claimed that number-one types tended toward this view. The rejection of the double negative is an example of how a number-one mentality works *inside* its own language as well.

Double negatives ain't no signal of an irrational mind. Double negatives occur in languages and dialects all over the world. In fact, they're so common that linguists have a name for them—*negative concord*. Negative concord is a simple rule of grammar that says, When you put a negative particle in one place, put it in this other place as well. The American English standard doesn't have negative concord; many American English dialects do. That's just how it is.

Saussure announced the difference between prescriptive and descriptive linguistics to avoid just this kind of confusion. He wanted to figure out the language that people actually used, not someone else's idea of what it should be.

///

The next move he made was unfortunate, because it set up the circle around language that I'm trying to erase. He made a distinction between *language* and *speech*. I wish he hadn't, but he did.

Speech is what people do when they're actually using a language. God knows what they're going to say or how they're going to say it. They'll probably make mistakes, use incomplete sentences, rely on objects in the context, slide their tone of voice around, chop the air with their hands. Not every speaker of a language will talk the same way, either. There'll be individual and social variation. Speech is a mess.

Language, on the other hand, is pure, clean, a steel skyscraper arising from the chaos in the streets. Language is an inventory of symbols with a system that ties them together. To get to language, you take a cleaned-up list of sentences, figure out the rules that label them grammatical, and congratulate yourself on a job well done.

The idea is as old as Plato's cave. The man in the cave could see only the shadows of things, never their ideal essence. Speech is the shadow, uneven and flickering. Language is the essence, sought after but elusive, approximated by a vision of the essence beyond the accidental details.

Linguistics can't account for speech, said Saussure. But it can use speech to get to language. Before speech can be used, however, it's cleaned up, taken out of the world of the speaker, laid out in a row of dressed-up sentences covered with makeup. Saussure drew a circle around language right at the beginning.

///

So if language isn't speech, then what is it? To answer this question, Saussure turned to a contemporary, a Frenchman named Émile Durkheim who was inventing the field of sociology. Society, said Durkheim, isn't just the sum of individual acts, not just the total of what all the individuals who happen to live in a certain place together are up to.

Instead, society is something that existed before a particular individual was born into it, and it will continue to exist long after he or she is gone. Society isn't what any particular person does; instead, society sets the limits on what a person *might* do. Society is like jazz. The musicians in the quartet agree on a musical structure as a frame of reference, but then each one of them blazes a personal trail through it with an instrument of choice.

Society is like a skier. Acres of mountain yawn out in front of him. Thousands of trails down the mountain are possible and he'll wind up taking one. But he can't ski off the edge of the mountain, and he'll always end up at the bottom near a lift.

There are limits on what one can do. I can't declare that henceforth students must wear a wet suit to my class. I can't park my car on the front steps of the building. I can't move my desk from my office into the hall and charge people a quarter every time they walk by. I can't set my watch five hours and twenty-three minutes ahead of everybody else and then claim that's the only time I'll recognize.

I *could* do those things, of course. But Durkheim's argument would shine by the response I received. When people cross the boundaries, go beyond the fences that the social facts define, then they're crazy or criminal or maybe both. They're no longer members of the group. They're locked into an institution until they are re-habilitated or, to put it another way, until they are brought back inside the fence.

"Social fact" fits Saussure's idea of language perfectly. Language isn't something that *predicts* what a person will say under certain circumstances. Instead, language defines the limits, the boundaries, the fence around the territory, and then sets individuals loose within those limits to do whatever they want.

Language, said Saussure, is just another social fact. Language doesn't tell you what will happen whenever speakers speak. That's *speech*. But it does tell you some of the limits that surround them every time they do. The poets explore the edges, and sometimes they fall off the cliff. By the time James Joyce got to *Finnegans Wake,* many readers thought he'd gone too far.

But most speakers and writers run well within the boundaries, and it is the job of linguistics to figure out what those boundaries are.

///

Saussure invented a linguistics for synchronic, descriptive studies, of language, not speech, with the goal of laying out a symbolic system as a social fact. But what did he actually study? What is the symbol? And what is the system?

The symbol, the unit of study, the thing one grabs on to and focuses on, Saussure called a *sign*.

A sign is a Janus-faced thing, a single creature with one face that looks outward and another that looks inward. Saussure named the two faces. The face that looks outward toward the public world of sound and fury he called the *signifier*. The inward-looking face, the face that whispers to the perceiver what that signifier meant, he called the *signified*. When a signifier and a signified are bound together, when the faces of Janus are complete, they make up a *sign*.

Let's say I travel to Yugoslavia to wander the Adriatic coast. Let's say I did this several years ago, before there was a chance I'd get shot. I hear streams of sound coming out of people's mouths. I can hear them as well as anyone can. They are public, out in the spaces between people, available to any person with normal hearing. But none of them are signs, at least not yet. The sounds *might* be signifiers, but they don't mean anything to me; they don't signify anything, so they can't be signs.

I walk up to an outdoor café on a hot day. I need a drink. I try "Beer," and the waiter nods and says, "*Pivo*." Of course he understands *beer*. It's like *Bier,* and half of Germany and Austria moves here for the month of August.

I've got a hypothesis. *Pivo* means "sure enough," or "another stupid tourist," or "beer." He brings a bottle, and I point at it and say "*Pivo*." He nods and smiles. Now a piece of those sounds has a meaning. *Pivo* is a signifier; *beer* is the signified. I've just glued together my first Croatian sign.

It's easy to get carried away and think that everything you can perceive *must* mean something. I'll tell you an anthropological story. It's about behavior other than language, but it makes the point. It occurred when I worked in a village in South India.

One day I noticed that the men wore two kinds of shirts. One kind had button-down collars and the other didn't. Since I lived there during the sixties, the button-down collar carried all kinds of symbolic value in my home territory, so I naturally assumed that the style difference meant something in the village as well.

It didn't. Try as I might, I received only confused looks when I asked why a person would buy one shirt rather than another. No, I was told over and over again, people bought shirts because of price, for the most part. Nobody seemed to care about the collar style.

The moral of the story: Not everything that is perceivable is the signifier you want it to be. But even with this caution in mind, the sign is still Saussure's unit of study, the thing to focus on, the element of language, the piece on the chessboard. When perceivable sound (a signifier) means something (a signified) to the people who perceive it, then the two together make up a sign, and the linguists are in business.

III

Not all signs are created equal. Saussure and the linguists who followed him are particularly taken with signs in which the glue between the signifier and signified is *conventional.* There's no necessary reason why the sound sequence *cat* signifies a four-legged furry creature that likes to get loaded on catnip. None at all.

The fact that human language pairs up sounds and meanings in an arbitrary way is one of its great strengths, something that puts it miles ahead of other animal communication systems. The good news about human language is that it takes a small set of sounds and hooks them up to a potentially infinite range of meanings. The bad news is that speakers and hearers have to learn what the hooks are on a case-by-case basis.

Other kinds of signs are easier, because something about the signifier *suggests* what the signified is.

A while ago, on that same Greek island where I met the Swiss architect who wondered about Americans and foreign languages, I sat in a *taverna* in a beautiful cove of pine trees, tinder dry in the summer sun. I talked with Yiórgos, "George" as he liked to be called, since he'd worked for years in Melbourne. His little girl was playing on the dirt road that ran down to the sea. She dropped the ball she was bouncing, stared up at the ridge, and started screaming "*Fotiá!*" I knew that *fotiá* means "fire," and when I looked up at the ridge I saw clouds of smoke pouring into the cove. Her observation started one of the longest nights I've ever spent.

For now, the only point I want to make is that the smoke *signified* that a fire had started somewhere, because the fire *caused* the smoke. When a signifier is caused by the signified, the sign is called *indexical*.

In English class in high school, the teacher eventually gets around to words that *suggest* the meanings they carry, the so-called onomatopoeia. If I wrote you a poem—I assure you it would be a bad one—and I put in the line "beezzz buzzing around the clock tick tock," I'd be using this time-honored technique. The *z* sound in "beezzz" and "buzzing" means to suggest the actual sounds of bees, because it *resembles* them. And the "tick tock" *suggests* the sound of the clock.

When signifiers suggest the meaning of the signified, because the sound *resembles* the thing that it means, the sign is called *iconic*.

But most signs are glued together by social convention and nothing else. The only way to understand the glue is to learn what the pieces that have been fastened together are. Gone are the helpful links of cause and resemblance. These arbitrary signs are called *symbols*.

Signs are the focus of linguistic study, most of them the conventional signs or symbols. But language isn't just a warehouse full of symbols. The historical linguists already knew that. What about the "system" part of symbolic system?

///

In Saussure's famous chess example, the system is easy. Well, I say easy. I'm a terrible chess player. When it comes time to play, I prefer something less cerebral, like racquetball.

But the chess system *is* easier than language, because a book of rules lays out the pieces, the moves, and the goals of the game. With language, nobody wrote the book of rules. Except the prescriptivists, who write the book after the fact, and they can't be trusted if the goal is description.

How do you figure out the system in which the signs participate? What relationships do different signs have to each other? Saussure offered an answer, another distinction, the most awkwardly worded of them all.

Language is a sequence of sounds that carry meaning, a linear string of words that make up a sentence. The trick to Saussure's notion of system is to step back, look at the flow of words, and ask two questions.

First, why did *that* particular word occur right there, in that slot? What other choices were available that were left behind? What else could have popped up in that slot but didn't?

"The dog threw up on the rug." What else might have occurred instead of "dog"? "Cat," "baby," "nuclear physicist"—a little weird, but plausible; "roach"—I don't know if roaches throw up, but still plausible. How about "plant," "microwave," "morning paper"? Maybe some poet skating on the edge of the social facts would say that, but it's not the sort of thing you'd usually hear.

The game is to look at a slot filled with something, and then figure out all the other somethings that might have occurred there but didn't. Saussure called this the *paradigmatic* relationship, the relationship that ties together a group of signs because they all could occur in the same slot.

In this particular example, a linguist would say we were discovering the difference between two paradigmatic sets, one consisting of *animate* nouns, the other of *inanimate* nouns. Animate nouns can throw up; inanimate nouns can't.

The second question you'd ask as the stream of sounds flowed by is, given that some choice is made to fill *one* slot, what implications does that carry for choices made in *other* slots? The example gives one answer already. "Throw up" is a verb—it occurs in a particular slot—that means that an animate noun has to be in the subject slot. Inanimate objects don't throw up.

We could have played the game a different way. "The dog threw up on the rug." What else could have occurred in the "throw up" slot? We all know what dogs do on rugs, but what besides that? "Slept"? Fine. "Crawled"? No problem. "Exploded"? No way, except in a Stephen King novel. "Marinated"? Maybe in some countries, but not here.

Animate nouns can sleep and crawl. They don't normally explode. They don't marinate, unless their name has changed from animal to food. Steers don't marinate, but steaks do. Saussure called this the *syntagmatic* relationship. When a sign in one slot means that something happens in another slot, the two signs stand in a syntagmatic relationship.

Syntagmatic and paradigmatic define the two basic relationships of the symbolic system. Signs are related either because they are both candidates for the same slot, or because if one occurs in one slot, it implies that something else will occur in another slot.

Syntagmatic and paradigmatic lie underneath most modern theories of grammar in one way or another. Much linguistic labor consists in taking a language and saying, Okay, here's a bunch of slots that can get filled to make a sentence in this language, so what can occur in each of the slots and what does one slot have to do with the others?

If you speak German or Spanish, the number and person of the subject tell you that you have to tack different endings on to the verb. *Ich geh*e, "I go"; *Du geh*st, "you go"; *Er/Sie geh*t, "he/she goes"; and so on. English doesn't do that much, except for third person singular present, where you tack on an *s*—"he speak*s*." The rest of it is covered by just *speak*.

In German or Spanish, the article has to match the gender and number of the noun it modifies. In English, you don't have to worry about it. *The* and *a* cover the territory. In German, the article routinely causes nervous breakdowns, because you also have to worry about case. There's an Austrian proverb about the articles that, shortened and paraphrased, goes like this: "*Der, die, das,* the hell with it."

English has a pretty simple grammar. All those linguistic collisions throughout its history—Celtic, Germanic, Latin, Danish, French—helped wash out the differences. English is a mongrel, one of the reasons it lends itself to world-language status. But the same history that created the simple grammar grew a vocabulary that's a monster, with words from all over the European map.

I wish I had a nickel for every time I heard an Austrian tell me: "You know, when I first learned English, I thought it was easy. But then the vocabulary . . . "

///

Saussure laid the foundation stones for modern linguistics. He was one of the key figures who sculpted the modern era out of the nineteenth century. But he set up the circle around language when he threw out speech in favor of language.

Saussure's ideas don't *have* to be limited by the circle. The trick—the one he himself suggested—is to let signifiers be something other than words, and let signifieds be something other than dictionary definitions. Why not take a synchronic, descriptive approach to signs other than words, and look at how they are paradigmatically and syntagmatically organized? Why not indeed?

For years I've escaped to the island of Cozumel off the Yucatán coast to scuba dive. A dive trip is organized in a certain way. As the boat leaves the town dock, the dive guide gathers the divers together and they discuss where they want to go.

The first dive is a deep dive. There are several reefs to choose from, such as Palancar, Santa Rosa, and Colombia. Then the boat pulls in to the beach for lunch. After lunch, the second dive is shallow, on any one of several reefs, including Chankanab, Paraíso, and Colombia.

I've just described a Saussurian structure. There are two slots, before lunch and after lunch. Different reefs are in the same paradigmatic set because they are deep dives or shallow dives.

What about syntagmatic relationships? Colombia is on both the deep and the shallow list, because different parts of the reef can serve either purpose. Let's say you notice that if Colombia is the deep dive, it is *always* the shallow dive, and that you do both dives and then go have lunch. If you make a choice in one slot of the structure, it has implications for the choices you make in the other slot. Syntagmatic, no doubt about it.

Colombia is way to hell and gone down at the southern tip of the island. It takes forever to get there, and once you're there the guides want to get the dives over with and head back. So, if the deep dive is Colombia, then, barring a revolution on the boat, it will be the shallow dive as well, and lunch will be late.

The underlying rule has something to do with deep versus shallow and close versus distant reefs, just as the language examples had to do with things like animate versus inanimate or masculine versus feminine versus neuter gender.

Diving in Cozumel, it turns out, is a Saussurian system.

///

So is ordering from a restaurant menu.

Near my apartment is a seafood restaurant decorated like something out of the fifties: wood paneling, heads of animals and mounted fish hanging from the walls, older-women waitresses who remind you that beauty parlors still exist.

When I go in to order dinner, I look at the list of main courses, but that's just the beginning of the job. I choose soup or salad, pick two out of five or six side dishes to go with the main course, and end with one of a number of traditionals—ice cream or apple pie.

The problem of ordering is another Saussurian structure, a symbolic system with several paradigmatic sets. Some of the sets are quite small—soup *or* salad in the appetizer slot, two side-order slots with only five or six choices, ice cream *or* pie for dessert. The main-course slot has more possibilities, though the odds are the choice is going to have something to do with seafood.

The paradigmatic relations among the food items that make up a "dinner order" are obvious. Are there syntagmatic relations? One simple one. There are two side-order slots, but you wouldn't put the same vegetable in both. I've said some ridiculous things in that restaurant, but never "For my two vegetables, I'll have green beans and green beans." Even gray-haired ladies have their limits.

Likewise, I probably won't order two starches to fill the two slots—baked potato in one and rice in the other wouldn't make any sense. I have some other syntagmatic rules—I won't order a salad in the appetizer slot and two vegetables in the side-order slots. One or the other, but not both. Enough green is enough.

That's about it, though. Don't put the same vegetable or two starches in the side-order slots, and enough green is enough. That covers the syntagmatic rules of my ordering system, at least at that restaurant. But the fact that it's simple doesn't hide the other fact— ordering a meal is a Saussurian symbolic system as well, as much of a social fact as language is.

///

The last example turns more complicated than dive trips or dinner orders. Consider fashion, clothes, the things we put on, as a Saussurian system.

If we actually took the notion seriously—and people have—we'd run into complications and ambiguities with the speed of light. For the present, pretend that we have identified a series of slots that make up the system. To keep it simple, let's call them head, upper body, lower body, and feet.

First, the paradigmatic sets for each slot might be laid out. Head—cowboy hat, turban, baseball cap, beret, football helmet, to toss out just a few examples for males. Upper body—tank top, T-shirt, sweatshirt, dress shirt, sweater. Lower body—jeans, shorts, swimsuit, slacks, jockstrap. Feet—sandals, cowboy boots, leather dress shoes, loafers, running shoes.

Are there syntagmatic relationships among the slots in the system? Obviously. A cowboy hat, tank top, jockstrap, and leather dress shoes would earn you some attention, as would a baseball cap, a dress shirt, a swim suit, and a pair of cowboy boots. They would earn you some attention because your choices would go far beyond the edges of the social fact fence.

Fashion approaches language a little more closely than diving or menus. Fashion begins to look complicated in ways that language will later in this book.

///

Saussure was a genius. In a world of historical linguistics, he crafted a set of lenses that formed the viewpoint for most approaches to language found today. The lenses he made let us see language as a symbolic system, a system used by a group of people in the here and now, one to be understood in its own terms rather than according to some outside standard. The system consists of signs that cement together a perceivable signifier with a meaningful signified. Those signs, in turn, are understood in terms of their relationships to other signs in the system, relationships that tie them all together into complicated networks of meaning.

Saussure founded inside-the-circle linguistics, a linguistics that narrows its view to grammar and dictionary, one that corresponds to the way most people think of "language." But, as you'll see shortly, he also founded a linguistics that erases that circle, a linguistics that connects inside-the-circle material with all those meanings outside. As we move along in this book, his fundamentals stay the same underneath the changes.

The changes to come are foreshadowed by our look at dive trips, restaurant orders, and getting dressed in the morning. In fact, Saussure helps anytime you come up against a perceivable surface—through sound, motion, taste, touch, or smell—and wonder what it means.

Saussure called his theory a *general* approach to the study of signs. He founded not only modern linguistics but *semiotics* as well. Semiotics is something you'll find in a variety of places. Film critics use a version of semiotic theory—what are the slots in a film, how can they be filled, how does filling one constrain choices in other locations? The world of fashion has already served as an example. Semiotics is everywhere. Advertising—what is an ad as a symbolic system? Architecture—how is a physical space a symbolic system? Washington politicians—how do I construct an image of profound credibility?

But semiotics isn't my job. My job is to erase the circle around language. Though Saussure is the grandfather of the circle, the growth of his ideas into semiotics shows that the circle wasn't necessary.

There's a problem that needs fixing. Semiotics does look outside the circle, but once it leaves, it looks at systems other than language—fashion, film, and so on. What I want to do is follow the other *linguistic* trail that Saussure blazed, the one that uses semiotic ideas to tie *language* inside the circle to the world outside.

Is there any reason why the descriptive, synchronic study of symbolic systems as social facts has to be limited to grammar and the dictionary? No, no reason at all. Saussure's vision of language stretches easily into a vision of culture. Hundreds of linguists and anthropologists since his time have made that case.

Culture happens when a problem in language has to do with who you are. It has to do with signifiers whose signification ties into identity. Consciousness *changes* when you think paradigmatically, when you imagine or encounter or learn other things that might have occurred. And once you imagine the new things, they have ramifications throughout the system because of the syntagmatic ties between the new things you've learned and the other aspects of your consciousness.

The circle around language isolates grammar and the dictionary, and Saussure helped to draw it. But his ideas, ideas that some linguists developed to help us see what was inside that circle, turn out to carry us beyond it as well.

The Circle and
the Field

FRANZ BOAS, the primary founder of American anthropology, didn't plan to draw a circle around language. He couldn't
have, because language was then just a *part of* anthropological fieldwork, and the point of fieldwork was to get to culture. Culture was
the destination; language was the path; grammar and the dictionary
marked the trail.

Boas talked about "culture" only as *what those people have,* as
a label for the shared beliefs and actions of some group. He had to.
In those days, he carried the burden of now-outdated notions of
science. He aspired to be the value-free recorder of objective facts,
facts just lying around waiting to be picked up with the right methods. In this view of science, the scientist disappears from sight. An
article or book had to be about *them,* not about *me and them.*

Me and them, of course, was what actually happened when he
did his work. When Boas sat down to talk with the Eskimos, he
noticed differences between himself and them, differences that
brought to consciousness ways of thinking he used to take for
granted. Boas started with "culture" *as a personal experience,* as a
problem in language that had to do with who he was. But then he
took the knowledge he created to extend his consciousness out to

understanding diff.

meet the Eskimos, and he called it "Eskimo culture." The trouble is, it wasn't theirs, nor was it his. It was *his-theirs,* but the science of those days didn't let him say that.

He said it in other places, though. In one famous passage, Boas wrote:

> In fact, my whole outlook on social life is determined by this question: How can we recognize the shackles that tradition has laid upon us? For when we recognize them, we are also able to break them.

This isn't Boas talking about the culture of the Eskimos; this is Boas talking about culture as personal experience.

Boas was born in Germany in 1858, a child of parents committed to the revolutionary ideals of 1848. He wrote a doctoral dissertation in physics on the reflection of light in water, but then he got interested in cultural geography. A Berlin newspaper sent him to work with the Eskimos for a year, and he returned an anthropologist.

At the end of the nineteenth century, he moved to the United States, where he granted the first American Ph.D. in anthropology. He eventually took a job at Columbia University and started his long career of research with American Indians. Among many other things, he founded the *International Journal of American Linguistics* and eventually wrote the *Handbook of American Indian Languages.* He died in 1942, heartbroken at what had happened in his native land.

///

Boas designed his version of anthropology in reaction to the excesses of the cultural evolutionists. Along with everyone else at the time, they were taken with the ideas of Charles Darwin, so taken that they extended them beyond the world of biology into the world of human society, along lines that Herbert Spencer had laid out shortly before Darwin published his famous *Origin of Species.*

If animals had evolved—from simple to complex forms, from instinct to intelligence, from grunts to the imperfect subjunctive—maybe cultures had, too.

The story of cultural evolution, like the story of historical linguistics, has complexities that I don't want to go into here. What I do want to discuss are a couple of key problems that Boas reacted to, problems that help explain how he came to think about language.

One problem, the one that horrified Boas, can be summed up in the chant *Bad Data*. Much of the raw material for evolutionary theory came from letters and books written by early explorers, soldiers, missionaries, and merchants—the usual litany of professions in the story of conquest: find them, defeat them, convert them, and develop new markets.

Competent as these people might have been at their chosen work, they weren't the most reliable reporters of cultural differences. They often suffered from the number-one problem and followed the deficit theory guidelines to keep culture at a distance. These people aren't like us; we're the best; so the unfortunates must be described in terms of what they *lack*.

Kinship is a perfect example of how things go haywire when the deficit theory operates. Many kinship systems around the world use the same term for father and uncle, mother and aunt, and brother/ sister and cousin. At worst, some early reporters concluded that "these people" didn't know who their own mothers or fathers or brothers or sisters were, probably—I'm launching into parody here, but not by much—because the "natives'" lack of Christian morality created so much confusion about who had slept with whom. The fact that anyone would admit he or she'd slept with anybody was a shock to some Victorian writers.

When deficit theory is the guideline, when the "natives" are evaluated only on how well they match the culture of the evaluator, it's no surprise to hear that a "different" culture would be ranked lower on the evolutionary scale.

Boas, like any other reasonable human being, understood that human societies had developed through history. Humanity started out hunting and gathering. An agricultural revolution led to settled communities; great societies arose in Iraq and Mexico and India, among many other places; colonialism and the industrial revolution transformed the world in fundamental ways; and now we speak of the information revolution and postmodernism.

Boas realized that this history could be investigated and analyzed to look for the ways society had developed. But turn-of-the-century cultural evolutionism was an embarrassment. A theory based on accounts of how "these people" weren't like us because they "lacked" the characteristics of the evolutionary pinnacle was about as loaded a game as anyone had ever played.

Boas labeled this error *ethnocentrism*, a term that has now passed into everyday speech. The early data on which cultural evolutionism was built was ethnocentric, because it measured a culture's position on a scale in terms of the culture of the one doing the measuring. The culture being measured had no chance to speak for itself, to reveal its own inner workings. If it tried, the merchants and missionaries refused to hear it, and they were the ones writing the letters and books.

Ethnocentrism

///

Here's a simple kinship example, taken from work I did in a village in South India, that shows the shift from ethnocentrism to the local culture.

In that kinship system, the father is called *baap*. *Only* the actual biological father is called *baap*. But the world of "uncles" is, from an ethnocentric point of view, a mess. Let's say the father's brother ambles by, and Nate Notebook, as I referred to myself then, asks what he is called. *Motobaap*, they say. The ethnocentric conclusion is that *motobaap* equals "uncle."

Another brother stops in, and the anthropologist, chest swelling with pride, points at him and calls him *motobaap*. The group members laugh, do the South Indian village equivalent of slapping their knees, and once again prove that the only reason Nate was ever tolerated was because of his entertainment value.

No, they say, he is called *kaaka*. I expect at this point that readers are having their own ethnocentric reaction.

Now, since a wedding is brewing, the *mother's* brothers show up from another village. Confused and perplexed, Nate tries *motobaap* and *kaaka* and gets that look like he just stepped out of a flying saucer. No, they are called *masi*. All of them are *masi*.

There are three types of uncles, *motobaap*, *kaaka*, and *masi*.

Since Nate was trained after Boas, he knows that the conclusion isn't that these people are confused, less efficient, or burdened with so much concrete detail that they'll never rise to the level of abstract intelligence. He knows that there is another system operating, one with its own logic, and that it's his job to figure it out.

And the system makes sense. *Motobaap* labels the older brothers of the father, and *kaaka* labels his younger brothers. *Masi* labels the brothers of the mother. It's actually more complicated than that, because the father's and mother's cousins come into the picture as well, but that's enough to make the point.

The point is that the father's line—the patrilineage—is labeled separately from the mother's line. And within the father's line, a distinction is made between uncles older than the father and those who are younger. The kinship terms differ from what Nate Notebook expected, because they dance with a system of inheritance he didn't know anything about. Property passes down the male line. The newly married couple live in the groom's village, not the bride's. The day-to-day social world in the village centers on the father and his line. And in a world where age makes a difference in terms of who has authority, a split between older and younger makes sense.

The mother's brothers, on the other hand, live over there somewhere. You don't see them much, and anyway they don't have anything to do with your inheritance or your authority figures. They're just a bunch of *masi*s.

The village kinship system is different for a reason. It is an alternative system that grew up with an alternative world of property and its inheritance. Nate figured it out—give him credit for that—though he tacitly assumed a male point of view, something that annoys contemporary women anthropologists no end.

Boas suspected that the early reports of "primitive people" often made ethnocentric errors and missed the point of the local system, just as Nate Notebook did at first. He started a "back to basics" program that looked with skepticism at the reports of the "natives" on which cultural evolutionism had been built. The key job of anthropology in the face of all the Bad Data was to go back to the field and get good data. Forget theory, at least for a while, at least until good information was available to build it on.

You still hear *Boasian* or (of course) *neo-Boasian* in the vocabulary of contemporary anthropology. It's a label for a position that emphasizes describing the culture of a specific group of people at a particular moment in time. Synchronic description, in Saussure's terms. It's usually not a compliment. In university life, structure is better than content, theory is better than description. It's one of the reasons universities are called ivory towers.

But when Boas founded American cultural anthropology, he looked at the evolutionists and saw the need for good data, for content, and that's the cornerstone he laid for the field I grew up in. His early students—one of the most famous was Margaret Mead—followed suit and built American anthropology.

Ethnography
= good data   ///   *Ethnocentrism*
= Bad data.

The business of going out and describing the culture of a particular group is called *ethnography,* a term whose Greek roots mean "folk description."

Boas's call was a call for good ethnography. He looked at his adopted country and called for an especially urgent kind of ethnography, not just because good data was necessary, but because the American Indians were disappearing.

Well, not exactly disappearing. The popular film *Dances with Wolves* has turned it into a cliché, but it's a truth all the same. The westward expansion of Anglo-Americans destroyed traditional Native American life.

Boas looked out at the reservations, at the kids herded into Anglocentric schools, and decided that an important agenda item for American anthropology was to record and preserve what was left of traditional Indian cultures. He sent his students off to interview older Indians about how it used to be; he wanted to build an archive of a way of life on the edge of extinction.

The early anthropologists set off, wire recorders in their Jeeps, to interview older tribal members about life before the White Man. In order to interview them, they had to talk with them, and in order to talk with them, they had to learn their language.

Saussure had worked with European languages, languages with a recorded history, a literature, and years of self-conscious prescriptive linguistic work. Boas and his students had no such luxury. The languages of the Indians were unwritten. They had to start from scratch.

And scratch meant starting with the stream of sounds the speaker produced, a stream that at first sounded like a continuous flow, as languages always do when you don't know them. Once the anthropologists had the sound system figured out, they had to tackle the grammar and write a dictionary. There were no grammar books to guide them. They had to build a synchronic description from the ground up.

For Boas and his students, linguistics was a means to an end. Linguistics was the work you did at the front end of fieldwork so that fieldwork would be possible at all. Linguistics was the nuts and bolts of the language—sounds, grammar, and dictionary—that enabled you to get on with your work. Margaret Mead wrote an article back in the thirties that told it like it was. She called linguistics a fieldwork tool.

///

Boas laid the foundation for *descriptive-structural* linguistics, the linguistics that became the American mainstream. This linguistics was etched in stone in Leonard Bloomfield's 1933 book, entitled *Language.* In that book, the circle around language was firmly drawn.

But in the shift from "fieldwork tool" to "linguistics," in the shift from linguistics as a part of ethnography to linguistics as a separate discipline, something important was lost—namely, the relation of language inside the circle to the world outside it.

Here's how it happened. In Boas's program, grammar was just the first step in a long-term ethnographic study. You figured out the grammatical rules and built up a dictionary, but that work was a means to an end, the end of learning about the speaker's *world.*

Boas was after culture; culture was what you learned from the older people who still remembered it; language was the way you talked with them and asked for their memories. The way Boas thought about language, the tie between language and culture was automatic. The tie was part of the research. Language was singled out for attention because it was a complicated problem that had to be solved before the job could get done.

But when Bloomfield wrote *his* book, language was ripped out of the ethnographic research program. The job of figuring out grammar was carved out of the ethnography and taken into its own private room. Linguistics became, primarily, the study of the sound system and the grammar.

Worse than that, Bloomfield ruled the study of meaning, *semantics,* out of the game completely. Semantics was the business of the experts. If you wanted to look at botany, you consulted with a botanist. If you wanted to understand society, you talked with a sociologist. Semantics was part of psychology, not linguistics.

Linguistics was about sound and grammar, not about meaning. American linguistics, right about then, drew the circle as tight as it ever gets. Even today, the tight circle is still the mainstream of most American linguistics departments. But more on this story, featuring linguists both inside and outside the circle, later in the book.

///

Not that there aren't interesting things to talk about within the circle. Ethnographers have published accounts of unique bits of grammar that highlighted the variety of languages on the planet.

Earlier I told the story of the pronouns for "you," *Du* and *Sie,* in Austrian German. It turns out that languages differ on the first person plural pronoun as well. In English, and other European languages, there is a simple pronoun, *we.* Other languages divide up the first person plural world differently. Ojibwa, an American Indian language, has one *we* for "you, he, and I," and another one for "he and I." Fijian has a *we* for "they and I," and another one for "you all and I."

Or consider the fascinating case of numeral classifiers. In many languages around the Pacific Rim, there is a bit of grammar that must be tacked on to numbers when you count things. The bit of grammar changes depending on the kinds of things you're counting. In Indonesian, for example, there are different numeral classifiers for humans, animals, large things, long cylindrical things, flowers, flat thin things, grounds or fields, grains and seeds, flat bladed things, sharp pointed things, long soft things, and things that can easily be torn or cut. So you can't just say "one knife"; you have to say "one-flat-bladed thing-knife." You can't just say "three guys"; you have to say "three-human-guys."

Cases like the first person plural pronoun and numeral classifiers show the variety of grammatical forms people have invented. So, even within the circle, the Boasian dream of showing the dangers of Bad Data came true. The results laid to rest forever any evolutionary approach based on the deficit theory, just as Boas intended. How could you rank a "primitive" language with complicated pronouns or numeral classifiers lower on the evolutionary scale than simple old English?

Boas used cases like pronouns and numeral classifiers to announce the principle of *linguistic relativity*. Linguistic relativity, and its more inclusive cousin, *cultural relativity,* summed up his critique of the Bad Data that the evolutionary approach had used. Grammatical differences existed, no question about that, but the presence of a difference didn't necessarily mean you could rank a language as more or less simple, as more or less "primitive," as more or less "evolved."

In fact, the difference might signal something, as in the case of pronouns or numeral classifiers, that was actually a corner of the system that was *more* complicated than the equivalent corner in the researcher's native language, even though the researcher supposedly came from a more "evolved" society.

The notions of linguistic and cultural relativity prevented simple evolutionary schemes. And they summed up the call to investigate differences as *expressions of alternative systems,* as the tips of different icebergs, rather than evaluating them against the American or European system of the researchers.

///

These principles of relativity annoy some people when they first hear about them, because they hear a call to *moral relativity* lurking underneath. If differences are just to be accepted, just to be investigated as an alternative reality, does that mean, for instance, that we have to accept the behavior of a Hitler as just another possible way of doing things? Is anything anyone wants to do okay, as long as it participates in an alternative system?

Of course not.

Linguistic and cultural relativity are *methodological* assumptions, a working stance to get the job done. They don't mean a person abandons all moral standards. They do mean that a person confronted with a difference investigates and understands its role in an alternative system, whatever he or she might eventually think of it in moral terms.

Hitler's a good test case, one of the monsters of history. How could he have happened? On a moral basis, you shrink back and condemn him to hell. But on the basis of methodological relativity, you start asking questions. Who was he? Where did he come from? In terms of what system did he act the way he did? In terms of what system did he gain power?

I lived through the Waldheim scandal in Austria in 1986. For forty years, the Austrians had considered Hitler too horrible to contemplate. He was locked in the historical closet. But then the presidential campaign of Kurt Waldheim, together with growing pressure from the postwar-born and their kids, dragged him out into the light.

It was a painful year. It was like dancing in a packed room full of people with freshly exposed nerve endings, their reactions depending on whether they or their kin supported, accepted, resisted, or were murdered by the Nazis.

In December of that year my Austrian "mother"—I'd been an exchange student with a family there in 1962—invited me to their vacation apartment near Innsbruck for a weekend. She started telling stories I'd never heard before, about being in the Nazi organization for girls, about her Jewish classmates disappearing, about bombs falling on Munich. I asked why she'd never talked with her own kids that way. Because, she said, they got so aggressive when the topic came up. After I returned to the United States, I learned later, she started talking with them as well.

When I next lived in Austria, in 1989, books, media, museums, and just plain conversations dealt with Hitler. Who was he, and how did Nazism happen? The new questions weren't all healthy, since Hitler-like sentiments surfaced as well. A formerly obscure political party, for instance, was taken over by a young German-nationalist type. He's no Hitler—far from it—but he says things that make a lot of people nervous. But at least the monster now appeared in language and the forbidden questions appeared on the street—how had it happened, all of it, including the Holocaust. Why had so many Austrians supported Hitler, and who were the unsung heroes, quiet all these years, who had resisted?

During that year a friend invited me out to a family house in a small town near Vienna. I'd met her during my previous visit to Austria, but now, for the first time, she explained that her mother was half-Jewish, that during the war she'd hidden in a town where people protected her from the Nazis. During adolescence my friend had started figuring out that she was part Jewish and finally got her parents to admit it. They'd kept it a secret until she forced the issue.

The family had held on to the country house, even though no one lived there permanently, to remind the townspeople of the Jewish relatives who had been arrested and sent to a concentration camp. We walked into a house full of ghosts, furnished out of the thirties, right down to the huge old radio that still worked. I asked if I could look through the place. I opened a drawer and lifted out an official paper turned brown with age. It certified the person's Aryan identity. I felt anger shoot through me and looked up at my friend, whose eyes were full of tears.

Even a Hitler, maybe especially a Hitler, warrants linguistic and cultural relativity, a recognition that differences between him and you reflect an alternative system that *must* be investigated and understood. But, for me and my Austrian friends and acquaintances—for most everyone—no understanding in terms of linguistic and cultural relativity warrants a *moral relativity*. There is no forgiveness for the sins Hitler committed.

///

Boas put Saussure to work in service of the study of culture. The study of a particular language was a means to an end, a step along the road to figuring out what the world of some group of people was like. Language inside the circle was left intact, but, by Boas's rules, you stayed inside just long enough to get comfortable with the details and then you stepped across the perimeter.

Boas represents the traditional anthropological way of thinking about language, language and culture or, sometimes, language in culture. Language—grammar and dictionary—stays *separate* from culture, and the only problem that remains is whether to hook it to culture with a conjunction of equality or a preposition of inclusion. Language is still something separate; the inseparable blend still lies off in the distance.

Keeping language separate, keeping the circle's edges clear and intact, allowed Bloomfield and the linguists who followed him to leave out the study of culture and go their own way. And go their own way they did, with a focus on sound and grammar and a neglect of meaning—even meaning inside the circle—that still defines the mainstream of American linguistics today.

Boas made inside-the-circle American linguistics possible, but he also set language into a relationship with the people who used it, a relationship that future linguists would develop into an alternative. What's still missing, though, is the *necessary* tie between language and culture, the tie that makes the awkward term *languaculture* an inevitable invention.

I know the term is awkward. Friends, colleagues, and my editor all squirm when it's used. I stole the term from linguistic anthropologist Paul Friedrich, who suggested "linguaculture," but that phrase keeps reminding me of pasta. I don't know what else to suggest. Everyone uses the word *language* and everybody these days talks about *culture,* a slippery concept if ever there was one that I'll try to catch in a chapter to come.

What I want to happen, what I want you to remember at the end of this book, is that whenever you hear the word *language* or the word *culture,* you might wonder about the missing half. That's the reason for the clunky term, as bad as anything Saussure invented. "Languaculture" is a reminder, I hope, of the *necessary* connection between its two parts, whether it's *theirs,* or *yours,* or, as it always is when it becomes personal, something that belongs to you both.

Cultural Signifieds

BOAS spawned two lines of descent. One of them bred the linguistics of the narrow circle, with offspring like Bloomfield. The other line of descent, the one I want to follow here with the work of Benjamin Lee Whorf, preserved the tie between language and culture. Whorf cracked the circle like the shell of a fallen egg, because he tied the grammar and dictionary into basic assumptions about how the world works.

Whorf was as eccentric a figure as the linguistics he invented. Born in 1897, he trained as a chemical engineer at MIT. He received only average grades, an inspiration to all students who never could figure out the relationship between classroom tests and intelligence. He worked all his life as a fire prevention engineer at the Hartford Fire Insurance Company, part of the same firm that nourished the poet Wallace Stevens.

I've often thought of applying for a job there. Maybe it's something in the coffee machine.

Whorf's personal adventure with culture started young. As a boy, he was fascinated with Mesoamerican prehistory and, like many before and since, plunged into that beautiful and mysterious system of writing used by the ancient Maya. Later in life, he slipped into a kinship with Buddha and Luther as well when his religion forced him into a concern with language.

Western history features conflict after conflict when scientific and religious accounts of how the world works differ from each other. Americans, for example, still argue over whether evolutionary theory, now around 150 years old, can be taught in schools, since it contradicts some Christian versions of human creation. Whorf decided that such conflicts were caused by bad translation of biblical texts, and that if he went back to the originals, the conflicts would disappear.

His work as a fire prevention engineer took him on the road all the time, and, the story goes, he would find the local library in the evening and work on the questions that so fired his imagination. Quite a difference from the contemporary road life—dinner in a motel restaurant, drinks in the bar, followed by hours of sitcoms on the TV.

Whorf paid attention to his own language as well. According to one famous story about his work as a fire prevention engineer, he went to investigate an accident at a factory. A fire started when someone threw a match into drums that had gas fumes in them. Over the drums was a sign, EMPTY GAS DRUMS. The word *empty,* Whorf concluded, caused people to think the drums were safe. A single word, one whose meaning lurked in the unconscious, had *caused* people to see the situation in a certain way.

He published his first academic paper in 1928 and decided to try for a grant to do research in Mexico. He figured he had the chance of the proverbial snowball in hell, since he didn't have a Ph.D., but his work had grabbed the attention of the academics and he won the award. The Hartford Fire Insurance Company gave him leave to do his research. Later, when he became better known, Whorf would receive offers from universities. He always shrugged them off, figuring he had a comfortable job he enjoyed, one that allowed him more independence to pursue his work than an academic position would.

When Edward Sapir, a student of Boas, came to Yale in 1931, Whorf took his course in American Indian linguistics. Sapir, a mystical figure, part poet, part scientist, deserves a book of his own; he wrote several and had several written about him.

For now, the important thing about Sapir is that the second

name of the famous Sapir-Whorf hypothesis appears. For Whorf, the important thing was that he entered the territory of anthropological linguistics. Up until then, he'd been self-taught. There are advantages to that, such as the development of a fresh perspective unhindered by the weighty jargon of the experts. But there are disadvantages as well, because one keeps reinventing wheels that are already available, if not discarded, in the shop.

Sapir got Whorf interested in the Hopi Indians, and he began working on the Hopi language with an Indian who lived in New York City. I always imagine the two of them, hunched over a notebook on a vinyl table in a coffee shop at Eighth Avenue and Forty-fifth Street, working out Hopi verb conjugations.

Eventually Whorf set up a series of visits to the Hopi reservation. His work with the Hopi language led him to the famous hypothesis that bears his name. He didn't stop there, though. Later in life he got interested in Hindu philosophy, founded a journal, and worked on nonmechanistic economic theories. This fascinating eccentric died young, at forty-four, in 1941.

I wish I'd had the chance to meet him. Funny, I don't have that feeling so strongly about Saussure or Boas, but I do about Whorf.

///

Whorf used the Hopi language in many of his most famous papers. He argued that Hopi was a "timeless" language. In fact, in one fascinating article he argued that had the Hopi the proper institutional support, they would have come up with the theory of relativity, no problem.

The Hopi, said Whorf, don't objectify time. Time isn't a thing or a substance that you can divide into units and count. The Hopi can't say "hang on a minute" or "see you in a couple of days." Time isn't a separate entity. It's part of the flow of events.

Whorf used several different parts of Hopi grammar and vocabulary to make his point. For example, he looked at Hopi verbs. When English speakers use a verb, they *have to* put on a tense marker. There's no choice. Did the event marked by the verb happen before, during, or after the time of speaking or the time of some other event that one is talking about? English speakers have to pay attention to *time* when they use a verb.

When the Hopi speak, they mark the verb with a bit of grammar, too. But, said Whorf, the marks they put on have to do not with *time,* but with *validity.* The Hopi don't care when the event happened with reference to the time they tell you about it; what they do care about is what the evidence is that supports what they say.

So, for example, one way a Hopi might say "he runs" is *wari.* But *wari* doesn't mean "he + run + present tense." *Wari* means "running, statement of *fact*." *Wari* could mean he runs, he ran, he used to run, as long as the statement was based on what the speaker and hearer both knew to be a fact.

The Hopi said "run" in other ways as well. *Era wari* means "running, statement of fact from memory." So "he ran" would change from *wari* if the hearer had seen the same thing to *era wari* if the hearer wasn't there but the speaker was. *Warikni* means "running, statement of expectation." In other words, given the flow of events, the speaker expects running to happen. As a final example, *warikngwe* means "running, statement of law." In other words, the person I'm talking about was in a race, so naturally when I say he's running it's true.

Because of their verb system, and the other areas of grammar and vocabulary that Whorf looked at, he argued that a speaker of American English and a speaker of Hopi live in different worlds. The American chugs along in his world of clocks and calendars, the Hopi in a world of events that happen.

The question that Whorf pondered is, *Are the two living in the same world at all?*

///

When I lived on a Greek island a few summers ago, I worked on demotic Greek. In the few months I was there, I only achieved the advanced beginner stage, but even to get that far I had to deal with *aspect.* Whatever tense you happen to be in in modern Greek, you have to worry about aspect, the difference between what the grammar books call perfect and imperfect.

Perfect aspect is a piece of grammar you hang on a verb to say that the event being talked about is a closed unit, a piece of action complete in itself. "I *wrote* this book." It happened, the whole thing, it's over and done with.

Imperfect aspect is a piece of language you hang on a verb to say that the event being talked about is something in process, something that's going on. "I *was writing* this book." It was happening, a part of an unfinished process, it wasn't done yet. There were days when it felt like it might never end.

Though both languages have the perfect and imperfect, modern Greek is more insistent on the distinction than American English. Perfect versus imperfect aspect is a part of the grammar that you have to attend to every time you use a verb, no matter what. Every time you speak, you have to choose between perfect and imperfect in order to pick the right verb form. There's no escape.

As I tried to learn Greek, I found myself attending more than usual to the aspect of the verb I was about to use. In other words, I thought more—at first consciously, then with time automatically— about the world that I was pushing into speech. Was I talking about a world of results or a world of processes, a finished world or an ongoing world? The answer told me which verb form to choose.

Perfect and imperfect aspect are classic pieces of grammar. Greek, unlike my native English, forced me to pay attention to the world I spoke of in different ways, because the grammar focused the choice for me. I started to look at things in terms of results and processes more self-consciously than I had in English.

The question that Whorf would ask is the same one he asked about Hopi and Americans, namely, if I compare me in American English with me in demotic Greek, *are the two ways of seeing the world that go with the language the same thing at all?*

But notice how the Whorfian question has changed. In the example of Hopi time, the question was, can two *separate* languacultures ever be connected? In the example of Greek aspect, the question turned into, can a person from one languaculture connect with the meanings in a second? Whorf thought in terms of the first question, in terms of distinct cultures, just as Boas had. And, just like Boas, he neglected the source of it all, his *experience* of the Hopi, in that imagined New York coffee shop as well as on the reservation. Slowly but surely, we shift to the second question: How does a *person* make the connections, when culture becomes *personal*?

///

Whorf still thought of language as grammar and vocabulary. But grammar and vocabulary took on a significance that ran well beyond the meanings that Bloomfield had stripped away. What they signified lay well outside the circle's edges.

Whorf looked at grammar and vocabulary, noticed the differences between one language and another, and said that they were more than just arbitrary differences that let you talk about the same, objective world.

The differences make you live in *a different world*.

This is strong, subversive stuff. The world can't be separated from the language used to talk about it. They're wrapped up together like hydrogen and oxygen in water. You can't pull them apart and still have water to drink.

Objective reality disappears in the mist. Two different languages aren't just alternative ways to talk about the same reality. Alternative languages carry with them a different theory of what reality in fact is. A shift from one language to another is a shift between two different worlds, where speakers of each one think their version is "objective," but they're both wrong.

As one of the most famous formulations of Whorf's ideas put it:

> Human beings do not live in the objective world alone, nor alone in the world of social activity as ordinarily understood, but are very much at the mercy of the particular language which has become the medium of expression for their society. It is quite an illusion to imagine that one adjusts to reality essentially without the use of language and that language is merely an incidental means of solving specific problems of communication or reflection. The fact of the matter is that the "real world" is to a large extent unconsciously built up on the language habits of the group. . . . We see and hear and otherwise experience very largely as we do because the language habits of our community predispose certain choices of interpretation.

These words are actually Sapir's, not Whorf's. By the time this famous quote appeared, the argument that language shaped the world rather than simply reflecting it had acquired its name, the Sapir-Whorf hypothesis.

///

After Whorf published his pioneering work, a minor industry grew up interpreting what it was he actually meant. One version of what he meant we can call radical Whorf. According to radical Whorf, you grow up in a language, and that language shapes the way you see the world, the way you think about it, the *consciousness* you have of it. The language you grow up with *determines* your view of things. This version of the Whorfian hypothesis goes by the name of *linguistic determinism*.

Language is a prison with no hope of parole. Translation and bilingualism are impossible. Even if you think you understand another world, you're just kidding yourself, because the very consciousness you think you have is constructed only insofar as the chains of your native language allow it.

There are some problems with linguistic determinism. The first problem is, how did Whorf write articles about Hopi, in English, if it's true? How can you talk about Hopi meanings in any other language at all?

The second problem is, if linguistic determinism were true, how would you ever test it? If you're trapped by your language, any test you devise would be trapped by it as well.

The third problem is that people do translate things and bilinguals do exist. True, perfect translation and perfect bilingualism might be difficult; at least I think they are, and I'm not the only one. But lack of perfection doesn't mean the task is impossible.

And finally, what about Whorf's interpretations of his data, like the Hopi verb example I showed you? Don't "expectation" and "memory" look a little bit like "future" and "past"? Aren't there similarities that weave the differences together?

So, death to linguistic determinism. If it were true, we could never know it, and there's plenty of evidence that it's not true, at least not as I've simply stated it here.

///

The weaker version of the Sapir-Whorf hypothesis is called *linguistic relativity,* the same term that Boas used. Language isn't a prison; it's a room you're comfortable with, that you know how to move around in. You know that the dress shirts are next to the socks in the third drawer down. But familiarity doesn't mean you can't ever exist in a different room; it does mean it'll take awhile to figure it out, because it's not what you're used to.

A friend of mine, a psychologist, told me how, in the frequent dilemma of modern American life, he and his wife wound up with jobs in two different cities. They shopped around until they found a second apartment that was as similar to their old apartment as possible. They furnished them the same, even put dishes in the same place in the cupboards, the TV in the same corner, and so on.

It's one of the reasons I never went into psychology. They standardize everything.

Linguistic relativity says that your language is the familiar room, the usual way of seeing the world and talking about it. Your language lays down habitual patterns of seeing and thinking and talking when you learn its grammar and vocabulary. But it doesn't *have to be* a prison.

Culture is the parole from the Whorfian prison. Culture is exactly what happens when you realize that the room you grew up in is only one of several, that other languages lay down other habitual patterns of seeing and thinking and talking and acting.

It's not impossible to move from one to another, but it's not easy, either. Bilinguals exist, but they say there are times when it's like living in two different worlds. Translators and interpreters can translate, but they complain about it a lot. In fact, one of their major complaints is that most monolinguals look at them as sort of advanced secretaries—"Here, put this into Czech for me, will you? I'll be back after lunch." What anyone who's done translation knows is how difficult it is to render the view of one world in terms of another. As far as translators and interpreters are concerned, monolinguals are terminal number-one types.

Differences in language and culture *are* tied together. But the differences, as they say in the divorce laws, are *not* irreconcilable. The differences can be connected, but forging the connections requires a change in consciousness. What Whorf didn't work out was, where are the points of connection? How can the connections be forged? True, he figured it out personally when he sat down with the Hopi Indian in New York and worked out verb conjugations. But he never made the experience part of his theory. Like Boas, he worked at a time when the researcher wasn't allowed to be part of the research.

///

One of the saner tests of Whorf's ideas was put together by Roger Brown, a social psychologist, and Eric Lenneberg, a neurobiologist. After they'd read Whorf, they were fascinated with the argument for linguistic relativity. So they designed an experiment.

I'm not wild about experiments. Generally, experiments are a hermetically sealed world of the experimenters' design. They lure people into it, assume they take it seriously, and ask them to do something ridiculous that they wouldn't ordinarily do in their daily lives if you paid them. Well, maybe if you paid them.

This doesn't strike me as the most direct approach to understanding the human situation. As someone, I can't remember whom, once said, "The greatest source of information about the real world is, in fact, the real world."

But the experiments Brown and Lenneberg did *are* a nice location to show how Whorf works. They show how Whorf works because the experimenters figured out a human *similarity* in terms of which differences in color perception from languaculture to languaculture could be compared. Brown and Lenneberg used a color spectrum, the rainbow squashed into a rectangle of color. The spectrum is divided into chips, so you can lift chips out and show them to people.

Then they invented two measurements that applied to each chip. One measurement they called *codability*. Codability means, how easy is it to name that chip in some language? Say you lift out a solid red chip and show it to me. I tell you it's called "red." Then you lift out a strange-colored chip and show it to me. I say, well, it's sort of the color of a sunset in Cozumel after it's rained. My language offered "red" for the one chip, but I had to make up a phrase for the second. The first chip is more *codable,* easier to say, than the other.

The second measurement they invented was *availability*. Here's

one way they measured it. You show me a chip. I stare at it, wondering what's the point. Then you take the chip away, toss it in a
cookie sheet full of chips, shake them around, and ask me to pick
out the chip you'd shown me earlier. How well do I do at this task?
The better I do, said Brown and Lenneberg, the more *available* the
concept. In other words, available concepts are right there, well oiled
and warmed up and ready to use.

So, by now you've guessed the results. Brown and Lenneberg said
that if Whorf is right, then the more codable the concept, the more
available it should be. If a language packages the concept in a neat
container that's easy and frequently used, like "red," that means the
concept is more available to the speaker of that language than others
that are more difficult to code.

As Whorf said, your language makes some things easier to do
than others. And that's the way it turned out. The hearts of the
linguistic relativists soared like eagles.

That first experiment was performed with native speakers of
American English. How would the test look in a different culture
where codability was different? Lenneberg teamed up with anthropologist Jack Roberts to find out. They took the original experiment
and transported it to the Zuni Indians in the American Southwest.

The Zuni have a single color term for the yellow and orange part
of the spectrum. In other words, the yellow-orange part of the spectrum is less codable in Zuni than in English. So, the experimenters
reasoned, if they did the same tests they'd done before, only this
time on a group whose color vocabulary was less *codable* in a particular area, then the results should show that the color category
was less *available* as well.

English speakers should do better in the yellow-orange area, not
because they are any smarter, not because they can see differences
that the Zuni can't, but just because their language makes those
concepts more available to them.

And by now it will come as no great shock to you to learn that
that's exactly what the researchers found. Even better, it turned out
that the monolingual Zuni had the lowest yellow-orange availability
scores, the bilingual Zuni-English came next, and the monolingual
English-speaking Indians had scores just like those of non-Zuni native speakers of English.

Language lays down comfortable ruts of perception, and people by and large stay inside them. They know the ruts, function quickly and efficiently within them. It isn't that they can't go outside them, but when they do, it takes some time and energy. And we all know how most people react when you ask them for a little time and energy.

Language carries with it patterns of seeing, knowing, talking, and acting. Not patterns that imprison you, but patterns that mark the easier trails for thought and perception and action. Linguistic relativity, the weaker form of the Sapir-Whorf hypothesis, soared skyward on the evidence.

///

Whorf thought of language as words and grammatical constructions, just as Bloomfield did. But Bloomfield banished semantics from linguistics, while Whorf stretched semantics well beyond the edge of the circle into the world of the speaker.

Whorf thought of culture as something "those people" have, just as Boas did. But Boas viewed language as a means to the end of culture, while Whorf wired language and culture into a single circuit. The way things worked in the grammar and the dictionary were the same as the way things worked in the world. *Meaning* became a thread that tied language and culture together.

With Whorf, the term *languaculture* starts to make sense. What Whorf studied wasn't just language. He used language as the signifier, but the signifieds ran on up to the basic assumptions about what is *significant* in the world at large. The two—language and basic assumptions—were bound up so tightly that it didn't make sense to talk about "language" in any traditional way anymore.

Saussure said that ways of studying language could be used to study other kinds of sign systems; Boas said the study of language was a means to the end of studying culture. But Whorf said that studying language and studying culture *were the same thing.*

Whorf showed that language—or languaculture, as I want to start saying now—shapes *consciousness,* shapes ways of seeing and acting, ways of thinking and feeling. When one realizes this truth, when one's own way comes to consciousness and alternatives become possible, then the concept of culture as something that happens to a person, instead of something "those people" have, starts to make sense.

Whorf didn't take that final step. The time wasn't right. To take it, to look at culture as what happens to a person when differences rear their fascinating heads, we still have the problem of *connecting* one languaculture with another, of finding the tie that lets one explore the new consciousness.

In the radical form of Whorf's argument, linguistic determinism, connections just aren't possible. In the weaker argument, linguistic relativity, differences exist, but they aren't insurmountable. But if two different symbolic systems, two different kinds of consciousness, two different languacultures, come into contact, how can they be connected?

The color studies hold the clue. The color studies used the color spectrum as an anchor for the comparison. The spectrum taps into something that comes with the human species, the ability to perceive colors. The spectrum, the human *similarity,* made it possible to investigate *differences,* the various color vocabularies that languages offer their speakers.

That's the secret, that's how languacultures can be connected, that's how a person can experience culture. The foreground of differences is organized against the background of similarities. You unravel the ways that you and they are *not* alike until you find a place where you and they *are* alike. When you find similarities, when you reach common ground, then you can start work on the bridge to cross the space between you and them—as long as "they" are willing to lend you a hand.

Similarities and
Differences

A WHILE ago I mentioned the kinship system in a South Indian village where I worked as a kid. I haven't told many
stories about that experience, and I won't tell many more, because
I did that work almost thirty years ago. At that point in life, I was
just trying to learn the basics of this languaculture business. The
ideas behind this book didn't take shape until much later.

But I remember that first day, standing on the edge of a village
that I would live in, watching the sights and sounds of a people
different from me doing things I didn't understand. The confusion
disoriented me. I felt like nothing I'd brought with me was of any
use. *Culture shock* is what it's called.

Then a village elder walked up, gestured like he was pawing at
the air, and led me to a wooden cot strung with rope and motioned
for me to sit. A woman walked out of the stone slab hut covered
with a thatch roof and handed me a hot cup of sweet tea laced with
milk. A man scolded a child and then picked him up when he started
to cry. Two women laughed as they strolled into the village with
clay pots balanced on their heads. A teenager walked by who looked
and acted just like my cousin back in California.

I relaxed. The people were different from anyone I'd ever experienced before. But enough had happened to teach me that our different selves had already touched, that connections were already there. The differences were overwhelming. I had a lot of work to do. But the similarities held out a welcoming hand. I sipped the tea and knew we had someplace to start.

The color experiments make the same point, only in a more focused way. Color is one of the favorite territories of the old linguistics textbooks. If you look at the classics, like Gleason's *Introduction to Descriptive Linguistics,* they often start out with color terms. Color terms are the great example to show how languages are different from each other. The same color spectrum, the books point out, can be divided up in many different ways. Nothing absolute about language. Each one has to be appreciated in its own terms.

What nobody paid much attention to until recently was that the yardstick used to measure the differences was a *universal.* Languages were shown to be different by hanging them on the same color spectrum. *Human differences were understood by holding them up against a human similarity.*

The standard human comes equipped with color perception. There are rods and cones and neurological circuits the likes of which I'm not going to try to describe. If you take any two chips from the spectrum, then if one human says he or she can see a difference, chances are any other human will be able to see that difference as well. Languages handle the differences in their own way, but when it comes down to just noticing, we're all the same.

Brent Berlin and Paul Kay, two anthropologists, wondered about the ties between the color spectrum—the universal yardstick—and the differences among languages. I remember them wondering. Kay was my graduate adviser, and Berlin one of the readers of my dissertation. I thought they were crazy, goofing around with people marking spots on a color spectrum. If I'd had any brains, I could have worked on a study that shifted how we think about language and its relationship to things outside the circle. I learned a valuable lesson—sometimes the research you don't understand turns out to be the most important of all.

Here's what they did. First they talked with a speaker of some language X and found out what its *basic color terms* were. A lot of blood has been spilled since their book came out about what makes a color term really basic, but for now just think of simple words that every speaker knows that serve generally to label colors. "Red" is basic; "reddish," "reddish-orange," "blood red," and "red of my face when I sneeze" are not.

Once they had the basic color terms for language *X*, Berlin and Kay laid a spectrum in front of the speaker. First they covered it with a sheet of plastic, though. Spectrums are expensive.

Say one of the color terms in language *X* is *garp* (with apologies to John Irving). They asked the speaker of language *X* to do two things: First, mark the single chip on the spectrum that is the best example of *garp;* second, draw a circle around all the chips that you could call *garp*.

Berlin and Kay did this with speakers of several different languages, and since their original work people have done the same experiment over and over again, with bilinguals in lab settings and with monolinguals in the field. The results surprised them. They surprised everybody.

Let's say a bunch of languages have terms that circle around an area of the spectrum that our first speaker called *garp*. Let's say that that area of the spectrum centers on areas that we would call red. I'll say RED here to mean it's not necessarily the same area that English would label with its word *red*.

It turns out that almost all languages do, in fact, have a basic color term that has something to do with RED.

So here's the surprise. When you asked speakers of different languages to point to the best chip, the strongest example of RED, they all pointed to the same one, give or take a few chips. If a language had a basic term that handled some part of RED, then the best example of RED was the same, no matter what the language.

What happened to linguistic relativity? Well, it turned out that, just as the classic linguistics books said, the range of chips circled to show how much territory RED could cover was different from language to language. *Garp* and *red* covered *different* amounts of the spectrum, but they had the *same* best example.

The heart of the color term was the same no matter what; the range of the color term varied from language to language. All those different words for RED zeroed in on the same best example, but the range of chips that RED covered was different.

Berlin and Kay made sense of differences between languages in terms of similarities that humans share. Before their work, linguists used the spectrum to highlight the differences. What Berlin and Kay did was to show how the differences showed up against the background of human universals of color perception, abilities wired into the eye and the brain.

///

In some ways things are different; in some ways they're the same. The trick is in figuring out which is which.

Consider the number-one types. They lean toward the "in some ways they're the same" side of the equation. The differences, they hold, are minor, unimportant. This comfortable assumption lets them stay firmly planted in the languaculture that molded their minds. Differences are trivial; really, they say, they're all just like me—and if they aren't, they've got some kind of problem. Culture stays locked out of the equation.

On the other hand, consider the strong version of the Sapir-Whorf hypothesis. It doesn't only lean, it plants itself firmly on the "in some ways things are different" side of the equation. Those different people live in a different world with no relationship to your own. You might understand it by becoming "at one with the people," an arrogant claim if ever there was one, but then you've severed the connection with your previous world, you've "gone native," as they used to say. Cultures remain detached; no possibility of connection.

Both positions make connections impossible, the one because everybody is just like me, the other because nobody is just like me. The truth of the matter lies somewhere in between. The truth of the matter recognizes differences and connects them in terms of similarities.

I remember wandering into my first anthropology class in 1964. I had no idea what anthropology was. The previous summer I'd worked for the California Department of Agriculture, checking grape vines for the dreaded Grape Leaf Skeletonizer. I'd driven into a ghost town in the hills around the Livermore Valley and pulled up in front of a restored wood frame house that a retired stockbroker and his wife lived in. First I checked the leaves on the few vines planted next to the house. Then the old man and I talked for half an hour, mostly about the growing civil rights movement. He made me promise to take an anthropology course when I went back to college. So I did.

I transcribed the first lecture and read it later. My notes told me of the truth of cultural relativity, which I think I'd profoundly noted as "how everyone did their own thing." But the prof also talked of what was then called the "psychic unity of mankind," that we were really all the same. Even then I wondered about what looked like a contradiction, but, you know, they were both in the lecture, so they both must be true.

They both were.

Differences exist, but connections *are* possible, and the color research shows how they can be made. Differences can be connected in terms of similarities, and the similarities exist because, at some fundamental level, we're all members of the human race. Your complexity makes you different, but your humanity offers you the chance to understand others, even to become different from what you were when you first tried to understand.

To experience culture, differences have to get personal. Similarities let you see through those differences and figure out what they have to do with you.

///

Whorf's descendants tried to make similarities more explicit. They took his truths and grew them into a way to use language to study culture. They did it by keeping his focus on dictionary and grammar and setting up some human similarities that let them approach different languages. I'm going to drag you through a couple of examples of how they worked, in part because they are my academic elders, in part to use some work from my checkered past, but mostly to show the powerful relationship of similarities to differences in a more precise way.

My elders revitalized Whorf because they ran across the same problem that Boas had, only half a century later. Boas, remember, criticized the evolutionists for comparing cultures before they really understood how they were organized *in their own terms*. His solution: go back into the field and find out how the world worked from the inhabitants' point of view.

But after a few years, people started to wonder. Eight million ethnographies later, after eight million studies of the local, internal details of some group of people, anthropology said, "enough already." Did we know anything *in general* about the human situation? Or were we condemned to pile study after study on top of each other and claim that cultural walls made connections impossible?

One person who took this question seriously was George Peter Murdock. He decided, in those days before the computer, that he'd take all the ethnographies that had been done, put them on microfilm, code them, and stand back and let the world of research ferret out the universal truths.

His dream went like this: Say you wanted to know something about housing. You'd go to Murdock's files, called the Human Relations Area Files or HRAF for short, and pull out all the cards coded for "Housing." Then you'd lay them out, look for the differences and similarities, and come up with a theory of how housing worked in the world of humans.

But then the problems reared their ugly heads. Different ethnographers paid more or less attention to housing. They looked at different things when they did look. They had more and less sophistication in what they knew about housing, both theoretically and practically, before they started their studies.

The results? Though HRAF produced, and continues to produce, some useful and interesting truths, it also showed that different descriptions couldn't be compared very well. There was no agreement on the similarities in terms of which differences could be understood. As a result, the differences couldn't be compared.

A lot of grad students worked on the HRAF project. They stumbled away with a Boas sort of attitude. The data were all over the place. You can't build general theories on data you can't compare. Ethnographers needed a theory of similarities to guide them so that they would collect data you could compare later on. Back to the drawing board.

The picture they drew was Whorfian. Culture, they said, wasn't what people actually made or actually did. It was what they *knew*. What they know, continued the argument, is a system of concepts and the links that tie them together. Concepts, goes the next step, are expressed in language in one way or another. Many of the concepts that are important, that are frequently talked about, acquire nice, neat linguistic labels. Think of the straightforward idea of "words" for now.

Words label concepts, and concepts are what you're after so that you can describe culture.

Pure Whorf. Words aren't just things you memorize whose meanings fit neatly into a dictionary. Words go well beyond that. They channel you into a way of seeing, of thinking, of acting. Words are the surface of culture.

[handwritten: → what it means is the signified.]

Pure Saussure as well. Words are the signifier. But now the signified stretches into culture, beyond anything that Saussure intended. And you look at the concepts in terms of their relationships with each other to put together a symbolic system, the kinds of relationships that Saussure had described years before.

And pure culture as well. Cultures are different, no question about it. But if you can just get a handle on a few of the words out there in the space between you, you can start into the concepts that travel with them. Everyone uses words—they're a human similarity. The words will lead the way into the differences.

Culture is a conceptual system whose surface appears in the words of people's language. That was the similarity against which differences around the world would be investigated. If everyone used the same framework for the similarities, it was hoped, then the results from different places could be compared.

My elders still thought of culture as something that "those people" have instead of as something that happens *to them*. They still thought of culture as a yardstick rather than a way to stretch consciousness when human contact happens. But they shined a spotlight on similarities and lit up some bridges across the differences.

///

Here's how it worked in practice. Say a Martian lands in an American town and notices that people talk a lot about primitive objects that move up and down strips of concrete. These goofy-looking things are obviously means of transport. Why they bother staying on the ground is beyond him.

Let's say he knows enough American English to get started. He hears a bunch of words used to label the objects. The list includes words like *vehicle, truck, car, Stud Macho Exterminator,* and *station wagon.* He's got a bag of words that label concepts, but he's not done yet. He doesn't know how they hook up together into a system, nor does he know what pieces might be missing.

Different kinds of links might hold the concepts together, and the links, like the concepts, will be expressed in the language. But instead of just words, links will be simple sentences that show how the concepts are hooked together. The star link that this new group of Whorfians used was the "kind of" link. A *car* is a kind of *vehicle.* A *station wagon* is a kind of *car.*

This link has a name. It is called the *taxonomic* relationship. X is a kind of Y. It's the same relationship you study when you learn taxonomies in biology. A dog is a kind of animal. A tree is a kind of plant. I can't do any better than that. I live in a city.

Why the obsession with taxonomies? Many of the people who founded this approach were interested in how traditional peoples conceptualized their natural environment. Traditional peoples, in general, live in a much more intimate and dependent way with nature than do those of us who live in Apartment 321 at 1850 Thirty-third Street. If you want to understand the "traditional" world, the world they see through their language, then the natural environment will be an important part of the picture. But for this example, since most of the readers of this book live in Apartment 321, including a lot of those former traditional peoples, I picked vehicles.

The approach I'm showing you here has a name. Actually, it has several, some of them unprintable. The name I'll use here is *cognitive anthropology,* cognitive because culture is viewed as knowledge. Among its other names are *ethnographic semantics,* semantics because it deals with word meanings, ethnographic because the point of studying meaning isn't to write a dictionary for second-language learners, but rather to learn about the view of the world that some group of people has. It was also called the *new ethnography*—an unfortunate term, because it implied that everything else was "old," but this is America, and "new" is always better than "old."

They called it "new" because it was supposed to replace the old ways of doing ethnography, the ways that had produced incomparable descriptions that frustrated the grad students who worked on the Human Relations Area Files. The new ethnography was supposed to ensure that ethnographies would be done in the same way so that their results could be compared. Taxonomy was a proposed universal human similarity in terms of which local cultural differences could be found.

Here the cognitive anthropologists differed from Whorf. Whorf laid out his ideas to put language and culture in an intimate dance, to show how language shaped the way one sees and acts. The cognitive anthropologists took Whorf's basic idea and developed a way to *discover* culture, a way to use the surface of language to get at and document the culture that it expressed. They changed Whorf from a theory to a method.

The method worked by using the links and the concepts to get more concepts. I take the taxonomy link, *X* is a kind of *Y*. Say the Martian, the one we left standing on the street corner a few pages ago, gets lucky and starts with the word *vehicle*. He asks, "Are there different kinds of vehicles?"

The person he's interviewing looks at him and says, "What are you, from Mars or something? There's millions of kinds of vehicles."

An ethnographer will tolerate most anything to get data. So he asks, "What are they?"

The person he's interviewing, it turns out, is waiting for a *bus,* so the Martian notes that term down. Since in most American cities public transportation lies somewhere south of neglected, the interviewee has an hour or so to kill. So he rattles off a list of words for different kinds of vehicles.

Once he's got his list, he starts with the "is *X* a kind of *Y*" routine. "Is a police car a kind of truck?"

The interviewee turns to another person at the bus stop. "You hear that? This guy with the green skin thinks a police car is a truck." He turns back to the Martian. "No, a police car is a kind of *car*." That, in simple outline, is how cognitive anthropology works. You use questions that represent links, words that represent concepts, and try to build a picture of a particular part of someone's conceptual system.

The study of folk taxonomies has a long and noble history that continues to this day. Since a lot of the anthropologists who used this approach were interested in how traditional peoples saw their natural environment, a taxonomy wasn't a bad way to proceed. It turned out that ordinary folks, just like biologists, used taxonomies to organize their experience, that taxonomies were apparently a structure that was wired into humans, ready to go.

Taxonomies tell the same story as color—you make sense of differences in terms of similarities. Humans all have words that express concepts and sentences that express links among them. Humans all organize some of their concepts into taxonomies. The actual words and sentences they use, and the way they organize them, are different from group to group. But just as with color, differences appear against the background of human similarities.

///

But then the complaints started. What about words that were linked up in ways other than the taxonomic ones? What about concepts that didn't fit into a word? And, most important, what did this neat diagram have to do with what people did all day?

That's the problem; that's always been the problem. Similarities are always too simple and differences are always too complicated. The academic tendency is to put together a framework of similarities and then go forth and understand the world in terms of it. With a good framework you can understand something of each piece of the world, no doubt about it. But each piece of the world won't *just* consist of *that* similarity; it'll consist of that similarity plus plenty of other things working within the system where the similarity is found.

The root contradiction of this languaculture business is that either you can go in with clear similarities and light up a piece of the world, or you can go in and figure out a lot of the world and lose control of the neat similarities you went in with. What people do is more than any similarity can handle.

As a student of some of the founders of cognitive anthropology, I was one of the complainers. I lifted up a piece of the world, held it up against the similarities I'd learned, and said that the similarities just couldn't handle the job. That's how it works with graduate students. They turn on you, sort of an intellectual Oedipus complex.

Some of my complaints started when I worked at what was then the main federal facility for the treatment of heroin addicts in Lexington, Kentucky. Therein lies a tale, but for now I'll just tell you that I landed at the treatment center in 1968, a newly commissioned officer in the U.S. Public Health Service, grateful that I could fulfill my two-year service obligation—against which I had no objections—without cooperating with the Vietnam War—against which I had many.

Like a good cognitive anthropologist, I started a collection of junkie terms, *junkie* being the term addicts used to refer to themselves, aggressively so in the face of straight people with a preference for euphemisms. I'd hear something that I didn't understand, get a paraphrase from someone, and put it on a note card. After a while I had maybe three hundred terms, words that weren't standard English that the junkies used a lot. I'd lay out the cards and look at them. The problem I had was that most of them weren't related to each other in any kind of taxonomic way. The similarity I'd learned didn't work.

Well, there were a few. One word, for instance, was *tie*. A tie was anything you used to wrap around your arm like a tourniquet to get the veins to stand out so you could inject heroin. There were different *kinds of* tie, like a nylon, or a belt, or a string, so taxonomy worked for that corner of the vocabulary. But most of the time, taxonomy just didn't apply.

On the other hand, the words obviously belonged together in some way. They were related to each other somehow. There had to be a more interesting thing to do than just alphabetize them into a list. So I figured it out a different way, a way that I stole from numerous others in cognitive anthropology and linguistics.

The trick was that most of the terms clustered around a *situation,* one that was unique to junkies, one they didn't share with the rest of us, the situation in which they injected the heroin into their veins.

How would you explain injecting heroin? "Well, I took this hypodermic syringe . . . " Except it's not really a hypodermic syringe; it's the top of a baby pacifier fastened onto an eyedropper with a needle slipped over its narrow end and a gasket of thread or paper to hold it tight. Wouldn't it be easier to say "I took the *works,"* because *works* is what that assembly is called.

Then maybe you'd say, "The heroin was so good, I decided to inject a little bit, then let some blood back up into the works, then inject a little more, and I repeated that for a while." Wouldn't it be easier to say you decided to *boot,* because that's what that process is called.

The junkies were just as Whorfian as the rest of us. Their language and their world grew up together in the same experiential space. Many of their unique words handled aspects of their unique situation. But how do you organize words around a situation?

Taxonomy is one similarity that helps understand differences, but its reach was too narrow to handle the junkie words. The solution to the problem is simply to add more similarities—new relationships, new links that tie together the concepts labeled by the words we're trying to understand.

One set of new links came from the grammar of Charles Fillmore. Fillmore argued that the way to figure out a sentence is to grab the verb first. The verb tells you what kinds of relationships different nouns might have to it. "John opens the door with a key." *Opens* is the heart of the beast, and *open* can take an *agent* who performs the action, a *patient* that is the recipient of the action, and an *instrument* by which the action is accomplished.

Here's how that all works out to make sense out of the junkie words. The general situation, the one within which the different terms play a role, is called, among other things, "get off." I'll ignore the problem of synonyms here. I'll also ignore that the term has other meanings in ordinary American English that you, the reader, no doubt are enjoying. In the junkie world, though, it labels the situation in which a junkie injects the heroin into his veins.

The ideas in Fillmore's grammar set up a new set of similarities to add to taxonomy, so that some of the other words fell into line. The *agent,* the one who does the action, is a junkie. The *object* on which the action is done is "stuff"—the heroin. The *instrument* by which the action is accomplished is the works. The *locations* in which the action can occur are a "shooting gallery" (a place you go to get off), a "crib" (someone's residence), or maybe just the streets. The *results* are numerous. You might OD or overdose, nod, get high, or just get straight, or maybe even get sick if the stuff is no good.

Laid out in a neat picture, Fillmore's grammar gives us this:

Get off	Junkie	Stuff	Works	Shooting gallery	OD
				Crib	Nod
				Streets	High
					Straight
					Sick
(verb)	(agent)	(object)	(instrument)	(location)	(result)

The words fall into line when they're organized as sort of a large-scale, high-level sentence that covers possible things that might occur in the situation.

I owed that one to Fillmore's grammar. Now, back to cognitive anthropology, where a few relationships besides taxonomy had been proposed. One of the neglected relationships was *stage-process*. One word labels a process, and other words label the stages that you go through to accomplish it.

When you cook, you buy the ingredients, organize the utensils, cut up the onions, brown the meat, and so on. When you go to work, you first wake up, throw the alarm clock against the wall, get dressed, drink coffee, get in the car, and so on. Cooking and going to work are processes that have different stages.

Getting off is a process that has stages as well. You cook the heroin powder in water, draw the mixture up into the works, tie off to get a vein to stand out, get a hit when the needle enters the vein, shoot the stuff into the vein, and maybe boot the mixture in and out a few times.

And since each of these stages is also a verb, they have instruments, locations, and the like that go with them. So we get this picture of the stages in the process of getting off.

Cook	Draw	Tie	Hit	Shoot	Boot
stuff (obj)	fix (obj)	tie (obj)	rope (obj)	fix (obj)	gravy (obj)
cooker (loc)	works (loc)		flag (res)	rush (res)	rush (res)
	filter (inst)		works (inst)	works (inst)	works (inst)

There's a couple of new words in there, *rope* for vein, *flag* for the blood that backs up when the needle hits the vein, and *gravy* for the blood-heroin mixture you get when you boot the stuff in and out.

A few words are still missing, some of which are in the taxonomy I mentioned earlier—there are different kinds of ties, like belts and nylons and strings. And a few other words are tied together by another neglected relationship from cognitive anthropology, *part-whole*. The works are a whole, as described earlier, that consists of the parts of a bulb, a dropper, a needle or spike, and a collar to fasten the spike to the end of the dropper.

///

This style of handling the dictionary isn't everyone's cup of tea, or cooker full of stuff, but the mix of Fillmore's sentence grammar and the neglected stage-process and part-whole relationships from cognitive anthropology tie together the list of junkie words I started with.

It's another example of using similarities—relationships among concepts that all humans have—to make sense out of differences, in this case, the difference between a junkie world where injecting heroin is the point of it all, and a straight world where no such situation exists.

But more than that, it's a story of avoiding the trap of *one* framework of similarities. When you travel into a new world, when you push against the edges of your own languaculture and start figuring out an alternative system, you *have to* use similarities. Otherwise, there's no way across the boundaries.

If you're a professional student of languaculture, you'll have a head full of similarities to use that you've learned already. If you're not, you'll still have a head full of similarities that you're using, but you might not be aware of them. So, the first problem, for the pro or the amateur, is, *What similarities are you using to see the differences with?*

The second problem, for pro or amateur, is to remember that any languaculture is much richer than any similarity can handle. If the similarity you start with gets you only so far, but not far enough, then add on more similarities, enrich the structure so that it can handle more.

The usual academic bias is to use content to check out the similarity, or, to put it another way, data to test a theory. My bias is *that content comes first.* If the similarities solve some problems but leave others confused, then fatten up the similarities. If they still can't handle it, then drag in the content anyway. Theoretically confused understanding is better than missing the point in a theoretically elegant way.

Chuck Frake was one of those students who worked with the

Human Relations Area Files at Yale and then went on to invent cognitive anthropology. He's been a friend and teacher of mine for years. He's the one who fooled around with relationships like stage-process and part-whole as well. After a few years, he watched cognitive anthropologists run off with a similarity and notice only what it would let them notice. It bothered him. He started writing about how the love of the narrow similarities got in the way of understanding what some group of people were all about.

Some time ago Chuck and I and another friend were sailing out of Abaco in the Bahamas. As we aimed into a narrow channel, we all studied the charts and planned our course into port. About halfway in, a sickening swoosh told us that the keel had run up onto the soft muddy bottom. We were aground on a falling tide.

Chuck looked at the chart and shook his head. "That's the trouble with cognitive maps," he said. Life is always more complicated than what they can cover.

///

The story of what happened after Whorf, at least this part of it, shows the solution to a problem: How do you connect languacultures? Cognitive anthropologists, frustrated by the different ethnographies they were supposed to compare, created a theory of similarities in terms of which different cultures could be studied. The similarity—taxonomy—worked, as far as it went.

Languacultures are different, just as Whorf said, and the differences lead their participants to see, think, and act differently from each other. Inside a languaculture, the way of seeing, thinking, and acting is the "natural" or "right" way.

But when a person from one languaculture starts seriously into another one, the culture half kicks in. At that point, with a self shaped by one languaculture and an interest in another, the problem of similarities and differences begins.

The new languaculture will be in some ways different, in some ways the same. The trick is to learn how to tell which is which. Similarities are where connections are forged, where the Whorfian barriers have their ports of entry. But differences are where the languacultural action is, where the barriers hold between two different versions of how the world works.

Similarities and differences work together to enable trips across languaculture boundaries. Confusing the two only supports pathologies, like that of the number-one types, or those who use a second languaculture to deny their own. Not everything is different when you go from one languaculture to another; that's the reason you can go from one to another at all.

Situations

THE diagram of junkie words a few pages earlier counts as a picture of junkie languaculture, a Whorfian picture that shows how language is the signifier of culture concepts. The picture works by tying together concepts of different types around a particular *situation* specific to that group. It also shows how a piece of junkie languaculture happened to me, how the use of similarities let me connect with and understand a world very different from my own.

Most important of all, it shows how vocabulary is *more* than a list of words you memorize. When people use words, they do more than just hammer out a sentence. Different words signal a different mentality, a different way of looking at things. In the case of the junkies, the family of words clustered around a situation I didn't know anything about. They highlighted a corner of the world that "those people" live in. No dictionary can give you that.

The circle around language broke when I hooked the words to the situation in which they belong. That's progress, but there's still a ways to go. The language was pried out of the situation *before* the picture was drawn. And the pieces that were pried out were those old, inside-the-circle standards, words and sentences.

Situation looks like an answer, but the question is off the mark.

The question is off because in situations people don't just talk in single words and isolated sentences. The *langua* part of languaculture needs to be stretched out, and situations are where the stretching gets done, naturally, by ordinary folks going about their everyday life.

Suppose two junkies are walking up the stairs in a tenement. They're going to get off, or use heroin. Here's what they say:

"Say man, you got your works with you?"
"Yeah, they're right here in my pocket. Don't worry about it."

There's a real situation for you, an example of what that neat picture of junkie words is supposed to be all about. What does the picture have to do with it?

A lot. From the picture you know what *works* are. You know why they're important. You can figure out why the two junkies might want to check and be sure they have them. That's what I thought, anyway, when I heard those lines. I figured it was sort of like a preflight checklist. "Works?" "Check." "Tie?" "Check." And so on.

I was wrong.

The junkies who produced those lines weren't worried about getting off. They were worried about getting *busted*. Works are illegal. Possession justifies arrest. When you're going into an enclosed space—like the stairs in a tenement—you don't have much time to run or get rid of evidence. When the enclosed space is an area frequented by junkies, you're asking for trouble, because every cop in the world knows you're ripe fruit waiting to be plucked. Illegal evidence plus no escape equals an easy bust.

The reason for the exchange quoted above is that one junkie is worried about a bust, and the other says that he can get rid of the works quickly if "the man" appears at the top of the stairs—they're right in his pocket.

The real situation isn't impossible to understand. The real situation isn't irrelevant to the neat picture I drew earlier. But the real situation and language are tied together in ways that the neat picture of words doesn't reflect. When I drew the picture, the situation was hauled in to explain the words and sentences after the fact. The problem is that the words and sentences were part of it in the first place.

In fact, the exchange between junkies in the tenement stairwell isn't *just* words and sentences at all. It's things that junkies said to each other while they were going about their business. Language in situations isn't the same as language in pictures.

///

Bronislaw Malinowski figured this out years ago. Malinowski was born in Cracow, in Poland, in the latter part of the nineteenth century. No sooner did he finish his doctorate in physics and math, complete with all the bells and whistles of the Austro-Hungarian Empire, than he went anthropological. He read Frazier's *Golden Bough,* a massive study of mythology that has inspired students ever since.

I don't know what it is about this field that attracts the science types. Boas was a physicist. Malinowski was a mathematician. I remember when I was a kid I went through all these phases—I wanted to be, God help me, an astrophysicist, and then I built a Heathkit amateur radio transmitter and bought a microscope. Out there in the dry hot California valley, I guess I was sort of a country-and-western nerd.

A few years ago, at a conference on computers and ethnography in England, a hard-core computer scientist from Australia stood up to give his paper. The thing about ethnography, he said, was that it was so rich, so complicated, so impossible, that it was the last interesting challenge for people of a systematic bent.

I guess that's it. The so-called hard sciences are really simple compared to any effort to figure out what "those people" are doing when you leave them to their own devices. It's the ultimate—impossible—challenge for a systematic mind. Plus, I think people are more interesting to hang around with than subatomic particles. Some of the time, at least.

So did Malinowski. He was famous for his interest in people. He moved in crowds. The crowds didn't always like him, because he could be direct and rude to a fault. But he had a gift, the gift of being a verbal backboard, a presence that inspired people to talk about who they were and what they cared about and why.

He had this gift, but he also had lousy timing. During his trip to do his first fieldwork, World War I broke out. When Malinowski landed in Australia, he learned that he was now the enemy, and the Australians informed him that he was stuck for the duration. But he convinced them that they should let him go and wander the territories, do a little ethno-exploring. He spent two extensive periods of time on a little string of atolls called the Trobriand Islands.

Malinowski became the patron saint of ethnography. He dived right in, lived with the "natives," and learned their language as they spoke it while they went about their everyday business. He talked about the goal of it all in romantic tones—"to grasp the native's point of view, his relation to life, to realize *his* vision of *his* world," or, as he sometimes put it, "to get inside the native's skin."

The name for his approach to fieldwork, a name that is now enshrined in the jargon, is *participant observation*. You don't just stand around and watch like a parody of a lab technician; you jump in and do everyday life with people to get a firsthand feel for how things go. At the same time, you keep a third eye at an altitude of several feet above the action and watch what's going on in a more distant way.

Never mind that this is difficult, to passionately commit to the flow of experience and keep your distance at the same time. The concept expresses the right contradiction. Besides, participant observation hides Malinowski's secret about culture. Like Boas and Whorf, he wrote about culture as what "those people" have. But participant observation carries with it a commitment to connect, to put your body and mind on the line, to engage what "those people" are doing and figure out why, at first, you didn't understand. Participant observation signals that culture *has to* get personal.

Given his gregarious nature in general and his devotion to participant observation in particular, it's no surprise that Malinowski came up with a theory of language that had no circles around it, none at all. How could he have? His first love was the real situations that made up the daily life of the Trobriand islanders. Language wasn't an isolated object that consisted of words and the rules for stringing them together into sentences. Language was the way that people came together in those situations and got things done.

Language was a means of practical action, and the way you un-

derstood a piece of language was to understand the situation it occurred in and the action it accomplished.

One shorthand term for Malinowski's theory of language, logically enough, is *context of situation*. Here's an example of how it
worked. A Trobriander actually said this:

Tasakaulo kaymatana yakida; tawoulo ovanu; tasivila
We run front-wood ourselves; we paddle in place; we turn

tangine soda; isakaulo ha'u'uya oluvieki similaveta Pilolu.
we see companion ours; he runs rear-wood behind their sea-arm
Pilolu.

To translate this, Malinowski says, he not only has to explain linguistic detail, like the use of "wood" as metonym for canoe; he also
has to tell you what the story is about, why the story is being told,
what situation it occurs in, and what activity it accomplishes in that
situation. As he put it:

Instead of translating, of inserting simply an English word for a
native one, we are faced by a long and not altogether simple process
of describing wide fields of custom, of social psychology and of
tribal organization which correspond to one term or another. We
see that linguistic analysis inevitably leads us into the study of all
the subjects covered by Ethnographic field-work.

It figures that he'd capitalize Ethnographic.

At its most radical, context-of-situation linguistics says you can't
translate, because language is so tied up with the situation in which
it occurs that you can't untie it. If you do try to translate, you have
to carry the situation with the language and find a corresponding
situation in the new language to carry over the same meanings.

As with Whorf, it's easy to get carried away, and, as with Whorf,
the caution against getting carried away is that translation is possible. Malinowski eventually explains, in English, that the Trobriander was bragging to his buddies after a trading expedition, the way
the guys usually do on the island.

The books he produced are still classics, beautifully written, rich
descriptions of a "primitive" people of the early part of the century.

And whatever sense of languaculture he'd developed growing up Polish in the Austro-Hungarian Empire, he refined it to a fine art. Like his fellow Pole, Joseph Conrad, he wrote in English, his second language, in a style so beautiful that it puts the native speakers to shame.

It's such a rush to perform in a second language for the first time. At the end of my year in Austria in 1989, I presented a lecture to the Austrian linguistics meetings. I'd written the whole thing from scratch, in German, for the first time. True, I asked a friend to look it over, but he knew my eccentric American/Austrian style by then, and I said that if it was understandable, leave it alone. He made only a few minor changes.

I had to read it—I wasn't good enough to improvise a one-hour lecture—but I remember thinking as I read, in German, "God, I'm in this weird secret code and these people actually understand what I'm saying. I'm *doing* something with this language."

Malinowski was the god I was referring to.

///

In the newspaper as I write this there's a Gary Larson cartoon, "The Far Side." In the cartoon, an ostrich sits at a bar holding a cocktail glass. He looks down from his long neck at the woman perched on the bar stool next to him. Here's what he says:

> Well, according to the dictionary, I'm just a large, flightless bird from East Africa. . . . But believe me, Doris—once you get to know me, you'll see I'm much, much more than that.

The ostrich might have been a reincarnation of Malinowski.

///

Malinowski didn't just break the circle around language by connecting words and sentences with culture, as Whorf did. He ignored the circle by dumping words and sentences back into the situations of their use.

Words and sentences have something to do with how we speak, though before the media coaches get to them, many of our politicians call even this fundamental assumption into question. But when people speak, they string sentences together, and some of them aren't complete, and there are all these other funny particles tossed around as well.

The other day I was walking across campus. Two young women of middle eastern ancestry were walking in front of me. They had obviously learned American English as their native language, and they dressed and acted like any other undergraduate students. Here's part of their conversation.

"So, like, you know, Ramadan?"
"Yeah."
"So I'm talking to X, you know, and like she goes 'Hey, Ramadan starts next week.' And I'm like, what do you say, Happy Ramadan, Merry Ramadan?"

Well, there are words and sentences going on here. Sort of. But you know, like, the first utterance has a bunch of particles and a noun, the second doesn't have much of anything, and the third has a string of things that I dare you to try to parse using a traditional sentence grammar of English. Yet the young women made perfect sense to each other, what I heard made perfect sense to me, and I expect most readers didn't even know there was a problem.

This kind of talk, and the Trobriand example from Malinowski I quoted earlier, and the sample of the two junkies in the stairwell— this is how people actually talk. Words and sentences aren't irrelevant, but they're obviously not the whole story, either.

Malinowski built a linguistics on how people actually talk, not on a sanitized list of words and sentences. Most of the time, most of us don't talk in clean words and sentences. And even when we do, there's a string of them, not a lone grammatical gem that hovers in the air. The way people talk in ordinary situations is called *discourse*.

You can see why Malinowski didn't catch on in the United States. He didn't just go cultural with words and sentences, as Whorf did. That was bad enough. No, he went on and said that words and sentences missed the point, that words and sentences, to repeat Boas's chant, were Bad Data. Any linguistics worth its salt would have to deal with discourse. Malinowski's celebration of discourse threatened the circle of language at its very foundation.

The Brits liked him, though. He took an appointment at the University of London in 1924. His ideas about language were taken up and institutionalized in the United Kingdom, preserved in a style of linguistics now called *discourse analysis* that we'll get to in some detail later.

Discourse analysis was laid out by J. R. Firth, based on Malinowski's work, and developed and refined by M.A.K. Halliday. The linguistics he founded takes social context and meaning for granted. I'm still thinking about what a different book this would be had I trained with him. I'm wondering, and will eventually learn, how it reads in the United Kingdom, since some of the book's arguments are taken for granted there.

This long struggle with inside-the-circle linguistics, with the way so many people think of "language," is about to come to an end. My hope is that the struggle against one languaculture will add something to the content of another, that working against mainstream American linguistics to arrive at a basic premise of Malinowski-inspired British linguistics will cast that premise in a new light. That's what this book is all about. Forging connections between two languacultures enriches the understanding of both.

///

The circle is erased. Meaning is back in, not just dictionary meaning, but meanings that stretch into the fundamental premises of identity. Language is reconnected to the situations of its use. Words and sentences are still around, but now they sit in the context of the discourse that contains them.

The *langua* in languaculture is about discourse, not just about words and sentences. And the *culture* in languaculture is about meanings that include, but go well beyond, what the dictionary and the grammar offer.

Here's an example of a bit of research that mixes all these changes into a single analysis of a critical Austrian German word. I know, I've got a lot of nerve talking about a "word" after the last few paragraphs. But as you'll see, what the analysis does is go beyond the word into discourse that exemplifies it.

My problem started shortly after I arrived at the Linguistics Institute at the University of Vienna in 1989. I wrote a letter back to my home university, and I remember that I closed the letter with a joke: "Well, I've got to go now and try to figure out which of two million verbs I want to use to say that I 'did' something."

I was forced into the problem because I was teaching a lecture course and two seminars for the Institute, and I was trying to teach them in German. Although I'd been an exchange student to Austria in 1962 for a few months, my classmates and I had spent most of our time discussing girls and soccer and rock and roll. Those vocabularies, it turned out, don't take you very far in lectures on linguistics and seminar discussions on political argumentation.

Some time later, my friend Helmut at the Institute—or should I say, formal Austrian rather than informal American style, my colleague Dr. Gruber—asked me to look over a lengthy abstract he'd written in English. He'd decided, for the first time, to write directly in English rather than having a German text translated, and the results were, in comparison to earlier translated texts he'd done, much smoother.

Our conversation turned to the difference between slipping into another language and staying there versus tacking back and forth between the two. I told him about my problems with "do." It looked like it should be a simple translation. *Tun* was of course available, and though it was sometimes the right choice, its use would often elicit a reaction that the expression was a bit crude or rough, if not imprecise or flat wrong. I had a choice among verbs like *schaffen, leisten, treiben, erledigen, vollziehen, durchführen, hinhauen, durchsetzen, zurücklegen, erlangen, vollenden, verwirklichen,* and *erzielen,* to name a few. I knew enough to appreciate that situations of use and webs of association hung powerfully around each choice, but not enough to produce and comprehend the right verb at the right time.

I often felt, and still feel, that inside of German, I am driving a powerful car on ice without chains. I move, but God only knows where.

Other English verbs are related to this list, translations other than "do" are available, and probably native German speakers will tell me I've misunderstood the verbs in the first place, which is likely and part of the point I'll eventually get to. But my intuitions were that going from English to German—in everyday speech, at any rate—often involved going from an English verb with broad reach to a series of partly overlapping German verbs with narrower reach. When I said that, Helmut (or should I say Dr. Gruber?) laughed and said yes, it was pleasant to take advantage of this going in the other direction. His intuitions, traveling from German into English, were the same as mine, that "do" could—excuse the expression—do a lot of linguistic work.

"Do" isn't the only problem. *Du* is another. The problem of choice between formal and informal second person pronoun, *Du* and *Sie* in German, isn't easy for English speakers, if you remember the stories from the beginning of this book.

Why am I telling you this? These anecdotes could go on and on. Anyone who's tangled seriously with languaculture has them. But the fact that they go on and on and that they are our common property is exactly the point. An anecdote is a brief narrative of a *situation.* An anecdote about language is interesting just because it sets up a problem that gets resolved in a mini-drama that involves some actors in some set of circumstances. The blend of information ties a bit of language into its situation of use, together with the conflict and resolution that bring to light otherwise tacit shadows of meaning. The anecdote, or more directly, the experience that it represents, shows how the proper speaking and hearing of language is in part a function of out-of-awareness interpretations that, if made explicit, would tie the moment into situations and webs of meaning that go far beyond what inside-the-circle language can handle.

Besides, I come by my confusion honestly. The emphasis, in my American training, was placed on the Whorfian tradition, the use of language—by "language" we usually meant words—as a publicly available source of expressions of underlying cultural concepts.

"Do" and *Du* are examples of words that jarred me with languacultural differences. They jarred me into another corner of languaculture, because I saw that my American English meanings weren't doing the job. I had to patch these signifiers into another system of signifieds. But to do that, I had to turn to Malinowski, turn to the situations in which people were talking to find the raw material for the new meanings I had to build.

Now I'd like to show how, for a particularly powerful Austrian word, the ghost of Malinowski lives. That maverick Pole, trapped on the Trobriand Islands by World War I, came home and argued that language was something people used to accomplish daily life, that culture—the sort of thing Whorf was getting at—was important, but that situation was equally if not more so.

We neglected Malinowski during my graduate student days, and after my experiences in Austria, I understand why. He was right, and his conclusions suggest that a proper understanding of languaculture involves so much background knowledge and reading of local detail that the claim to understand what somebody says becomes much more challenging.

Things like "do" and *Du* forced me to think of discourse and situation, just as Malinowski would have wanted. But I'd been trained into Whorf, with a love of words and all they could teach me about culture. So in Austria, I decided to try to split the difference. Sort of like a convert to Catholicism who just makes the old god a saint.

///

When you encounter differences, when you experience culture, some connections are fairly simple to find. Others, in contrast, are striking by their difficulty. The English verb "do" and the German second person pronoun *Du* are examples of contact points that catch an English speaker's attention just because they are problematic when trying to speak German. The concept I'm about to discuss, that of *Schmäh,* makes these earlier examples look easy. At the other extreme, many points of contact between English and German are no problem at all. An ashtray is an *Aschenbecher* and that's that.

The problem is Whorfian, with a simple twist. Unlike Whorf, the argument about differences is not a global one, that two languacultures, *in general,* constitute an insurmountable or difficult barrier, depending on which version of the Sapir-Whorf hypothesis you hold to. Instead, the argument is that points of contact vary—some, perhaps most, are easy jumps, some are traversed only with difficulty, and a few are almost impossible to connect. Rather than a Whorfian wall, a Whorfian Alps would be a better image, a mountain range with plenty of valleys and trails and a few vertical cliffs.

When two languacultures come into contact, *yours* and *theirs,* the most interesting problems, the ones that attract your attention, are the vertical cliffs. These cliffs are difficult because—on one side of the barrier or another, or perhaps on both sides—the problematic bit of language is puttied thickly into far-reaching networks of association and many situations of use. When one grabs such a piece of language, the putty is so thick and so spread out that it's almost impossible to lift the piece of language out.

I need a name for this location, this Whorfian cliff, this particular place in one languaculture that makes it so difficult to connect with another. I'll call it *rich,* with the connotations of tasty, thick, and wealthy all intended. Interestingly enough, this word and the connotations I intend work pretty well with the German *reich* as well, not to mention the Spanish *rico.* Maybe some European, or perhaps even universal, patterns of connotation are around?

The *rich points* in a languaculture you encounter are relative to the one you brought with you. The juxtaposition of English and German highlight rich points that a juxtaposition of English and Hopi wouldn't. And a native speaker of Austrian German might be struck by different rich points than I would be if he or she set out to study how people talk in a Viennese neighborhood.

One rich point that grabbed my attention was the word *Schmäh.* It had registered when I was in Vienna three years earlier. I'd heard the term, but in the flow of language that flies by I'd tagged it with a rough gloss of "put-on"—a concept that in itself would take a while to analyze—and left it for a future date. But in rapid succession after my arrival, I heard it several times, saw it used in a book review and a newspaper article, looked it up in a couple of dictionaries, and read about it in a guidebook. It looked central, slippery, and interesting, and I had no idea what it really meant.

I was assigned a lecture course at the Linguistics Institute, and I decided to pick a rich point, show the students some of the ways an ethnographer would go about looking at it, and then turn them loose. I considered the concept of *Schmäh* as a candidate. I decided to try it out. At a lunch with some Austrian friends, I told them I was thinking about looking at *Schmäh* in my class. You can't imagine the laughter, which of course was the first sign that I'd made the right choice.

Everyone at the lunch said it was a good idea. I asked if they knew what *Schmäh* meant and they all looked at me like I'd asked if the sun rose in the morning. Of course they did. But then, as we discussed it, all kinds of disagreements followed. *Schmäh* was Viennese. No it wasn't, it was Austrian, or universal. It was something men did. No it wasn't. It was more characteristic of the lower classes. No it wasn't. It was telling jokes, picking up a woman in a bar, manipulating a situation, what politicians did, a way of life. No it wasn't. Yes it was.

I sat back and listened and realized that *Schmäh* was about as rich as a rich point could get. I learned that richness wasn't just reflected in the difficulties in connecting it with my native languaculture, but also in the disagreements among native speakers when they discussed it. Because the putty was so thick and broad, different native speakers would take different interpretive trails through it, and that meant that they would then disagree over what *Schmäh* meant. The confusion of the outsider signals a rich point, but so does immediate native-speaker recognition followed by wild disagreement.

I asked the students in my course to do three assignments (how would I translate "do" if I said that in German?). I'll describe them briefly. In general, they constitute an ethnographic approach to a rich point, one that mixes Whorf and Malinowski:

1. A systematic interview in the tradition of cognitive anthropology around the concept of *Schmäh*. Such interviews take some similarities, like a taxonomy or the sentence diagrams in the junkie example, place the concept in the center of them, and then pose questions that represent relationships and place the answers to those questions in the appropriate slots.
2. A collection of anecdotes of *Schmäh* use encountered in everyday life. The notes that result are like the field notes traditionally collected in participant observation.
3. An informal interview about *Schmäh*. Such interviews allow native speakers to discuss the concept in whatever way they choose. Methods of discourse analysis can be applied to such data to make explicit the underlying folk theory that contains the concept.

The students were beginners, and so was I, so I make no claims to a finished study. But from our discussions over the semester and the oral reports that the students delivered at the end, I'd like to summarize what we found out.

Schmäh is first of all a basic cultural premise, a Whorf-like way of looking at life, a general attitude; and it is in this sense, I think, that one talks about the Viennese *Schmäh*. A notion that repeatedly appeared in interviews and conversations was that *Schmäh* was a way of looking at things, often described by contrast with the expression that it was *nicht ernst,* not serious, but a not-seriousness of a particular kind. *Schmäh* as worldview rests on irony, on the fact that things are not as they appear, on the difference between dream and reality, to use another Austrian cliché. And reality is cruel, full of harmful events and ill-intentioned others.

Several interviewees mentioned that *Schmäh* was a way to deal with grisly reality, a way to convert this reality into humor, a release of hardship—real or imagined—through laughter. In this sense, *Schmäh* has something to do with *schwarzes Humor,* black humor, and several people mentioned this. But the difference is that, while a particular *Schmäh* attitude at a particular moment might also count as an example of black humor, black humor isn't used to describe a general orientation to life. *Schmäh* is.

At this general level, *Schmäh* isn't directly connected to particular bits of discourse. Rather, it labels a wide-ranging premise with implications for numerous situations that do connect in a more intimate way.

But the term doesn't just label the basic premise; it labels two specific situations as well. In the first kind of situation, *Schmäh* is a humorous comment or exchange that arises from the details of the moment. Many interviewees emphasized that not everyone can do a *Schmäh;* it is a skill requiring intelligence and wit. And several mentioned that it is not "telling jokes"—a description that people sometimes give at first—because jokes are prescripted and *Schmäh* is not.

Peter Nosbers, one of the students in my class, turned in several examples, and I'll copy one of them here just as he wrote it in his paper. A teacher walks into the room with a heavy purse.

COLLEAGUE 1: *Hast da Goldbarren drin?*
TEACHER: *I oarbeit.*
COLLEAGUE 2: *Weißt eh, das is ihr Schminkkoffer.*
TEACHER: *Das, was du brauchst, hätt ich gar nicht reinbekommen.*

Translated loosely, for humorous effect rather than accuracy:

COLLEAGUE 1: What you got in there, gold bars?
TEACHER: I work for a living.
COLLEAGUE 2: I know, it's your makeup kit.
TEACHER: The amount of makeup you'd need would never fit.

Here's a second example. I was talking to a colleague from another university. He told me a story about an American who taught in German. One day a student came up and said to the American, "You know, your English has gotten much better since you came to Vienna." I laughed and tried my new expertise by calling it a *Schmäh,* and my colleague laughed in return, surprised that I knew the term, and said that was exactly what it was. A *Schmäh* on that American, and probably a *Schmäh* on this one as well.

There were arguments in class and disagreements among interviewees as to whether the *Schmäh* is *bösartig* or *gut gemeint,* roughly, done with good or bad intentions. It is easy to understand why. The exchanges walk the line between the two. *Schmäh,* in this instance, reminds me of the verbal game my friends and I used to play in high school called "cut-lows." My impression is that *Schmäh* is more improvisational, that is, that *Schmäh* exchanges must be more tightly bound thematically, whereas cut-lows required less tightly linked statements, in part so that certain set pieces could be used and reused. But both *Schmäh* and cut-lows rest on the ability to form statements that attribute a negative reality to the other, and they all walk the line between humor and insult.

I can't resist an anecdote that is particularly appropriate for the recent two-hundredth anniversary of the French Revolution. Among the histories of *Schmäh* that interviewees offered, one mentioned the Austrian wife of the French king, Marie Antoinette. When told that the poor had no bread, she uttered her famous line, usually translated into English as "Let them eat cake." The interviewee pointed out that Maria Theresa's daughter had just uttered a *Schmäh,* but the French, as history has shown, didn't see it that way.

A second use of *Schmäh* is to label a lie, again with disagreement over whether it is ill or well intentioned, a lie that is linked to some personal, instrumental end. Again the folk history is interesting, since interviewees claimed that this version of *Schmäh* had roots in the monarchy—the same one that inspired Franz Kafka—where one often had to manipulate people with authority over them to get something done. This *Schmäh* is something different from the first type. Such a *Schmäh* may or may not be funny, and the listener may or may not know that a *Schmäh* is in progress. One student, for example, told stories about how she used *Schmäh* all the time to deal with the university bureaucracy.

Another example, one that is funny, obvious to the listener, and an illustration of how a *Schmäh* may be nonverbal, goes like this. A man pulls up and parks in a loading zone. A policeman tells him he can't park there. The man walks into the coffee house, brings a chair out, and puts it in the car, drives around the block, parks again, and carries the chair into the coffee house. In this case the policeman laughed and let him park. The lie was obvious and humorous, but the goal was achieved all the same.

A final example. In my other two classes at the Institute, seminars dealing with political argumentation and institutional discourse, we used the transcripts from some legislative hearings as data. The hearings centered on a political scandal in which several Austrian government officials were implicated in the cover-up of a case of insurance fraud. When I told friends and acquaintances outside the university that I was lecturing on *Schmäh* and studying the scandal in the seminars, the inevitable result was laughter and a suggestion that I had organized things well, since the scandal was a good example of *Schmäh*. In retrospect, I understand that they meant *Schmäh* in this second sense, the *Schmäh* as a lie told to achieve personal ends.

To sum it up, *Schmäh* is a view of the world that rests on the basic ironic premise that things aren't what they seem, what they are is much worse, and all you can do is laugh it off. Such an attitude is hardly unique to Vienna. What is unique to Vienna is that the premise, with all its complicated strands, is puttied into a single piece of language, and that rich piece of language is, in turn, used as a badge of identity.

The *Schmäh* worldview finds expression in at least two different situations that are both labeled *Schmäh*: one, a humorous exchange growing out of the moment that is based on a negative portrayal of the other; two, a deception designed to attain some instrumental end. Both specific examples fit the general philosophy—things are not what they seem, what they are is bad, but the fact that the difference exists is not to be taken seriously.

The reason this piece of language appeared so rich—in other words, appeared so problematic when brought into connection with my American English languaculture—becomes clear. Over the course of the semester the students and I played a game repeatedly, trying to link a specific example of *Schmäh* with an American English equivalent, or with other German-language varieties like the *Schnauze* from Berlin or the *Schmoos* from Cologne.

Such links are possible, on a situation-by-situation basis. Assume I equated one *Schmäh* example with my old high school verbal game, cut-lows, glossed another as a con, and then linked the worldview with New York City. (I tried to link it with Washington, but the "humor" part doesn't work; people in Washington take themselves too seriously, though since Clinton's election I'll have to admit things have loosened up.) Would I have understood the concept? No, I would have destroyed it.

The reason I would have destroyed it is what this book is all about. I would have destroyed it because I would have taken a rich point, cut the putty at different levels in different ways, and reputtied the different pieces I'd cut into another language in a way that not only was piecemeal, but didn't quite match, or didn't match very well at all. *Schmäh* isn't really like the cut-low game; *Schmäh* as con isn't the right fit either; and though New Yorkers may be *Schmäh*-like in their worldview at times, they don't encode it in a word and celebrate it as a badge of identity. The glosses might work to get by a single example, but in general they'd add up to confusion and distortion.

And that would only be the beginning of the damage. When *Schmäh* is lifted out of the language, the putty that comes with it drags along the raw material for a complicated but coherent set of meanings with links to history and culture. The ease with which it is used in Viennese discourse to characterize situations and persons and verbal and written expressions is a testament to its centrality and power, as are the disagreements when people discuss what it means. *Schmäh* is a laughing surface laid over an ugly world, a way of seeing and at least two different ways of talking within it.

To use an expression I learned, one that you now realize is ambiguous as to whether I am denying a lie or denying a joke, *Des is' ka' Schmäh*. "That ain't no *Schmäh*." Some of this, anyway, is both serious and true.

///

Rich points signal where the languacultural action is. Rich points don't *just* happen in language. The other night I ate dinner in a Japanese restaurant. A tour group from Japan partied in a separate room near my table. When they left, they filed out, and the owner and waitress stood near the door. The bows—I'm telling you, it was a symphony of bows, different in how much, how long, degree of head tilt, direction the bow was aimed. Richer points would be hard to find.

But I'm focused on language, and language is loaded with rich points, since language carries most of the rich and complicated symbolic freight that humans exchange.

Rich points are easy to find. They happen when, suddenly, you don't know what's going on. Several responses are possible. You can ignore it and hope that the next thing will make sense. You can number-one it to death, take it as evidence that the rich point only confirms that whoever produced it is deficient in some way.

Or you can wonder—wonder why you don't understand, wonder if some other languaculture isn't in play, wonder if how you thought the world worked isn't just one variation on countless themes. If you wonder, at that moment and later as well, you've taken on culture, not as something that "those people" have, but rather as a space between you and them, one that *you're* involved in as well, one that can be overcome.

Rich points aren't just the territory of professional students of languaculture. Rich points happen to all of us, all the time. The pro might take a well-worked-out academic framework for similarities and jump into the space with it. The color experiments and the junkie vocabulary served as examples of how this was done. Similarities, to the extent that they work, save you a lot of time. But when most people encounter rich points, chances are they won't drag along a spectrum or a taxonomy. That doesn't mean there's nothing they can do.

Schmäh took me all over the Austrian German map. The most important data came from the informal interviews—translate that as talking with people about a rich point—and participant observation in daily life—translate that as going out into the world and actively engaging it. I do that more systematically than most people when I do a bit of research. And I write it up to make a convincing case to skeptical outsiders who weren't along for the ride. That's my professional job, to *document* and *report* in a credible way. But *anyone* who stumbles across a rich point—inside or outside their native languaculture—can, in principle, do the same thing. All you have to do is talk and listen and engage a different world with languaculture in mind.

Talk to people who produced the rich point and go out and sample their world. Nothing mysterious about that. If you work, and continue to work, with the people who intially surprised you with a rich point, the understandings that you craft, with their help, will grow more and more complicated and interesting. And when you take that new understanding and try it out in another moment of talk, their reactions will telegraph, loud and clear, whether you're on the right trail or not. When you figure out rich points, the grades come back directly, right away. The people who produced the rich point are the judges, the ones you're learning to communicate with.

If what you're learning doesn't fit neat similarities, if you accept the principle but let the narrow frameworks go, what are you left with? What are you building, if not a taxonomy or a picture of a situation? You're building new knowledge born of personal experience, a new awareness, a new connection between you and them that can take any number of shapes. You're building *culture*.

Culture

THE ghosts of Malinowski and Whorf guided us from the study of language to the study of culture. But "culture," what is that, really? It's two things, so far in this book. It's what *those* people have—Austrian culture, Mexican culture, Trobriand culture. But it's also what happens to people when they encounter differences and change their consciousness to figure them out. The two aren't so far apart.

Boas, Whorf, and Malinowski described the culture *of* some group of people. But to accomplish that, they drew from their own personal *experience* of a group, from the rich points *they'd* run across. Out of that experience they built a connection between them and the group of people, with their help. Without the experience, without the contact, without the personal struggle, without the help, they couldn't have built culture at all. Rich points crop up on the surface and signal the vast wealth below. To mine it, to build the new meanings to learn a corner of a new languaculture, *culture* is where you have to go.

What is this culture that you experience? And once you experience it, what is it that you've built? What is it made of, and how does it change you? How does it grow as you learn more and more?

How does it surface in language so that the term *languaculture* makes some kind of sense? Culture is doing a lot of work. It's time to deal with this conceptual monster. What *is* culture, anyway?

///

You'd think by now we would have figured it out. I remember when I was a graduate student, shortly after electricity was invented, I thought I'd take a break from reading articles about a burning issue that I couldn't make any sense out of.

I walked over to the *International Encyclopedia of the Social Sciences* and looked up "cultural anthropology." I approached it with all the arrogance born of insecurity that my grad student life was full of, crystal ego wrapped in barbed wire, figured I'd snicker at the *Reader's Digest* version of what I was studying and feel superior. The *Encyclopedia* went on about fieldwork, about a comparative perspective, about a holistic point of view. "Yeah, yeah," I muttered, as I returned to the serious stuff.

But just before I slid the volume back onto the shelf, I noticed that the piece had been written by the very graduate adviser I was about to leave, David Mandelbaum.

I'd been tinkering with what we then called "formal models," elegant steel structures of axioms that tied to multiple realities and cast universal humanity into stark relief. The goal was to build fine-tuned theories of similarities, with all the strengths, and all the limits, that you saw in the previous chapters. I was chasing Euclid's ghost, chasing the elusive badge of science, with background cheers from post-Sputnik America.

Some of you mutter, "What the hell is *Sputnik*? A Russian expletive that comments on the effects of *perestroika* and *glasnost*?" You're younger, and in America yesterday is history and last year is archaeology. One expression I hear all the time is "you're history," a phrase that condemns its object to irrelevance and insignificance. It's a phrase I've heard only in American English, a phrase that flags our short-term, fast-food approach to life.

Back then we were in a "space race" with the Soviet Union, sprinting to see who could be the first to sling a little steel ball so high that it would run circles around the earth. In 1957 the commies beat us, sent Sputnik up, and we stayed up late to watch it chug across the night sky and listen to its insolent "beep beep beep" on the radio humiliate us into technological inferiority.

So I grew up in an educational system that shifted into screaming scientific and technological overdrive, a system dedicated to "closing the gap," and with that competitive urge for science, aping Euclid looked pretty admirable.

David Mandelbaum, on the other hand, cast a jaundiced eye toward such an enterprise, an eye trained on images of India, where he'd worked for years. For those who haven't been there, India is a place where, just as you've hammered together a fragile generalization, you walk into the street and run into ten fascinating counter-examples.

He kept telling me that "formal models" were really quite interesting, that he'd always thought you could do a formal analysis of, say, sports. In retrospect, I realize he was teasing a bit, highlighting the limits of formalisms for those of us who aspire to understand the human situation. To me, master of truth that I then was, his advice smacked of sacrilege. The same man who scorned formal models had written this golden book of what cultural anthropology was. It made sense to me.

A couple of years ago, after two decades of silence, David wrote me a letter. He'd heard a radio program that featured a study I'd done on American independent truckers. The letter was loaded with congratulations and pride. I wrote back, told him how I'd learned from the weekly lunch meetings he'd held with his graduate students. I'd heard he'd been sick and was grateful that kismet had thrown me an opportunity to thank him, to make things right, in some way. A short time later he died.

Today I think the letter exchange was more cosmic than accidental. I think David's spirit had returned to haunt me because mine had finally grown closer to it. That spirit looked with amusement at elegant formal definitions because they couldn't handle human complexity. And, therefore, the field that took on that same complexity, cultural anthropology, could be built only with a list of concepts as massive and opaque as a row of sealed refrigerated vans of the sort I'd stared at during my study of truckers.

No one knows what's in those sealed vans. No one's figured out how to open the door. My own field of anthropology, the one I'm supposed to be trained in, is full of rich points as worthy of study as all the other concepts in this book, and *culture* is one of the richest.

///

The last anthropology meeting I went to, in New Orleans, I was hanging around the ground-floor Hilton bar. Why a field that identifies with the underdog and tends to the left insists on meeting in Hiltons is beyond me. But I'll have to admit that the bar was built right for people who prefer to loiter in crowds rather than listen in orderly rows of seats. It was open, easy to move around in, with a clear view of the escalator and the entrance lobby.

I landed on a bar stool, and a young anthropologist landed next to me. She'd given a paper earlier that day in a session on German reunification where I'd been the discussant, a good paper from someone who actually lived in the new Germany. A discussant's job is to read the papers at the session, study them carefully, and present an overview that ties them together and shows how, really, none of them are quite as good as he could have done. I enjoy it. It's a license to talk about something on your mind without reading from printer-paper pages crinkled and stained with apple juice from the airplane tray.

The two of us, presenter and discussant, talked about the session. Several anthropologists had presented their views of what German reunification was all about. The papers were intelligent and interesting. But, twenty-some years after reading David's article, I got it again in answer to my question:

"So, I mean, the thing I'm wondering about, did y'all . . . "

The meeting was in New Orleans, and I needed the second person plural that Yankee English doesn't provide.

" . . . really say anything about reunification that any group of intelligent people wouldn't have said? Did it matter that you all were anthropologists?"

She looked at me, then looked around the room, probably for someone she could go say hello to to get out of the conversation.

"Well, yes."

Then she read me the pages out of the *International Encyclopedia of the Social Sciences,* the pages that David Mandelbaum had written. She talked about how she'd used a comparative point of view, not only comparing East and West Germany, but those two nations with other societies she'd lived in and read about.

"You know, that's not in the paper, but that's how I thought to get to the paper."

She talked about how she'd made connections between things rather than tearing them into pieces, a holistic point of view rather than an analytic one. She described how ideas came from numerous conversations she'd had with "natives" from both East and West, the fieldwork aspect, the personal experience of culture.

"So I think anthropologists would see it that way, and other people wouldn't."

The striking thing was the litany, the sacred chant—comparative, holistic, fieldwork. She was right, right in the same way David had been twenty-five years before.

///

At one of my first anthropology meetings I put myself on the meat market. I went with the usual spoiled attitude: "Which major university will I allow to rent my body and jump-start my career?" We'd been spoiled by the sixties boom in anthropology enrollments. In a period when students looked at their own culture and shuddered at the sight of greed and aggression masking as values to aspire to, anthropology looked pretty good. Don't like your culture? Join anthropology, bask in cultural relativity, and head to the field to stretch out and explore some alternatives.

New faculty positions sprouted all over the campuses. But in 1970 the first drought hit, a drought that peaked in the Reagan era when greed and aggression won. A recent survey showed that, for the first time in history, more than half of the new Ph.D.'s in anthropology were working outside the university.

My first university job, the one I got at those fateful meetings in 1970 when the market started its downhill run, was at the University of Hawaii in Honolulu. People always assume you go to Hawaii for sun and fun. True enough, I jumped into the ocean, became a sailor and diver and bodysurfer about five minutes after I landed.

But one of the reasons I'd picked Hawaii was because Gregory Bateson was there. The late Gregory Bateson is one of my few heroes. I realize now that he is a hero in Joseph Campbell's sense, because he left the ordinary world on a quest, an inner quest, and then returned to the benefit of us all.

He was tucked away in something called the Oceanic Institute, not far from Makapu'u, one of the best bodysurfing beaches on the island. When I landed in the department, after I'd borrowed a schedule from the secretary and looked up my new classes to find out where they met and what they were called, I asked a colleague who will remain nameless for reasons about to become apparent where Bateson was.

"Well, he's not around the department."

"Why not?"

"He works at the Oceanic Institute. Besides, he's only got an M.A., you know."

Well, I thought, I'll just call him myself. Me? Call Gregory Bateson? I found his number and stared at it for a while. I picked up the phone and dialed, hoped that maybe the telephone lines had rotted from humidity or something.

"Hello."

"Can I speak with Gregory Bateson, please?"

"Speaking."

I said something intelligent.

"Mphnglrb splakldorf."

"Pardon me?"

I spoke with a nervous speed that he could decode only because he'd been working with dolphins. I told Bateson that, though this of course would never happen—watching a TV sitcom would be more interesting for him—I'd sure like to just listen to him read the front page of the Honolulu newspaper or something.

Ah for the days of heroes.

His book *Steps to an Ecology of Mind* was in galleys, and he gave me a copy of some of the original selections. He'd drawn on cybernetics, which he'd helped invent, to cast this elusive anthropology into a clear general light. True, he was a tad on the side of Euclid himself, but that of course suited me just fine.

We talked about anthropology, or rather, he talked and I listened. He said some things that I later found in his new book. He started the book with an essay describing his struggle, and I want to quote one passage at length:

Gradually, I discovered that what made it difficult to tell the class what the course was about was the fact that my way of thinking was different from theirs. A clue to this difference came from one of the students. It was the first session of the class and I had talked about the cultural differences between England and America—a matter which should always be touched on when an Englishman must teach Americans about cultural anthropology. At the end of the session, one resident came up. He glanced over his shoulder to be sure that the others were all leaving, and then said rather hesitantly, "I want to ask a question." "Yes." "It's—do you want us to *learn* what you are telling us?" I hesitated a moment, but he rushed on with, "Or is it all a sort of example, an illustration of something else?" "Yes, indeed!"

But an example of what?

But an example of what? An example of a comparative perspective, of holism, of fieldwork. An example of all the twisted complicated meanings packed together inside those sealed concepts.

///

One of the reasons I'm obsessed with culture lies in my own struggle to find home in the postmodern fog. Linguistics, once upon a time, was one of the "four fields," a sacred chant that anthropologists use to divide up their professional world: "cultural, linguistic, physical, and archeological" anthropology. Linguistics offered up a way to convert into a grammar an incomprehensible stream of sounds among the nonliterate unstudied people you approached. Earlier I mentioned Margaret Mead's article that called it what it was, a fieldwork tool. Since you can find a grammar of almost anything now, demand for this trick has dropped considerably.

Then Noam Chomsky converted linguistics into an elegant mathematical theory that aimed at explaining mind. The messy world of bumbling speakers and hearers hammering out reality and getting through the day with language disappeared. Linguistics, in the United States, pulled away from anthropology and joined the ranks of mathematical neurophysiology.

It's a long story. I'll tell part of it later. But twenty years ago or so a critical mass of interdisciplinary, international people discovered that they had something in common; namely, discourse, language as it naturally comes, Malinowski's sort of stuff.

The meetings of the discourse crowd are fascinating. They pull together people from different national traditions and professional angles of vision around how to make sense out of what people do with language, how they get it done, and how an outsider can make sense out of their accomplishment.

A few years ago, I went to my first international meeting of this new linguistics in Antwerp. Among the hundreds of unknown faces were many of my old colleagues from linguistic anthropology. The thing that fascinated me was that the papers by the anthropologists were different.

I'd come to the meetings to find the "new" linguistics, to escape the routine I'd fallen into. Instead, I wound up listening to the voice of David Mandelbaum's ghost. Why were the anthropology papers different? They were more comparative, more holistic, more field-work based.

During a break between sessions I stood in the hall and talked with my old teacher John Gumperz. He's one of those people who say something that five years later resurfaces in an idea you think *you* invented. A European friend of John's walked up, talked about how interesting the meeting was, and then asked him a question.

"John, how do you tell which ones are the anthropologists?"

He grinned. "It's easy. They're the ones who never say 'culture.'"

The joke unearths a truth as embarrassing as the one I'd found in David Mandelbaum's article. The banners of holism, comparison, and fieldwork mark the path to culture. Not only are the road signs blurred, but so is the destination. "Culture" is the reason that "cultural" anthropology exists, an identity built of, and on, sand.

> Culture consists of patterns, explicit and implicit, of and for behavior, acquired and transmitted by symbols constituting the distinctive achievement of human groups, including their embodiment in artifacts; the essential core of culture consists of traditional (i.e., historically derived and selected) ideas and especially their attached values; culture systems may, on the one hand, be considered as products of action, on the other as conditioning elements of further action.

That's how Clyde Kluckhohn and Alfred Kroeber, two deities of American anthropology, summed it up in their report in 1952. They'd clambered through the looking-glass history of anthropology and tried to find the common denominator in dozens of definitions of "culture."

The definition fogs up the problem, like the fog that David Mandelbaum produced in his encyclopedia article. Ironic, in a time when "culture" is a concept that pops up everywhere like a spring-loaded surprise to explain the dilemmas of modern life and their solutions.

Every institution of the modern state is littered with problems of "cultural differences": education, health care, business, housing, law enforcement, and the list goes on. And intercultural training rivals computer chip production as a growth industry. Those about to depart these shores to buy and sell, either goods and services or American public policy, learn the ten things to remember about where they are headed in one week's time. Culture isn't so easy. Culture is a complicated concept with a hundred years of history behind it.

///

German trains give me a sense of calm and order and speed, all at the same time. In 1989 I sat in one and shot into the gray reaches of northern Europe to attend the applied linguistics meetings in Göttingen, Germany. "West Germany," we said then. The featured theme was "intercultural communication." Academic German contains a cliché for "theoretically grounded concept," so I figured maybe *they* would have figured out what *culture* meant.

There's a joke, told to me and a German colleague by an Austrian. An American and a German go off to study elephants. After a year, they both return. The American hands over a short essay titled "How to Use an Elephant." The German, on the other hand, presents a twelve-volume work entitled *Introduction to Elephant Science*. The German and I pointed out that it was significant that an Austrian hadn't made the trip, probably because he couldn't get organized.

Well, the Germans didn't know what *culture* was, either. I tried to start discussions around the issue.

"Look, everybody's using the word *culture* without defining it.

They're using it where the two participants in a conversation are from different national and linguistic traditions, like Turks and Germans. But some of the Turks might be second-generation German residents, and two Germans might have differences when they talk that are cultural, too. In fact, a Prussian and a Bavarian might have more trouble communicating than a resident Turk talking with his German neighbor in Munich."

The example worked especially well if the listener was Prussian or Bavarian.

The discussions never landed on the theoretical ground. The Germans hadn't brought culture under control any more than American anthropologists. In fact, they were worse off; they had no idea what a mess they had landed in with a concept that was supposed to *solve* their problems. Which of course is why John Gumperz joked that everybody *but* anthropologists uses the word *culture*.

///

Maybe the concept has outlived its salad days. Maybe when we pretended you could isolate a small community in space and assume traditional continuity in time, maybe then *culture* worked to tag the description of that hermetically sealed research space. Maybe with the disappearance of that fiction—both because we've figured out the lies it was built on and because the real communities that inspired it have all but disappeared—maybe the concept should just be left in the hot sun to dry and wither and blow away.

But then . . . Not long ago I gave a paper in the United Kingdom that involved an analysis I'd done in Austria. (I realize I'm talking about meetings a lot, but meetings are where you do fieldwork to find academic rich points.) An Austrian showed up. We chatted in Austrian German, talked the politics of the chaotic Second Republic, exchanged reasons why we were on the planet, specifically at that conference.

When I gave my paper, I noticed that he laughed, groaned, frowned, and later argued in ways that no one else there did. Naturally. And I knew, at least had a plausible guess, why. What I wondered then was, what would I have had to tell the English speakers from Australia, the United Kingdom, and the United States so that they would have reacted like he did, or at least understood his reactions? The answer to that question has something to do with culture.

So did the answer to another question years ago. When I landed at a hospital for narcotics addicts in the late sixties, I watched a young Black addict from one city meet an older White addict from another city, watched them meet for the first time and talk immediately about several things in a way I couldn't make any sense out of. Here were native speakers of American English I couldn't understand, and the difference between me and them, I knew right away, had something to do with culture, too.

Junkies aren't usually thought of as having anything to do with culture. Many would say they don't deserve one. I used to hear often, still do occasionally, that an anthropology of junkies isn't really anthropology. The hell it isn't. What was that similarity among different people and difference among similar people if it wasn't culture? When I encountered them, I found rich points all over the place and had to change to figure them out. What was that if it wasn't the kind of experience that I'm calling culture?

///

When Kroeber and Kluckhohn struggled with that philosophical nightmare of a definition, they opened with the word *pattern*. Maybe that common everyday word holds a secret that unlocks the relationship between the sacred litany—comparative, holistic, fieldwork, the cloudy concept of "culture," and the mysterious anthropological perspective.

The reason I think *pattern* might be so important is because of a cosmic experiment I tried once, a disciplinary null hypothesis, in both the scientific and the existential senses.

When I did a study of American independent truckers in the early eighties, I wondered what, if anything, I could add to what the world already knew about them. Here was a group about which mountains of information were available. Government agencies, corporations, lobbying organizations, and faculty from business schools and economics departments had studied truckers to death, and their own spokespersons from unions and professional organizations regularly offered up images of themselves as well.

What could an anthropologist add to this endless trail of paper?

After a study of the type I knew how to do, what would I be able to say about truckers that hadn't been said before?

I found out at the national transportation meetings when I gave my first paper there. I thought of the meetings as just another form of fieldwork, a chance to see how the corporate and government types—there weren't many truckers there—talked about the industry. But then I gave my paper and, to my surprise, found out I was a hit. I was surrounded by business folks, dragged off to the reception, and fueled up for the numerous questions to come about my methodology.

I wish I could claim personal credit, but the paper simply did something any anthropologist would have done—hooked together bits of material from separate sources to show what they had to do with each other. Different domains of trucker life, different bits of American history, different pieces of the trucking industry—the rich points I'd encountered, wherever I found them, I'd wired them into the same fuse box.

The answer to my cosmic null hypothesis was clear. Everyone in the transportation field had *variables* and *lists*. But I, like any other anthropologist with a comparative, holistic, field-oriented perspective, had built *patterns* out of my encounter, and patterns were news.

///

The second edition of the unabridged *Random House Dictionary* lists several definitions for *pattern*. The term *pattern* is rooted in the Latin for "patron," which is itself anchored in *pater,* the term for "father." The first couple of definitions center on the idea of "decoration." But here are some of the rest of them.

1. a combination of qualities, acts, tendencies, etc., forming a consistent or characteristic arrangement.
2. an original or model considered for or deserving of imitation.
3. anything fashioned or designed to serve as a model or guide for something to be made.
4. an example, instance, sample, or specimen.
5. to make or fashion after or according to a pattern.

There are other definitions that have to do with shotguns and sewing that I ignore. The point for now is that this select list echoes Kroeber and Kluckhohn's definition of culture, as it should. They started out, "culture consists of patterns . . . "

And the echo reverberates with confusion and ambiguity. Pattern is both prescriptive and descriptive, ideal and real, organization or a single thing, theoretical and practical, and, by a stretch of the imagination, rich in connotations of male authority, as well as connotations of "decoration" that underlie the first meanings that I didn't cite. Dumping jargon and shifting to ordinary language won't clear up the problem. "Pattern," like "culture," is a mess.

///

Anthropologists know that "culture" is a mess. They've known it for years. Culture is so basic, so fundamental, so important, and no one can quite figure out what it is. But then most things in the human situation that are that important are also mysterious. That's the secret that David Mandelbaum knew.

Whorf said Hopi language is about a different sense of time. The junkie example said language is about a different kind of situation, and the *Schmäh* example is about a principle that says the world is basically ironic rather than literal. If time, situation, and interpretive stance aren't *cultural,* what is?

In other examples I've used, the language was less cosmic. Numeral classifiers lead you to look at objects in terms of certain shapes and types; demotic Greek with its emphasis on aspect leads you to think more in terms of states and processes. But, although less cosmic, if seeing objects as related and thinking more of states and processes isn't *cultural,* then what is?

One day, after a long period of life in Austrian German, I walked down the Kärntnerstrasse in Vienna. Any reader who's been there knows the street. It's a traffic-free pedestrian mall with lots of fancy shops that speak English. As I walked past groups of Americans, their language slapped me across the face. They were shopping, many of them, so naturally they were talking about prices. But more than that, the number of money metaphors struck me: *What's it worth to you? Never sell it. Too high a cost. Million-dollar idea. Wouldn't give you a nickel for it.*

They weren't talking about objects to buy; they were talking about places, people, activities. I remembered how when my Austrian family and my American family met for the first time, the Austrians asked about what they'd done and the Americans asked about how much things cost. I thought about how "marketing" had become an Austrian German verb.

Americans are materialistic, goes the cliché. As I walked down the Kärtnerstrasse, I began to believe it. If a tendency to evaluate the world in terms of its material worth isn't part of *culture,* then what is?

///

Culture means something, but what does it mean?

The problem with *culture* is where it came from. In the good old days, anthropology invented an idea of what it studied. It studied small groups of people who lived in some bounded space. These people didn't read or have TVs. They produced what they needed to live. Maybe they were tied to a couple of other groups to find spouses, and maybe there was a small market town nearby where they went to get the few things they didn't produce themselves. But by and large, the circle around the group pretty much included all the things they did.

And what they did was *traditional.* It was based on a fine-tuned way of doing things that had endured for generations. Parents taught it to their kids, who in turn taught it to their kids, and so on forever. The tradition was replicated from generation to generation. It never changed.

This is an oversimplified parody, but not by much. The old-style unit of study was small and bounded in space and time. Anthropologists crawled inside of this space and explored it, everything from religion to subsistence down to the recipes for the evening meal. That description, the results of that exploration, counted as a description of *their* culture.

The idea was a fiction then, because small groups weren't *that* isolated and traditions changed from generation to generation. And it was especially a fiction because it left out the way the personal experience of culture led to the results. But it was a fiction that was close enough to reality so that the cracks between real and ideal didn't rupture the concept.

Anyone who approaches the current world can't maintain that

fiction any longer. True, there are still small groups isolated in space. But information and the consequences of political and economic events move through them and divide them and tie them to the world outside. The globalization of markets and the media and music, tourism and migration and war, the continuing growth of English as a world language—that's just the beginning of a long list that explains why the gap between fiction and reality is greater than the Grand Canyon.

Culture grew up as a concept to cover the description of isolated traditional communities. Now I want to use it to describe why two people who are different in some way have trouble communicating and what they can do about it. *Culture* needs to be hooked on to *langua*. If the concept is to have a chance, it has to be changed.

///

Here's two ways of changing it. First, abandon the heartbreak of a closed space that you're going to explore. There aren't any closed spaces anymore.

You'd think I would have noticed a long time ago, when I started working with heroin addicts in 1968, but I didn't. Not really. Instead, I was making a common move among ethnographers at the time. We accepted that things were more complicated than the good old days. But instead of taking the next logical step, we tried to find the closest equivalent to a village, a band, or a tribe in the modern world.

Herbert Gans wrote a book in that era whose title captures the move perfectly, *The Urban Villagers*. I did the same thing. I looked at junkies like a tribe, a band of hunters and gatherers roaming the urban tundra like Eskimos. If they were from Buffalo, they even dressed that way.

I didn't make the leap. But at the time, I was still held captive by the traditional idea of culture, what it meant to me and how I used it. Whorf and Malinowski applied to my use of the jargon just as much as they applied to anyone else using their language. My languaculture led me down its well-worn paths.

Junkies weren't the only example, in retrospect, that should have taught me a lesson. Years ago I sat at an outdoor table at a café in Italy, sipping espresso and trying to figure out which of four thousand kinds of pasta to order. I looked up and saw an old woman dressed in black. Ah, I thought, a traditional village woman. As she approached, I noticed that she had a peculiar rhythm to her walk and held her hand to her ear. When she got closer, I saw that she was holding a transistor radio. This was before the Walkman, which will prove how old this story is. As she passed in front of my table, I heard the music. It was "We All Live in a Yellow Submarine."

Or, a few years later, I was standing at the bar in a progressive country music club in Houston. A man stood next to me, enjoying the music. He was a person of color, but I couldn't place his ancestry. During the break, we struck up a conversation. After a while, I asked where he was from.

"I'm an Australian aborigine."

I was speechless. Australian aborigines had been "the natives" in numerous articles and books I'd read as a student.

He asked me, "What do you do?"

"I'm an anthropologist."

I've never seen anyone so happy at my professional tag. His eyes brightened with hope. "You don't speak . . . "

I shook my head. "No, sorry, I don't know any of the aboriginal languages."

His momentary disappointment faded. He was delighted that he was talking to somebody who at least had some idea of who he was. His uncle had migrated to the United Kingdom, then later to America, and set up a business in Houston. When he died, he left the business to my new acquaintance, so he'd relocated from Australia to run it.

Even back then the world was telling me that the old days were going fast, that the old anthropological image of an isolated group of "primitives" was fading into the global village. Tradition didn't just disappear, but it entered into strange and new combinations with all the other ideas and activities floating around the planet.

If what *culture* used to label is gone, then *culture* has to label something else. And whatever it labels, it won't be a closed, traditional society in which an individual always and only participates.

///

A second way to change the culture concept is to refocus on what kind of problem we're trying to solve with it. Since the old problem doesn't exist, what kind of question are we trying to answer? The question asks, when you run into rich points, when you assume they're an expression of some different languaculture, what do you do next?

We're trying to find some answer other than the number-one-type answer—these people, or this person, isn't like me. The conclusion—they are deficient; they lack something. We're trying to find an answer that takes differences and does something more than that.

Differences. Think differences. Culture is supposed to explain differences, to take rich points and make them understandable. And it's supposed to explain those differences by hooking them to a common human denominator, to similarities, to the human bridge between you and them. It's supposed to be a guide to the personal experience of culture, a guide that shows how to stretch consciousness to include an understanding of rich points that puzzled you at first.

In the old days, the differences were assumed to be complete and coherent within isolated traditions, something that those people had, independent of who came into contact with them. That's not true anymore. But there are still differences, and "culture" is a convenient tag to hang them on. But then that's dangerous. Got a problem? It's culture. Named, tagged, and bagged. Culture names the problem, and therefore the problem is solved.

Recently I worked as a mediator between Mexicans and Americans in the development of a new Mexican company. There were plenty of rich points. But once a Mexican customer didn't want to send a deposit up to the United States; he wanted to wait and check the order first when it arrived in Mexico City, and then he wanted thirty days to pay. The Americans didn't want to send the shipment until they had a deposit to cover their original costs.

The problem was handed to me. Obviously it was a cultural problem, right? Wrong. That particular problem had everything to do with two business guys, who operated in exactly the same frame of reference, trying to cover their backs. The difference wasn't a rich point; it was two different agendas within the same way of thinking about doing business.

A more serious example is the "culture of poverty" debate in the sixties. Oscar Lewis had written a book where he argued for the existence of a culture of poverty, a culture that people "had" no matter where they were, just because they were poor. His argument led some to say, Why do poor people act that way? Well, it's their culture.

Nonsense, said Charles and Betty Lou Valentine. Most of the poor act that way to adapt to a world they're born into, locked into, and offered no way out of. Poverty is about what society has to offer, not about a "culture."

Culture is supposed to be an answer to the problem of understanding differences. But it's supposed to be an *answer,* not a label that hides the question. Not all differences are cultural, because people do things differently *within* the same languaculture. Sometimes, the reason they do things differently has to do with who owns the store and who has the guns, not with what languaculture they grew up with.

/ / /

The other day I went to happy hour with a bunch of friends from the university. An Asian-Indian woman and I walked up to the serving table to grab a free taco. We stood there, filling up the shells on our paper plates with ground meat and greens and sauce. She looked around and wondered why there weren't any plastic forks. Forks? I said, "We'll eat it with our hands, a direct relationship with the food, like in India."

In India people often eat with their right hand, pulling things together into interesting piles of mixed tastes before lumping them together with rice or scooping them up with a folded chappati. It's an interesting way to eat.

We laughed and she looked at me and smiled. "Thanks for reminding me of my culture."

Styles of eating are a major difference. I'm remembering a dinner I had with an Austrian friend. I'm a sloppy eater—junk all over the plate, huge forkfuls of food, occasional displays of the half-chewed mess in my mouth while I talk. Traditional Austrians, on the other hand, eat like surgeons, carve things up into tiny pieces, line them up like a regiment, then have them disappear into closed mouths.

There's a difference for you. Is it cultural? It looks like it. But in what way? The Indian woman at the bar and the Austrian I had dinner with are like me in a lot of ways. We all wear jeans, we all like jazz, and we all enjoy talking about Gabriel García Marquez. We're all members of a sort of amorphous culture vulture category, the one that raises Senator Jesse Helms's blood pressure. In that way we're the *same,* not different. Rich points aren't a problem.

But when it comes to food, there are differences. When I first encountered them, in Austria and later in India, my "natural" way of eating no longer made any sense. Are the differences cultural?

The way I explain them is. I explain them by linking the differences to an *identity:* American, Indian, Austrian. One of the things that makes an explanation cultural is that a *difference* between something X and Y do or say is linked to a different *identity* that X and Y have.

That isn't enough, though. The number-one types do the same thing. "Look at that, will you? Oh well, what can you expect from an *X?*" The number-one types link difference to identity all the time. It's called ethnocentrism, chauvinism, racism, sexism, and several other isms as well. That's not what I have in mind, though the slippery boundary between *isms* and *culture* should make you nervous. It makes me nervous, for reasons I'll get to in a later chapter.

///

Difference plus identity isn't enough to figure out a rich point. Remember the *Schmäh?* That was a difference between me and the Austrians. But understanding it required more than just an "Oh yes, there's that *Schmäh* again. Just like the Austrians." I tied *Schmäh* in with ways of talking, ways of seeing the world, history, politics, and I'd only just begun when I left.

I'm still a beginner at Mexico. When I arrived I knew that things weren't going to go at an American clip, and several American "old Mexico hands" had chanted it repeatedly: "Everything is slow down here." They'd noticed a rich point, hooked it up to difference plus identity, and left it at that.

But I was still surprised when I got into the game. Negotiations with a customer started as if we'd never talked about the issue before, and they never reached a firm conclusion. Things felt like they were dragging on forever. I was at the point that the old Mexico hands had told me about.

Then I started noticing *other* rich points. A Mexican friend joked about the way they'd handled an American who'd come down and wanted several appointments in one day to close deals. The Mexican friend just held his hands out to the side, waved them back, and said "*Olé!*"

Later, a Mexican lawyer told me on the way to a meeting that we'd *capotear* a little. What's that? *Capotear,* he explained, was what the toreadors and the matador did with the bull, waved the cape and controlled his charge and watched carefully how he behaved.

I remember reading things anthropological about the bullfight, symbolic things about life and death, male and female, and several other oppositions from a structuralist's dream. And I remembered the first time I saw a bullfight, in Spain several years ago, how I thought the point of it all was that the question wasn't if you were going to die or not, but rather how well.

But suddenly I started seeing the bullfight differently. It was a metaphor for how to handle aggression and directness, the behavior of a doomed and stupid, though perhaps noble, animal. It charges, you control it, and then just pass it by. And we all know how the bullfight usually ends.

Mexico is an example of how I took my first step beyond the simple link of difference with identity. I took the step by noticing ties between two differences, one in the pace of business negotiations and one in a metaphor from the bullfight. I started to put together something *coherent,* something that started to show how one difference tied in with another, something that launched me into a series of questions, as yet unanswered. The two rich points—slow pace and bullfight metaphor—moved me beyond identity plus difference. They started me on a journey to change my consciousness, to see alternatives to my "natural" way to do things, to understand that I needed to build something new to understand business negotiations in a fundamentally different way.

Difference wasn't just attributed to identity. Instead, it was investigated as the visible tip of an invisible iceberg. The trick is to find out how the difference is related to other differences, to assemble a coherent picture of how they all fit together to make up a grand difference between you and them, a difference that leads to a different way of seeing and doing things.

That's the beginning of the culture half of languaculture, but just the beginning, because the ties won't go just from negotiations to the bullfight, but to other things as well, things I don't know about yet. The point is that I did *fieldwork* in which I found the rich points, *compared* slow negotiations and *capotear,* and *tied* them together, the holistic point of view.

Whatever it is that you build to start making sense of rich points, whatever story you tell to show how those differences cohere into a different way of seeing and acting from the one you brought with you, you could call *culture*.

You call that culture? It's weird compared to the old way the term was used. Culture isn't something a group of people "have"; it's something you make up to fill in the spaces between them and you. Culture isn't an exhaustive description of everything inside a closed space; it's something that handles rich points and uses similarities to organize them. Culture isn't tied just to the kinds of identities that anthropologists used to deal with, like Australian aborigines; it might be tied to any identity, including occupation, ethnicity, leisure time activity, or gender.

And culture, once you make it up, doesn't leave you where you were when you started. When you're done with the job, you're aware of something about your own identity that used to lurk on the edges of consciousness as the natural order of things. And you understand an alternative to who you are, and now imagine that probably there are many more.

If you hit a rich point, think you've solved it, and haven't changed, then you haven't got it right.

///

Culture is something you create, a coherent connection of differences. What in the world is a "coherent connection of differences"?

The junkie vocabulary offered one example. Some words *differed* from ordinary American English. The different words were wrestled into *coherence* by showing how they were related to each other, so that all the little differences turned out to be a big difference in terms of a situation, namely, injecting heroin. *Schmäh* was another example. Austrians used the word in all kinds of different ways. But the different ways turned out to cohere into a common theme of irony.

Once you trip over a rich point, you stand at the door of the culture half of languaculture. Say you figure out what that difference *means*. That's not enough; you only wind up with a long list of differences. Long lists of disconnected things keep you on the surface, keep you from the deeper threads that tie the differences together. There's no pattern, and without pattern, there's no coherence, and without coherence, there's no culture.

Instead, what you do is *compare* the difference you've just figured out with other differences, other rich points that come up. You start fooling around with what one has to do with another, start playing with the old Saussurian notions of paradigmatic and syntagmatic, start toying with a model of a piece of another symbolic system. Coherence is what happens as you move from lists through connections to system.

As I revise this book right now, I'm sitting in Cozumel, the same island that produced the dive example I used in the discussion of Saussure. Last night I had a drink with a friend, a Chicana who does business here. She told me a horrible story about problems she's had with local officials as the business started to take off.

Her story reported *differences* between our shared American notions about how the world works and what the officials had done and why. In a nutshell, she'd come in from outside, prospered with the flow of tourists, but unknowingly stepped on too many traditional toes in the generations-old system of power on the island.

Other differences came to mind as I listened to her, some from my work last summer in Mexico City with a new Mexican-American joint venture, some from things I've read and heard in both Mexico and the United States. I thought about the old notion of *envidia,* envy, that I had read about in traditional Mexican ethnographies.

As I walked back to my place, the skies flashed bright with a streak of coherence. A massive struggle is under way, a struggle between ways of doing things in a Mexico economically isolated for years and a Mexico crouching into the starting blocks of the world economy. Historical mountains of differences stand between the old and the new, hundreds of them, but all part of the same continuous range.

At the moment I'm not judging. I'm not sure which side of the mountains is better or worse, from my or anyone else's point of view. But my friend's story was a difference, a rich point, that, when compared with other differences, backlit a pattern. I'd built a piece of culture—not "Mexican culture" in any traditional sense, but rather a "culture" that helped me understand many of the rich points between me and them so I could make more sense out of what I read and hear in Mexico today.

///

This thing you're building and rebuilding and remodeling as you wander ever deeper into the new languacultural forest—are there any guidelines for how it should look? Is there any way to talk about it? What are you building as you hammer together the pieces of a new languaculture to handle the rich points you stumbled across? What are the *similarities* in terms of which you're organizing the *differences?*

One way to think about it is to steal the idea of a *frame*. A frame, as the name suggests, sets a boundary around the details and highlights how those details are related to each other. Frames were invented by the artificial intelligentsia, those abstract thinking people who program computers to do intelligent tasks.

Back in the sixties, when they first started making robots, they noticed that robots were actually pretty stupid. Say this little metal guy rolls into a room. He takes in images from his lens and starts to figure them out.

> Let's see. There's a rectangular area of a higher light intensity on that vertical plane, and there's some kind of object over there with two perpendicular planes on top of four sticklike objects.

The poor robot is lost in thought for hours just trying to get from geometry to a window and a chair.

Wouldn't it be better to give him some hints before we turned him loose? Why not tell him—or her, I guess, I don't know how to tell with robots—that there's something called a *room,* and that when he rolls into a room he can expect certain things to be there, like windows on the wall and chairs on the floor. Now all he needs to do is figure out he's in a *room,* and then he's got some ideas about what he might run into.

He has a *room frame.* The frame tells him what the room will look like, what will be in it, what sorts of things he can move and what things he can't. *Room* now means more than what he could look up in his dictionary. The signified of *room* stretches into what matters in the world and what actions he can do in it.

But life, even robot life, consists of more than rooms. Suppose you want to tell the robot a story before it goes to bed. You plug a keyboard into the computer the robot carries around inside and type:

> John walked into the restaurant. He ordered a hamburger. When he finished, he started to leave, and the waiter shouted, "Hey, you forgot something." John pulled out his wallet.

The stories computers can understand aren't going to win any Nobel prizes anytime soon.

So now you want to check how the robot's going to do on its SAT test; you want to test its comprehension of the story. You type in, "Why did John pull his wallet out?"

Since the robot's computer has a *restaurant frame* as well as a room frame, it knows that certain activities occur once you're inside. After you eat, you ask for the bill and then pay it. That crucial step is missing from the story. The "something" that the waiter refers to must be "paying," and since the next thing John does is pull out his wallet—which from the dictionary the robot knows contains money—John is about to pay. Case closed, using some simple reasoning that even the robot can handle.

Now the robot can answer the question. John pulled his wallet out because he forgot to pay the bill. The answer wasn't in the words of the story you typed in. The answer was in the combination of the words and what the restaurant frame told the robot it could expect to happen in restaurants.

The restaurant frame handles discourse—a story instead of isolated words and sentences—and it hooks the discourse into meanings that go beyond dictionary definitions. Frames look like they might work in ways that this peculiar notion of languaculture does.

Where does the robot get the frames? The artificially intelligent researcher gives them to him. The researcher has to do a self-ethnography, figure out what he or she already knows under the terms *room* and *restaurant,* and shovel it in.

Once the machine finds the right frame, it's way ahead of the game. Now it can make several intelligent guesses about where it is or what it's having typed in through its keyboard. It can make these guesses because the frame *makes connections* among the differences between itself and the world it's in. It shows how those differences *cohere.*

Frames show coherent links among several differences that came up in language. That's what languaculture is supposed to do.

///

Frames don't fit David Mandelbaum's *International Encyclopedia of the Social Sciences* article on cultural anthropology so badly, either. Frames are *holistic*—they tie different things together and show their interrelationships. They are *comparative* in two ways: They're put together based on a comparison of what we know about rooms and restaurants and what the computer knows, and they're also based on a comparison of different rooms and restaurants to find out what one can usually expect. And they're *fieldwork* based, in a self-centered kind of way, because researchers explore their own experience of rooms and restaurants to find out what to put in the frame. And then the robot modifies the frames, depending on how well they work through experience.

Frames go well beyond the circle around language. They tie into language, since *room* and *restaurant* are what started the problem for the robot. But they carry meaning outside the circle, since the frames guide the robot to what's significant in rooms and restaurants and what he can do in them.

Frames stretch language beyond the circle, and frames act like culture. Frames take language and culture and make them insepa-rable. The "and" disappears, and we're left with *languaculture.*

///

Right after I arrived in Vienna in 1989, I was awakened by the door buzzer in my apartment at seven A.M. I staggered to the door and opened it. An older man with some official metal clip on his shirt looked at me, annoyed at the disorder I represented, and said, "*Stromrechnung.*"

Even though my German was rusty, I knew that *Strom* meant "current," and *Rechnung* meant "account."

My precoffee mind twisted this into "accountable for the current," and all I could think of was, why am I for some reason responsible for the Danube? I asked the man what he meant and he explained that he was there to collect the payment for the electricity bill.

My idea of an electricity bill was something you got in the mail and wrote a check for and mailed back. Austria's idea was a guy who showed up at dawn and handed me a strange piece of paper that I had no idea of what to do with. I gave him cash and he stamped the paper a couple of times and went away.

I'd just run across a rich point. I couldn't very well haul out a number-one response and decide that Austria didn't know the proper way to bill you for electricity. Not if I wanted to run the coffee pot and play my Mozart in the morning.

It turned out that bills and banks were different in Austria. Bills were weird pieces of paper you took to your bank and wrote your account number on. Money was transferred from account to account without checks. In fact, I received checks for my account that I later learned—with some embarrassment—I couldn't cash anywhere but at the bank. So I used cash most of the time or relied on those funny pieces of paper. Turned out most Austrians did exactly the same thing.

I ran across a rich point when that bill collector came to the door. By comparison with how I usually paid bills, it didn't make any sense. So I had to build frames to organize the differences, frames that started with that piece of paper and eventually linked up to banks and to any other situation where my money was going to move from my account into someone else's. The links grew with time to include the general observation that Austrians used cash and bills more than checks or credit cards.

The frame hooked an electricity bill up to institutions and then to general preferences for cash transactions in stores and restaurants. It connected to language all the time, whenever I was in the bank, or in one of those stores or restaurants. It organized some differences between me and them in a coherent way. The frame turned into an important part of living in Austria, of being *communicatively competent,* part of what any immigrant to Vienna had to learn. The frame hooked to a social identity, so, from my point of view as an American formerly hooked on credit cards and checks, it counted as part of Austrian languaculture.

If you don't think paying the bills is an important part of languaculture, you're still thinking of *culture* as something that applies only to hunters and gatherers. If you don't think paying the electric bill is part of languaculture, you're going to spend a lot of time sitting around in the dark.

///

The meanings that frames organize are *expectations,* not certainties. In the jargon of the computernauts, such expectations are called *default values.* Most computer users know the term by now. When you fire up a word processor, it sets the page for 8½ by 11 inches and 66 lines unless you tell it otherwise. Those are the default values for a page in the United States. When I lived in Austria, I had to reset the default values to handle that strange A4 paper that Europeans use. One of my colleagues claimed that my thought processes, conditioned by an 8½ by 11 mentality, would be destroyed.

Frames contain default values. Default values aren't what you find *all* the time. There are rooms without windows and restaurants where you serve yourself. There are bills in Austria you have to pay in cash and credit cards are starting to take off. When default values don't work, you have to decide if it's an exceptional case or if you're using the wrong frame or maybe if the frame has to be changed.

When you move into a situation, find the right frame, and start using it, you're in a *top-down* mode. The frame works, so you apply it to organize the world around you and act within it. When you move into a situation and frames don't work, you're in a *bottom-up* mode. You take in the differences and work to build a frame that shows how they're all related.

Number-one types are top-down to the core. If their frames don't work, frames they probably aren't conscious of at all, then the problem is that those other people are deficient because they don't have the right frames. If their default values aren't met, then the world must be wrong, because they never are.

Culture, the experience of it, starts when you go bottom-up. You're struck by differences you don't know how to make sense out of. Your default values aren't met, but instead of holding the world responsible, you figure maybe there are other frames out there with other default values that *are* being met, and you try to figure out what those frames might be. Once you've built a new frame, you go into top-down mode and carry it around and apply it to new situations. You *compare* the situation you built it in with new situations where it should work. If it doesn't work, you go bottom-up again and fix it, then go top-down and try again.

This trampoline approach characterizes how you experience culture—culture as the frames that coherently organize rich points you find in discourse.

When the frames coherently organize several rich points that work with people of a particular social identity, be it nationality, ethnicity, gender, occupation, or social style, then you've built a *languaculture* of the identity, from your point of view. I have to add "your point of view," because culture isn't something that "they" have; it's something that fills the spaces between you and them, and the nature of that space depends on *you* as well as *them*.

What happens if you change the "you," change the nature of the space between by changing the one doing the frame building? Then the frames might change as well. This is as subversive as anything Whorf ever said. It's enough to make an old-time scientist break out in a rash. There is *no* unique set of frames that organize the differences between people. There are some that work and some that don't, and the trick is to figure out how to tell the difference.

If you're a researcher, the trick isn't so easy, because you have to obsess over research method. If you're a person just doing the best you can to learn a new languaculture, the trick is, you try what you've learned, and if it doesn't work, the confused look or sympathetic help or stifled laugh from the person you've just said something to lets you know that you'd better go back to the bottom-up drawing board.

If you want to tackle a new languaculture, you have to get used to making mistakes. If you're not making mistakes, you're not learning anything.

///

The artificial intelligentsia use *frame* in a mathematical sense. Everything in the frame has to be laid out explicitly, ready to feed into the computer. The computer that understands the restaurant story can't slide around in a fog of loose ideas and associations. It's not *that* intelligent.

Restaurant scripts are mind-numbing in their detail. Walk in, if there's a host/hostess wait to be seated, if not go to an empty table, sit down, waitperson brings a menu—and like that. Then "host/hostess" is the top of another frame that hooks into the script—a person who works in the restaurant who comes up when you enter the door, who may or may not have a list of customers on a table, who may or may not take five bucks to put you on top of the list, and like that.

Humans who handle rich points don't need all that detail. Unlike a computer, they already have some frames that will be useful. They just need to know about the *differences*. Humans share similarities in terms of which the differences can be understood. Computers don't.

I've never walked into a restaurant anywhere in the world and wondered what the tables and chairs were for. Well, places with thirty kinds of forks in the table setting make me wonder, and a dive where dogs are licking the plates makes me wonder my way out the door. But I've never been lost in thought because there were tables there and I wasn't sure why.

When you start work on rich points, when you start to put together a new languaculture, *you don't try to build complete frames.* You build enough to get you from where you started to where you end up when you can understand and operate in a new world. That's all. That's enough. That's a lot.

///

Frame is a general idea that includes some of the similarities already described in this book, like taxonomy or Fillmore's sentence grammar. Those are specific examples of frames, examples of two particular shapes that a frame might take.

The problem is that the academicians develop one kind of frame and then ride through languaculture—or whatever other field they're in—and try to solve rich points in terms of it. The solution may work, or at least help out, but at best it's only part of the story.

Frame is more general than that. It doesn't tell you *how* you have to hook things together; it just says that hooks have to be there, and that eventually the hooks have to land in language. It doesn't tell you that the hooks *always* work; it just says that you can expect certain hooks to tie one thing to another. It isn't *static;* it lets you build and rebuild and wire frames together as you learn more and more. And it isn't just a *passive conclusion;* instead, it's a resource that you draw on to participate in a new languacultural world. When you participate, you check it out and change it.

Frames let you go where you need to go to put things together to understand a rich point. If you're a professional student of languaculture, you'll pull together bits and pieces of different well-worked-out similarities already available in your field, and then add some more. Your field will call you "eclectic," not a good word, because you haven't stayed on a particular theoretical trail, but that's the pro's problem, not yours.

People who encounter a new languaculture do the same thing. It wouldn't hurt if they knew the academic similarities, because it'd save them some time. But even if they don't, people have been learning new languacultures and changing for as long as there have been people. What *frame* gives them is a way of thinking about what they are doing, a guide to the trip from rich points to understanding, a sense of what the experience of culture is all about.

When you encounter a new languaculture, when you start to build up new knowledge, stretch your consciousness to meet another, frame-building is what you're up to. The key things to remember about them are in David Mandelbaum's article about culture—fieldwork, comparative, and holistic. Frames will be partial; they will be about expectations, not certainties; and they will take you wherever you need to go to figure a rich point out, as detailed as a small piece of language, as grand as the sweep of history that carries the speaker along. *Frame* gives you the culture half of languaculture.

///

Culture as a system of frames. It sounds pretty strange. Culture can't *really* be a system of frames. It's not. What it really is, is a problem, if you remember the discussion of my quest for the meaning of culture at the beginning of this chapter.

No one knows what culture *is*. It has some characteristics, like holistic, and comparative, and fieldwork based. It happens to you. You have to get out there and talk and live with people to find it. You figure it out by comparing rich points that happened at time one with rich points that happen at time two, and comparing those two with others that happen in other spheres of life, with other groups, with yourself. And whatever culture is, it shows patterns, the connections among different things.

Frames have all those characteristics. Frames aren't the same as culture; they're a metaphor for it. Frames are like a systematic poem about culture. No one knows exactly what culture is, so they use metaphors that resemble culture because the metaphor has some characteristics that they think culture has.

If I were writing fifty years ago, I couldn't have used the metaphor of frame, because the idea didn't exist. If I were writing fifty years from now, I might use a different metaphor that none of us knows will exist yet. And if I were someone else writing this book, I might use some other metaphor that exists now.

But *frame* strikes me as a useful metaphor, not because culture is *really* made up of frames, but because frames work to guide me toward a coherent understanding of differences in terms of similarities, and that's what I want to do to understand rich points.

Culture is something you create, something you invent to fill in the differences between you and them. It's something you manufacture in your conscious mind. It's an intellectual object. It doesn't include just intellect, though. It includes emotions. And it isn't logically pretty. It includes contradictions and ambiguities.

But what you make up is based on contact, on comparisons between you and them, and on ties that show how different rich points are related, one to another. Frames are a useful fiction to show what you're after and what it is when you get there. Culture isn't really a system of frames, but a system of frames is a useful way to think about culture. When you build frames to solve rich points, to build an understanding of what happens in discourse, you've entered the world of languaculture.

Speech Acts

THE Austrian *Schmäh,* rich a point as it was, strong a guide to diverse frames as it proved to be, as far into languaculture as it might have led me—it's still a word. So are *room* and *restaurant,* two rich points for the robot that led the AI researchers to donate some frames to its memory chips. But since Malinowski, a couple of chapters ago, words and sentences only make us applaud with one hand. They don't go far enough. Malinowski went beyond them into *discourse,* language as it naturally comes, language as people actually *use* it in real situations.

Words can be rich points. What about discourse?

Here's an example. I'm still thinking about restaurants, partly because of the restaurant example in the previous chapter, partly because I'm hungry right now. I wrote that I've never had any trouble walking into a restaurant, noticing that there were tables, and wondering why they were there. On the other hand, I *have* wondered who should pay the check.

My friend at Maryland Erve Chambers and I grew up in similar worlds at similar times where the custom is one guy pays one time, one guy pays the next time, or else you flip coins and match to see who pays. In Mexico, an assumption often floated around that since

Americans are richer, they'll pay. A group of Croatian friends took turns being the host and hostess, making sure everybody had what they wanted, and then the host/hostess paid. Austrian waitpersons do up a check after the fact, one for each customer, so they assume that everyone will pay for him or herself. Several faculty I know, including me, have a personal rule that students should never pay. When I invite an American woman out to dinner, negotiating who pays how much can turn into a political conference.

Sitting down at a table in a restaurant is pretty much the same anywhere in the world. But discourse that deals with who pays for a meal is a *rich point* that you need to build a frame for. And discourse it always is—a discussion, a conversation, an announcement, an argument, but never single words and sentences.

///

Even before you worry about who pays, the conversations you have over dinner aren't the same way everywhere, either. I grew up with a saying, "Never talk about sex, politics, or religion." Such topics might upset people, cause trouble, start arguments. The most important thing was to keep it smooth, keep everyone happy and friendly.

It took years until I felt comfortable with Austrian conversations, because they talk about sex, politics, and religion all the time. And they don't coat their contrary opinions in sugar, either. They start with things like *"That's wrong."* When this happened, even though I was right along on the ride as far as grammar and vocabulary were concerned, I'd feel uncomfortable, as if the social event were on an express train to hell.

American conversations emphasize servicing the relationship; Austrian conversations assume the relationship is fine and go to direct debate. For the Austrians, a contradiction is not a threat to the relationship; for Americans, it is. Americans worry about the "I'm okay, you're okay" aspect more than the Austrians.

The result is that the Austrians stereotype the Americans as superficial. Americans never get any interesting debate going. The Americans stereotype the Austrians as arrogant. They just jump right in and tell you you're full of waste material and that they know better.

Learning to converse in Mexico City was easier for me in one way, more difficult in another. It's easier because, more so even than Americans, Mexicans service the relationship. They worry that everyone in the conversation is "having a good moment," and, if someone gets upset, everyone works to make him feel better. But the conversation doesn't move in a straight line. It's "aboutness" drifts around, both in the topic and in the way Mexicans will play with words, even invent them.

One evening in Mexico City I walked into the lounge next to my hotel lobby. A Mexican and an American businessman walked in and sat at the table next to me. The American was selling pulleys to the Mexican customer.

The Mexican started talking about business, and then slid—I'm not sure how—into the full eclipse of the sun that was going to happen in a few days. He spoke with enthusiasm about the Aztec notion of the fifth sun, how this was a new sun, how important and mysterious an event it was, how people had different "superstitions"—that's the word he used.

The American sat back, impatient, and looked down at his spreadsheet. Finally he looked up and said, "An eclipse is science, that's all, the moon crosses in front of the sun, it's a natural event. Now, can we talk about these pulleys?"

The Mexican slouched down and the American turned animated as he discussed prices and quantities.

For the American, the conversation had a topic, and he wanted to take a straight line through it from beginning to end. For the Mexican, the conversation started with one topic, but conversations have permeable membranes, and if another interesting topic seeps in you ride it around for a while. Sticking to the first topic is less important than having an interesting conversation. In fact, you may never get back to the original topic, but then there's always tomorrow. That's a horrible cliché about Mexico, *mañana,* but in my experience, anyway, it came in handy. In fact, a Mexican friend, when I was having trouble opening a bank account, joked, "In Mexico the week has seven days, Monday, Tuesday, Wednesday, Thursday, Friday, Saturday, and *mañana.*"

So *conversation* is a rich point, too, just as much as picking up the tab in a restaurant, just as much as any of the word examples used earlier. When I landed in conversations in Austria or Mexico, some of my American English frames didn't work. It wasn't any particular word or grammatical construction that produced the rich point; it was something about the way things were going, something about people's ideas about *how to do* a conversation.

A couple of years ago Karin Aaronson, a Swedish colleague, told me about frames she'd built for Swedish businesspeople about to go to the United States. She'd been an exchange student to the United States and knew us well. She explained that the Swedish conversational ideal was represented by a championship skier who was interviewed on TV. When asked how he managed to ski so magnificently, he didn't launch into a discussion of his childhood, his training, and his technique. Instead, he shrugged his shoulders and said, "You just do it."

Her biggest problem, she said, was to teach the Swedes to lace their conversation with self-promotion—here's who I am, here's why I'm good at it, here's why you should pay attention to me. For the Swedes, this kind of talk was like walking into a party and putting your cigarette out in the onion dip. But it was what the Americans expected—an answer to our orienting question, and I've heard it phrased just like this on occasion: "Who in the hell are *you?*"

Conversations can be rich points, no doubt about it. To handle the rich points, old unconscious ways of doing things are dusted off, new ways are built up. To converse in the new way, you have to experience culture and manufacture some frames. If you don't figure out the frames, you might speak grammatically correct German or Spanish or Swedish, but what you communicate will differ from what you intended.

In the eyes of the number-one beholders, you won't *just* look like your conversations are off. The beholder will interpret what you're doing in ways that go beyond the grammar and vocabulary you use. Way beyond them.

To an Austrian you'll be superficial; to a Mexican you'll be unimaginative; to a Swede you'll be a fathead. From an American point of view, the Austrian will be arrogant; the Mexican will never get to the point; the Swede will lack self-confidence.

So important are conversational frames that I'll make a heretical linguistic prediction. Say your Austrian, Mexican, or Swedish acquaintance knows English grammar and vocabulary, but doesn't really know America very well. And say you don't know their grammar and vocabulary, but through years of reading and friendships and travel you've learned a good bit about the differences between you and them. You'd be better off speaking to them, in English with the right frames, than another American would be speaking with them in their own language, without those frames.

As far as communication goes, the culture part of languaculture can be more important than the language part.

///

Picking up the tab and having a conversation are rich points that you need a frame for. The languaculture game has changed, in the following way: For most of the book until now, I've talked about the circle around language, the circle that promoted grammar and vocabulary to the privileged position of what language *is*.

The way out of the circle was to build frames for vocabulary and grammar that went well beyond its edges. Vocabulary and grammar, it turned out, contained some rich points that signaled massive differences. Nothing wrong with any of this. In fact, it's a good general principle: *Grammar and vocabulary contain rich points that require frames for their understanding.*

But, with examples like paying the tab and having conversations, it looks like words and grammar aren't the only places where you find rich points. What in the world are paying the tab and having a conversation? They're not words or grammar. What are they? They're *discourse*. They're things you *do* with words and grammar. They're language as a means to accomplish something, just as Malinowski said.

This is a different breed of language cat. The rich point isn't some particular word or grammatical rule; instead, it's something people are doing *with* them. The rich point isn't sitting out there in public; usually you can't point to a single word and find the problem; the problem isn't a word; the problem is you don't know what's happening or how to do it.

You have to know it's time to pay the check, how it gets paid, and what your part in paying it will be. You have to know a conversation is going on and how to talk inside of it. You have to know how to *speak* and *act* at the same time. Learning a new languaculture isn't just words and sentences and frames; it's discourse and frames, or *speech acts*.

///

Take a *lie*, for example. How do you speak and act a lie at the same time? Ordinary folks, and some linguists, try to keep lies inside the circle. A lie? It's easy. You just say a sentence that's not true, a sentence that doesn't correspond to the reality it represents.

Human hair is made of wire.

Back in the old days, in high school in the late fifties and early sixties, the junk that girls sprayed on their hair might make you consider that sentence an accurate description, but it's just not true. It's a lie.

Human hair is a petroleum product.

Back in those same old days, the junk we boys smeared on our hair to keep the wings combed back and the flattop upright might have led you to believe that, but it's a lie.

Those are classic lies—sentences that are false. But what about the famous social lie? You know, you go to a friend's house, and he's just learning to cook, so he serves something green that you have to carve with a hacksaw and it pulls off a tooth cap when you chew it. But his hopeful look is more than you can stand, so you say, "Man, this er um dish is really tasty."

A flat-out lie.

But somehow the social lie isn't as big a sin. Something about the circumstances, something about lying to your friend who's trying his best to overcome the heartbreak of a history of culinary incompetence makes the social lie less of a lie.

Lying, it turns out, is more complicated than what's in the sentence and the words. Whether it's a lie or not depends on *what the speaker is doing in that particular discourse*. Lying isn't just words and sentences that don't correspond to the world; lying is also what people are doing when they talk. Lying is a speech act.

///

A friend and colleague at Maryland, Linda Coleman, took a look at lies together with Paul Kay, the faculty adviser we shared in graduate school. They're both linguists, but they never cared much for the circle around language. They're the sort of linguists you're going to meet more of from here on out. They started out their research on lies by wondering what the circumstances might be that would make something a lie or not.

Well, one thing you can't get away from is what everyone thinks a lie is; namely, that you say something that's false.

But there's more. The person who's speaking has to *believe that the sentence is false.* Suppose the person tells you that the interstate is the quickest way to Baltimore, so you jump in your car and head up I-95. But it turns out that an hour earlier the highway crew closed off three of four lanes as a quirky little April Fools' joke. You're stuck in traffic long enough to go through your entire cassette collection. Did the person who told you to take I-95 lie when they said it was the "quickest" way? They *said* something false, but most people wouldn't think what they *did* was a lie.

Another condition: The person who's speaking has to *intend to deceive you.* Say you walk into the office and report that you just had a wreck, that the police called and your kid has been arrested as a terrorist, that the IRS just froze your accounts, and that the dentist made reservations for a vacation while he told you that you need five root canals. The person in your office—there's always one—whose job it is to trivialize problems says, "Oh, it's not so bad." While such a statement might be grounds for justifiable homicide, it isn't exactly a lie. What the person said was false, no doubt about that, but they didn't intend to deceive you. They just wanted to make you feel better, to console you.

So, there are three characteristics of an *act* that tell you whether a lie occurred or not: 1. The sentence is false; 2. The person knows it's false; 3. The person intends to deceive you. A lie isn't just what's in the discourse; it's also what's in the circumstances of the *act* of speaking, like the knowledge and intentions of the speaker.

But is what Coleman and Kay said, you should excuse the expression, true? To find out, they made up stories and asked people to tell them if they were lies or not. The stories mixed up the three conditions, so that sometimes just one of them held, sometimes two, sometimes all three.

Here's one story:

> Moe has eaten the cake Juliet was intending to serve to company. Juliet asks Moe, "Did you eat the cake?" Moe says, "No." Did Moe lie?

Damn straight Moe lied. He said something false, knew it was false, and meant to deceive Juliet. When Coleman and Kay asked a sample of people to evaluate Moe, they agreed. On the old seven-point scale, Moe got an average score of 6.96, about as perfect as a measure of anything ever gets.

Here's another story:

> Dick, John, and H.R. are playing golf. H.R. steps on Dick's ball. When Dick arrives and sees his ball mashed into the turf, he says, "John, did you step on my ball?" John replies, "No, H.R. did it." Did John lie?

No way. John is the man Diogenes was searching for. He said something true, knew it was true, and intended to express that truth to Dick. John got a 1.06, which is about as close to the perfect truth score of 1 that you can get.

Things get more interesting, and complicated, when some of the conditions hold but others don't. Consider this story:

> One morning Katerina has an arithmetic test she hasn't studied for, and so she doesn't want to go to school. She says to her mother, "I'm sick." Her mother takes her temperature, and it turns out to Katerina's surprise that she really is sick, later that day developing the measles. Did Katerina lie?

Most people thought so. Katerina got a score of 5.16. But several people didn't agree. She said something *she* believed to be false and she did intend to deceive her mother, but it turned out that what she said was, after all, true.

What about if only one of the conditions holds, instead of two as in Katerina's story?

> John and Mary have recently started going together. Valentino is Mary's ex-boyfriend. One evening John asks Mary, "Have you seen Valentino this week?" Mary answers, "Valentino's been sick with mononucleosis for the past two weeks." Valentino has in fact been sick with mononucleosis for the past two weeks, but it is also the case that Mary had a date with Valentino the night before. Did Mary lie?

Well, Mary said something true, and she knew it was true, but she did mean to deceive John. She got a score of 3.48, less of a liar than Katerina.

I won't repeat all the stories here. There are eight of them, one for each possible combination of the three conditions. The example of a social lie in the data, by the way, got a score of 4.70, worse than Mary, but better than Katerina.

Coleman and Kay went on, did some fancy math I won't drag you through here, to find out which single condition was most important. The single most important condition, the one that tended to make you a liar more than anything else, was *intent to deceive.* The least important condition, the one that had the least effect, was *whether the sentence was literally true or not.*

The thing that most people would say makes a lie—the sentence is false—turns out to be less important than the speaker's knowledge and intentions. The thing that's most important in figuring out whether something's a lie is *what the speakers were trying to do,* not the literal truth or falsity of the words and sentences that they said.

What's in the words and sentences matters, no doubt about it. But what people are doing with the discourse matters more. People do things with words, and what they do is to *act,* and how they act differs from one group to another as much as the words and sentences themselves. Words and sentences can be rich points that inspire frames, but so can *speech acts.*

///

The concept of *speech act* lets you talk about what language is doing. It has a noble history. The philosophers developed one version of it, based on Wittgenstein's idea of "language games," situations in which people use language to accomplish social activities.

Wittgenstein fascinates me, in part because he came from my own second city, Vienna, a city I enjoy because of its contradictions. The cliché is that Vienna is a city of German surfaces and Slavic souls, and that's before they get to the Hungarian and Italian influences.

Wittgenstein was as contradictory as they come. He was the son of a rich man from a Jewish family turned Protestant who gave away his money. He was gay but played it straight. He went to England and revolutionized philosophy with a brilliant treatise on logic, which he criticized when he wrote his later book setting out the idea of language games, a book that revolutionized philosophy again. Vienna and Wittgenstein hated each other, but he couldn't break the bond and kept returning.

In the twenties, after he'd written that first book, Austria leaned into educational reform in its uncomfortable new identity as the tiny fragment of a former empire. Wittgenstein signed up as a schoolteacher in a mountain village south of Vienna.

Philosophers consider these his lost years, but my ethnographic nose smells an experience that changed him profoundly. Imagine one of the world's greatest philosophers living in the sticks, spending his days teaching kids math and reading. I'm not sure who learned more.

A few years ago, a Wittgenstein scholar rented a car and drove to the villages where he used to teach. He walked into a *Gasthaus*, spotted an old woman cleaning the floor, and asked her if she'd ever heard of Ludwig Wittgenstein. She mopped her brow. "Oh yes, the teacher. Whatever became of him?"

What became of him is that he returned to England, read mysteries and went to the movies, and told his students philosophy was a weird way to earn a living. He also wrote a book, called *Philosophical Investigations* in English, in which he showed that language wasn't an abstract entity to be contemplated in terms of the truth or falsity of its sentences. Instead, it was a living, breathing thing that formed a part of everyday life.

What Malinowski learned from the Trobriand islanders, Wittgenstein learned from those grammar school kids in the Alps. At least that's my guess. Tentative guess, because he didn't like them much. Besides, even at the end of his life, after years of residence in England, he talked about how difficult it was to live and work in English, his second language. Maybe it was life in two languacultures that moved him toward language games.

At any rate, the difference between Wittgenstein's first book on logic and his second book on language games is exactly the difference between how people usually think about lies and how Linda Coleman and Paul Kay showed that lies actually work. It's the difference between lies as false propositions and lies as knowing, deceitful acts.

Wittgenstein broke the circle around language just as Malinowski did. His ideas were picked up and turned into an approach to philosophy. The British philosopher John Austin told it like it was in his book title *How to Do Things with Words*. And the American John Searle just called his later book *Speech Acts*.

The problem with these guys is, well, they're philosophers. They wanted to talk about things like promises and commands in a new way. Are promises and commands true or false? Well, neither, really. Like lies, promises and commands depend on conditions about the *act* of promising or commanding. If the conditions are fulfilled, the promise or command is "felicitous" or "happy." Really, that's what they called it.

But the philosophers obsessed over single sentences that were examples of single speech acts. I'm obsessing over discourse that exemplifies several frames. Speech acts are a step in the right direction, but there's a ways to go.

///

Dell Hymes took a different angle on speech acts that fits what I'm trying to do here better. No surprise, since he's one of my elders in the linguistic anthropology tribe. Hymes's approach to speech acts is usually called *Ethnography of Speaking,* and he proposed it, in part, to counter what the Chomsky revolution was doing to the study of language.

I remember, during my graduate days, reading Chomsky's *Aspects of the Theory of Syntax*. God what a beautiful book, what elegant arguments and intricate models. Chomsky is a genius, and the linguistics he invented is much more interesting than the old chop-'em-up and sort-'em-out kind of grammar that existed before him.

But he stayed inside the circle. Did he ever. Here's an excerpt from the first page:

> Linguistic theory is concerned primarily with an ideal speaker-listener, in a completely homogenous speech-community, who knows its language perfectly and is unaffected by such grammatically irrelevant conditions as memory limitations, distractions, shifts of attention and interest, and errors (random or characteristic) in applying his knowledge of the language to actual performance.

I suffered the classic case of mixed emotions. Chomsky's beautiful, elegant book had little to do with what I, as an ethnographer, wanted to do with language. In fact, as I think about it, reading Chomsky was the first time that I felt the conflict that made me sit down, twenty-some years later, and write this book.

Hymes couldn't stand it either, and he set out to define another kind of linguistics, one that grew out of the same tradition of Whorf and Malinowski that I'm trying to stand on the shoulders of. He wanted a linguistics that filled in the gap between what Chomsky did and what ethnographers did when they moved in with a group of people and started to learn their languaculture.

The idea of speech acts served as the bridge. Hymes distinguished among several different levels of them, but the general truth remained the same. Language is more than words and sentences. Understanding language involves more than what the words alone carry. You have to understand the *acts* that language is part of. You have to understand what the language *counts as*. And once you know that language *counts as* paying the bill, having a conversation, or telling a lie, you have to figure out if paying the bill, having a conversation, or telling a lie is the same kind of *act* that you have always assumed it was, because chances are, it's not.

Chomsky spoke of *competence,* the ability of a speaker to produce grammatical sentences in his or her native language. Hymes took the term and extended it to show the difference between what Chomsky was doing and what he wanted to do—he wrote of *com-*

municative competence, a term I've already used in this book. Consider the example of a child crawling into its languaculture:

> Linguistic theory treats of competence in terms of the child's acquisition of the ability to produce, understand, and discriminate any and all of the grammatical sentences of a language. A child from whom any and all of the grammatical sentences of a language might come with equal likelihood would be of course a social monster. Within the social matrix in which it acquires a system of grammar a child acquires also a system of its use, regarding persons, places, purposes, other modes of communication, etc.—all the components of communicative events, together with attitudes and beliefs regarding them. There also develop patterns of the sequential use of language in conversation, address, standard routines, and the like. In such acquisition resides the child's sociolinguistic competence (or more broadly, communicative competence), its ability to participate in its society as not only a speaking, but also a communicating member.

Hymes's ethnography of speaking and his concept of communicative competence are banners under which those of us trying to erase the circle around language still march. Communicative competence is the difference between the master of grammar and dictionary and the person who has built the frames necessary to communicate.

Hymes built a model of human similarities for speech acts. Like the taxonomy of the cognitive anthropologists, it sets out one kind of frame that gets filled in with the local details, wherever you go. He summarized the similarities with the acronym SPEAKING.

Say you walk into a situation where people are talking. People, by definition, are wrapped up in a speech act. SPEAKING alerts you to characteristics of the situation that might be important. *S* stands for the *setting,* *P* for the *participants,* *E* for the *ends* they strive for, *A* for the sequence of *acts* engaged in, *K* for the *key* or tone in which the talking is done, *I* for the *instrumentalities* or tools to get the job done, *N* for the *norms* that apply, and *G* for the *genre* of talk they're engaged in.

Here's an example of how SPEAKING might work: The other day I drove to the gym for a game of racquetball. I arrived at 3:45. The parking rules changed at 4:00, but I needed time to change clothes before the game. When I came out, my car had a twenty-dollar ticket, issued at 3:55. Since faculty at Maryland haven't had a pay raise in years, and since budgets are so tight we can't do most of the things we're supposed to without using our own money, faculty morale is somewhere south of the ninth circle of hell.

So when I slid the ticket out from under the windshield wiper, let's say I focus all my aggravation on the overzealous ticket writers who tear around campus, and I head for the traffic office.

With SPEAKING as my guideline, I would describe the setting—the reception desk, the tacky carpet, and all that. I could describe the participants—the receptionist and me; the ends—fix the ticket; the acts—walk in, wait my turn, go up to the desk, etc.; the key—formal understated outrage; the instrumentalities—the ticket itself; the norms—a greeting, a statement of the problem, etc.; the genre—kind of a mini-courtroom argument.

SPEAKING helps organize my work, helps me start into a speech act to figure out what frames I need to build. But I wouldn't necessarily want to follow up on *everything* that SPEAKING called for. Instead, I want to focus on the rich points. And the frames those rich points call for might have to do with the SPEAKING model, and then again they might not.

It's the same problem that came up before, the same gap between elegant similarities and the details of particular rich points that one wants to understand. Some who use SPEAKING, like some who use taxonomy, figure that SPEAKING is everything you need when you stumble on a rich point. Fill in the blanks in SPEAKING and you've figured it out.

Not true. SPEAKING helps you see *some* of the *potential* things outside the circle of language that *might* help create frames, but it's not the whole answer. Dell Hymes never suggested that it was. On the contrary. In the parking ticket example I gave you, SPEAKING would miss one important piece of a frame—actually, the key to what the speech act was all about in its heart and soul.

If you were after the languaculture of the University of Maryland, the story I told about *why* the ticket was so aggravating would be the most important clue, a clue to a thread that runs through how faculty feel about the institution they work for, one that would help you understand, not just the ticket incident, but also what people do when they talk in a variety of situations all over campus.

Maryland, like all large organizations I've ever been associated with, frustrates action with bureaucratic ritual, and the frustration intensifies when demands increase in a time of severe budget reductions. That's a piece of a frame that would purchase you a lot of understanding around campus. Unfortunately, nothing in SPEAKING would direct you to it.

So SPEAKING, like taxonomies and the color spectrum, has its limits as a guide to human similarities. But Hymes's vision of language lies behind what I'm trying to do here. Hymes set up a view of speech acts that dissolved the circle, just as Malinowski did with context of situation, just as Wittgenstein did with language games.

///

I'm in the process of building frames for speech acts right now for Mexico. I'll never finish—frame building never stops unless you force it to. Since I'm in the beginning stages, I want to show you an example that's different from others because it's the start rather than the conclusion. My apologies to Mexicans and those outsiders who are communicatively competent in Mexico, because I'm sure I don't have it right yet, but the story will show you how frame building looks in the beginning, how encounters with rich points lead to the first fragile frames.

The subject, again, is lies. Anglo-Americans stereotype Mexicans and say that they lie more than Anglos expect. That's not a pleasant thing to report, but people say it all the time. You hear it from tourists who only superficially know the country, from Anglos who've lived there for a while, and from Mexicans describing Mexico to Anglos.

A classic number-one response. These people don't talk as I expect them to. In this case, they don't tell "the truth" where I'd expect, so they must be deficient in some way. They must *lack* the ability to tell the truth. The result—a negative picture of an entire nation of speakers. Difference plus identity isn't enough.

A little experience in the languaculture game and you recognize the number-one script right away. The alternative, the one I'm laying out in this book, leads you along a different path. You recognize the differences, the rich points, and you wonder if there aren't other frames that show that what you think are "lies" might actually be another kind of "truth."

John Condon wrote a book called *Good Neighbors: Communicating with the Mexicans,* and one of the communication problems he takes on is lies. He quotes a Mexican businessman:

> You Americans, when you think of a banana, you think of only one kind of fruit. But when you come to Mexico and visit a market, you see there are so many kinds. Some are big and solid and used for cooking, like potatoes. You never heard of such a thing. Others are tiny as your thumb and sweeter than candy. You never imagined such a thing. And I'll tell you, my friend, here in Mexico we have as many kinds of truth as there are kinds of bananas. You don't know what you've been missing.

Notice how the Mexican emphasizes different kinds of "truth," not lies. Condon goes on to write, with a pun in the introductory phrase that I wonder if he was aware of:

> Though his analogy is strained, the point is well taken: what we expect and how we define "the truth" or "a lie" is a cultural matter. When Americans and Mexicans work together, it can become a source of intercultural confusion and conflict.

I've been as fascinated with lies as Condon or Coleman and Kay, who did the study of lies I described earlier. I grew up in a world where a common phrase to characterize ordinary conversation was "telling lies." As I got older and caught culture, I wondered about this phrase that didn't exactly mean what it looked like it did. What I think my native dialect says is that when you put a rich piece of reality into language, you *have to* notice some things rather than others; you *have to* talk about some of the things you notice, but not all of them; and you *have to* choose one of hundreds of ways to put the language together to talk about them. Any talk has to be telling lies, or partial truths, if you'd prefer a more generous phrase. That's the *truth.*

So, when I got to Mexico, as far as I was concerned, people just "told lies" or "told the truth" *differently,* and I wondered how and why. These new "lies" were rich points that I needed some new frames for.

As the Mexican businessman said, there are a lot of different kinds of bananas. One kind of "lie"—Condon mentions this one, too—is captured by the phrase *pasar un buen momento,* "have a pleasant moment." In the story of Mexican conversations I told you earlier, I mentioned that if someone gets upset, everyone rallies around to make that person feel better.

One joke I make all the time in English, one that a lot of Americans creaking into middle age make as well, centers on wisecracks about getting old. The wisecracks didn't work in Mexico. The first time I tried it in Spanish, before I finally edited it out of my joke repertoire, the person I was speaking with didn't laugh at all. Instead, he talked about how the important thing was the spirit, that one could stay young no matter how old the body.

The point of conversation is to keep the moment pleasant, to construct a positive sense of life; that's why my Mexican friend reacted that way. It's more important to maintain that feeling than to "tell the truth" in some literal sense of the term. If the choice is tell the literal truth or maintain the pleasant moment, you tend to maintain. Forget a "frank exchange of views." George Washington was an inconsiderate fool for telling his parents he chopped down the cherry tree. All he did was upset them.

A related kind of "lie"—Condon mentions this, too—is to emphasize the positive and avoid mentioning the problems. In Mexico I have a business partner named Luis. Luis and I made several trips together to a customer for the new company we were both working with. On the drive to the customer's office, Luis would always say that everything was arranged, that we'd sign the order on this visit, that the customer was enthusiastic about the product and ready to work with us.

Then we'd arrive and a problem would come up that would block the order. On the ride back, Luis would say, "It's normal," and then explain what had happened. The customer had problems with the prices and he hadn't checked them before. The purchasing agent was messing with us because he didn't want a new supplier from outside his network. The director shifted things around and then forgot to follow through.

The explanations after the fact suggested that Luis anticipated the problems, but the picture before the fact was that they wouldn't occur. It happened all the time, with Luis and everyone else. Draw on the positive to characterize an event that is about to happen and leave out the negatives. They'll be bad enough when they come up. Why dwell on worst-case scenarios before the fact?

These two frames I'm hammering together fit into a common superframe. The first one keeps the current conversation smooth and pleasant; the second keeps the future rosy. There's a thread of coherence that hooks them together. But here's a third kind of "lie" that's a little different, one that Condon talks about under the concept of "time."

Lots of things get planned. We'll do this at eleven, that on Thursday, and this weekend we'll take a trip to Cuernavaca. Instead, it turns out we do this at five, that on Monday, and the trip to Cuernavaca is canceled. Multiple events are scheduled with certainty and then shift around or disappear. For the plan-oriented gringo, the shifting agenda can make you crazy.

What I eventually learned was that no one expects things to work out all the time. Problems come up and other activities become possible. An event will be suggested and scheduled. But what actually occurs at any given moment might draw from the planned events, or then again it might not. The important thing—here comes the tie to the superframe, the first tentative try at coherence—is to have a pleasant moment, not to follow a schedule you set up a week ago.

The rule I currently use is that you don't have to do anything you said you'd do, but you should call the host or hostess or organizer and let them know you're not doing it. If you just don't show after you've promised to appear, that's a bit rude, but if you don't show and let them know you're not going to, even a couple of hours after the event started, nobody bats an eye.

Like I said, these frames are fragile, first tries, the initial effort to build frames that move beyond the difference summarized in the American stereotype—Mexicans lie—into an understanding of how to tell the "truth" in Mexico.

The so-called lies are speech acts, rich points that call out for new frames. The language part is the discourse that exemplifies them, the sorts of things I just told stories about. I could tell you the stories because they represented experiences from *fieldwork*. That's where I found them.

The culture part is frames. They're *holistic*. There are hooks. They connect with attitudes toward people, toward conversations, toward future events, toward the way the world works. I listed three kinds of "lies," but I also started hooking them up together to get a superframe that shows their interconnections.

I'm working to build a coherent connection of differences, just what "culture" says you should go after. I'm working on it by *comparing* in a number of ways. I'm comparing my idea of lies with what I find in Mexico, and learning that what I originally saw as a lie is, in fact, a truth. I'm also comparing lies with truth in Mexican discourse, comparing different kinds of lies and truths with each other, and comparing different examples of the same kind of lie or truth. Building the new frames is comparative at its heart.

The frames contain *expectations,* not certainties. My frames are guidelines to what I can usually expect, based on my experience so far. But I know that, once in a while, people say cruel true things to each other in conversation, predict that a situation will be a disaster, and get angry if you don't show up on time. I know that, sometimes, people self-consciously fabricate something with bad intentions; they intend to deceive. With more work, I'll build more frames to figure out how to understand these exceptions, or maybe learn that the frames aren't complete, that the exceptions aren't exceptions at all.

The frames are *dynamic,* not static. I'm showing you what I've built so far. When I arrived in Mexico City, I was about at the level of "Mexicans lie more than Anglos expect." In five years I could write you an encyclopedia of lies and truths in both places. Frames develop and change with experience, or they should unless you give up and pull up the number-one shield.

The frames are *active,* not passive. They're not just things I build and admire and show slides of. They're resources I use to move toward communicative competence. Frames are tested continually in the laboratory of social life, and if they don't work, misunderstandings and mistakes will flash warnings the next time I talk and listen. And with that, we've come full circle back to fieldwork, to the source of the discourse that produced the rich points in the first place, and the cycle starts anew.

///

Truth in Mexico is different from truth in the United States, or at least my version of it. But the differences, the rich points, aren't impossible to handle. The experience of encountering Mexican "lies," the experience of culture, forces out the old frames. You tinker with them, assemble something to make sense out of how the "lies" weren't what they seemed. What's missing, still, is the kind of coherence I presented with the Austrian example of *Schmäh,* but then I'm an old-timer in Austria and a newcomer to Mexico.

Some coherence showed up in the general positive tone, the optimistic social attitude, that the so-called lies maintained. So I can't resist a little speculation, even though I don't yet have enough experience to back it up. Consider it a hypothesis, another example of how frame building looks in the early stages.

Coleman and Kay, remember, worked with Americans. They emphasized *individual* knowledge and intentions in their frame for the speech act. What appeared as lies in Mexico might say something that isn't true, and maybe the speaker knows it isn't true, but maybe he or she doesn't intend to deceive. So, from an American point of view, Mexican lies are "sort of" lies, like social lies, with two out of the three conditions present.

But then again, the Mexican examples I described are *normal* ways of talking, ways of maintaining the pleasant moment or formulating plans in a world where things don't always work out. The Mexican examples—at least the ones I described—*aren't* just departures from default values in an American frame. Instead, they're how one normally talks, what's *expected,* for reasons that make sense in terms of other ideas about how the world works.

The philosophers who invented speech acts emphasized *speaker's intentions* as the most important raw material for frame building. They would. They worked out of languacultures in which the individual is the center of the universe. That's the tradition that Coleman and Kay followed, and since they worked with Americans in their study, it worked well. It would be interesting to give some of their stories to Mexicans and see what *they* call a lie.

Mexico, on the other hand, is a place where the social unit is more important, especially the family. Even the Mexican constitution mentions the family dozens of times. Maybe to understand Mexican discourse, you need to think socially, not individually. Maybe individual intentions miss the point. In fact, a lot of what happens that Anglo-Americans think of as "lies" aren't really lies at all. They're just normal, proper *social* discourse, discourse that considers group members more than American discourse does.

My suspicion is that the Anglo-American emphasis on individual intentions misses the point for Mexico. And that suspicion tinkers with a change of the most fundamental kind, a change from an individual orientation to a social one. That's a change on a par with time among the Hopi and irony among the Viennese, a new frame that connects to so many different moments of discourse that it alters how you think and act and who you are.

///

Where in the surface of discourse do you look when something goes wrong with your expectations and you suspect new frames hold clues to the solution? With words it's easy. There are some technical problems with *word* that turn fascinating if you dive into linguistics, but on the whole everyone knows what a word is.

Discourse is different. Discourse is language as it naturally flows in a situation. How do you look at discourse? What do you look for? We're at the edge of a huge field, one that grows in the number of people, journals, and books every day. It's got different names. It's called discourse analysis, text linguistics, pragmatics, and a few unprintable things by its students.

Under whatever name it's called, the field includes the cast of characters you've met so far—linguists inside and outside the circle, anthropologists, sociologists, artificial intelligentsia, and philosophers. It also includes psychologists, literary critics, second-language teachers, intercultural communicators, translators and interpreters, and professional-school types who've figured out that discourse and frames are what make business, law, medicine, and politics go around.

I don't want to write an encyclopedia of that field. Not here. Not now. You don't want to read one, either. So what do I do instead?

A few years ago I worked on an article for *Smithsonian* magazine. The magazine assigned a photographer to shoot pictures for the story. When we met at the airport, he had cases and bags stacked on a cart. He joked about how he hated writers, because all they needed was a pen and a notebook.

Once we got on site, he taught me about his gear. He had several cameras, each with several different lenses. He had stacks of filters to change the way light came in through the lens. He would often shoot something from several different angles.

The analysis of discourse is like that, too. A piece of discourse can be looked at with different lenses, from different angles, from different distances, with different filters over the lens. Each combination of a lens and angle and distance and filter is something you can find several articles and books about.

Let me back up to a general principle: *The kinds of rich points you notice in discourse depend on the kinds of expectations you have, and the kinds of frames you build to solve the problem will depend on which expectations need changing.*

There is *no* combination of lens and filter and so on that will be right for every shot. What you do is look at what you want to shoot, and then figure out what to do from there.

In the examples in this book, I've shown how words, grammar, and speech acts are all possible rich points. And in some of the stories I've told in this book, I've shown you prefabricated frames— taxonomies for vehicles, Fillmore's sentence grammar for junkie vocabulary, Dell Hymes's SPEAKING for language in use. The prefab frames were all useful in some cases, but none of them covered all the territory.

The languaculture business is like that, possibilities that you put together in some way for each encounter you go through. What you do will be different from one time to another. It's a tinkering kind of field. Car won't start? Let's see. Plugs firing? Yep. Must be the fuel. Gas in the tank? Yep. How about . . .

Scenes in Tom Wolfe's book *The Right Stuff* come to mind. He wrote that the test pilots would report even as the experimental aircraft headed straight for the ground. "Well, I've tried this, and I've tried that, and . . . "

To learn the languaculture game, you need to work on different problems, store up the various cameras and lenses and filters so that you have the right ones to recognize and fix a specific rich point when you get to it. People do this all the time. You don't have to be a pro.

But I want to show off a couple of pieces of professional equipment, equipment that'll give you some ideas about how to look at discourse. I'll pick a few that illustrate some of the most powerful lenses in the camera bag and give you an idea of who invented them and why.

///

Discourse rich points, like the rich points found with grammar or words, call for frame building. When you bridge the difference between the speech act you brought with you and the speech act you stumbled over, you've moved into a new languaculture.

The number-one types act the same way with speech acts as they do with words and grammar. Mexican lies are a good case in point. Many Anglo-Americans will tell you that Mexicans lie. What they mean is that they lie more than their own Anglo-American frames lead them to expect. And of course from their point of view, they're correct. They're in the starting gate of culture. They notice a difference and attribute it to a social identity.

But if they maintain number-one status, they stay within their own frames to solve the problem. They never leave the gate. "Mexicans lie more than I expect, given my frames. So I guess they just lie a lot." Number-one types never wonder if the problem isn't in *their* frame. They just figure that anyone who doesn't live up to their frames is deficient in some way. The deficit theory rears its ugly head again—*explain others by what they lack*—good old-fashioned ethnocentrism.

The worst problem is that the number-one types probably aren't aware that they have any frames at all. They're buried in patterns of unconscious habit, lost in the lessons of childhood that drill in how the world works until a kid forgets and figures that's how the world *naturally* works. Culture happens when one realizes that something "natural" is actually just a frame, that the way one always assumed things were isn't always the case.

True number-one types won't change their frames, probably won't admit that they have any, since they're not aware of them.

Even if they do get a glimmer of them, they'll see them as a momentary revelation of how truly superior they are. Number-one types are epoxied into their social identity. They won't drag frames into consciousness and consider alternatives. That's calling into question who they are, perhaps in a fundamental way. The terror such changes inspire among the number-one types rivals that of a Stephen King novel. What are they afraid of? The answer to that question would change the world.

Whatever the answer, the number-one types, wherever they are, can't figure out rich points that pop up in discourse. The more extreme cases can't even *see* them. The best they'll ever do is learn a grammar and memorize a vocabulary that they'll just paste onto the bottom of their own speech act frames. They'll *talk,* but they won't *communicate.*

To take the next step, to experience culture, to become aware of speech acts and start construction on frames for new ones, two promising areas to start are speech act *structure* and speech act *content,* and that's what the next chapter deals with.

Is it me.

Speech Act Lumber
and Paint

RON and Suzanne Scollon worked for years in Alaska with Athabaskan Indians. Right from the beginning, they noticed that when Anglos and Athabaskans tried to communicate, the verbal landscape was littered with rich points. And, they argued, most of those rich points pushed up from speech acts, not from language inside the circle.

> Recently we have begun to see that the main problem in interethnic communication is not caused by grammar. Although languages use grammar as the system of expressing ideas, in interethnic communication it is the discourse system which produces the greatest difficulty. It's the way ideas are put together into an argument, the way some ideas are selected for special emphasis, or the way emotional information about the ideas is presented that causes miscommunication. The grammatical system gives the message while the discourse system tells how to interpret the message.

The Scollons noticed, as do most Anglos, that things didn't work right when Athabaskans and Anglos talked, even though both sides might use grammatical English. Unlike most, the Scollons set out to find the rich points and fix the frames.

Problems started right at the beginning. Anglos almost always spoke first. Athabaskans, it turns out, think it's important to know what the social relationship is before they talk with someone. So, when Athabaskans meet an Anglo, they wait and see what happens. Anglos, on the other hand, figure that the way to establish a relationship is to talk a while. So, when Anglos meet an Athabaskan, they start chatting away, usually by asking a bunch of questions.

From this problem follows another. The person who speaks first introduces a topic. That fact is painfully obvious, but much frame building simply makes the obvious explicit instead of unconscious and then spins out the consequences. And the consequences here are dramatic. The person who introduces the topic controls what the talking is about. A friend of mine jokes all the time: "Let's talk about *you* for a while. How do *you* like my new hairdo?"

Since Anglos speak first, they control the topics. The results are a conversation about what the Anglo wants to talk about. Ironically enough, the Scollons report that a frequent conversational opener that the Athabaskans use is translated into English as "What are you thinking?" In other words, even if Athabaskans talk first, they often invite the other to introduce a topic, rather than introducing one themselves.

The next problem comes when it's time for a new person to take a turn. When we talk among ourselves, we read all kinds of cues without even thinking about it. The cues tell us when a speaker is closing down, when there's an opportunity for someone else to take the floor. Those cues vary wildly from group to group.

One cue is a pause. Athabaskans allow a slightly longer pause than Anglos do, maybe half a second or so, but enough to make a difference. The results—an Athabaskan will wait patiently for the speaker to continue when an Anglo has already decided that the speaker is finished.

You can imagine what a mess this makes. The Anglo talks, finishes what he is saying, then waits for the Athabaskan to take his turn. But the Athabaskan is still waiting for the Anglo to finish. The Anglo decides that the Athabaskan has nothing to say, so he just moves right along and says something else.

Or consider it from the opposite angle of vision. The Athabaskan talks and then pauses between thoughts. But before he starts up again, the Anglo figures that the Athabaskan is done and jumps in with whatever he has to say.

There's another difference in how long one should talk. Athabaskans have a general idea that once someone starts talking, you leave them whatever time they need to say what they're going to say. From an Anglo point of view, this can start to look like a monologue, since the Anglos expect shorter turns when they talk with each other.

And finally, the idea of how a conversation should close is different. Anglos want to sum things up and make some kind of evaluative comment on the conversation, even something as simple as "Well, been nice talking to you." Anglos close off the conversation and set up future conversations by expressing pleasure at what's happened.

Athabaskans don't close conversations like that. In fact, from an Anglo point of view, they don't close them at all. They don't like to make predictions about the future, and most closings are designed to do just that for Anglos, leave open the possibility of future contact.

The Scollons write about many more differences between Anglos and Athabaskans than these. They use a variety of cameras, lenses, and filters. But just this list of differences makes the point about two different *structures,* structures that differ across a number of different speech acts.

First, things that seem "obvious" or "natural" aren't at all. Who talks first, who talks next, who opens and closes conversations and how do they do it—these sound like rich points that could wipe the enthusiasm out of a lottery winner. But there's nothing obvious or natural about them. On the contrary, they vary all over the place.

Second, the circle around language doesn't appear. In fact, the Scollons tell us that the differences they've described show up whether the two speakers are using English, Athabaskan, or so-called village English. Even if one uses the grammar and vocabulary of the other person, he might *still* use the frames from his own languaculture. Grammar just isn't where the action is.

Third, the differences make a huge difference. Anglos and Athabaskans do things that don't meet the expectations of the other. Buried frames about how speech acts are structured, frames that started growing in the unconscious in childhood, give them different instructions. The metric is off, the rhythm doesn't work, there are two conductors for the same symphony.

From a number-one Athabaskan point of view, Anglos talk before they know you, just talk about what they want to talk about, don't wait until you are done, and flirt with bad luck by guessing about the future. For a number-one Anglo, Athabaskans are reticent, never have anything to say, and would let a conversation drag on for centuries if you didn't finish it for them.

The interpretation one has of the other isn't just that a problem occurred, that the talk isn't working right and it's the other's fault. The interpretations are that the other is deficient in some way, that he or she lacks the qualities that hold people inside the boundaries of normal behavior.

What the Scollons do, by way of contrast, is to take the rich points, find the frames, and fix them. They document the rich points and bring the alternative frames to awareness. They built frames that filled in the spaces between. That was their academic job, and they did it well. Based on that work, they then tried to repair the damages by working in situations in which Anglos and Athabaskans came into contact, situations like the schools and the courts. I don't know how well they did, but at least they tried.

///

Back in the seventies the National Indian Board on Alcohol and Drug Abuse hired my friend Dick Stephens and me as consultants. Four Indian sites—that's what the Native Americans all said, "Indian"—had received grants to set up culturally appropriate programs to treat drug and alcohol problems. The Indian sites were failing by Anglo agency standards, so they hired us to come in and help them figure out how to tell the agency about what they'd done right.

Here's one way they "failed."

An Indian program director in Montana showed us some videotapes. In the first tape, a group of Indian men sat in a circle on folding chairs. The therapist asked questions about how they felt, about their drinking, about what problems they solved when they were drunk.

They weren't Athabaskans, but their way was more like the Athabaskans' than it was like the Anglos'. You can guess what happened. Nothing. Nothing at all. The Anglo model of group therapy rested on Anglo frames of how to talk, not on their Indian frames.

So the program director tried an experiment. He asked each member of the group to pick out an Indian historical figure and research him. Then the director set up the group like a TV talk show. He'd interview the group member in his character as the historical figure.

He'd start out with questions about his tribe, when he was born, and other basic biographical data. Then he'd start in with some loaded questions, like "So what did you think when they moved you onto the reservation?"

All kinds of personal feelings started coming out through the historical figure's mouth. It was more powerful than I can express to you here. I left the viewing angry, angry at America, and at anthropology, for idealizing the Indian past and neglecting the Indian present.

But once I cooled down, I understood that the program "failure" was a failure by Anglo expectations that didn't allow what the program *did* do to count as a success. The Indians were angry because they were damned if they did and damned if they didn't. They were told to develop cultural programs, but then to submit to an evaluation in Anglo terms. When they got down to the details of therapy, the contradictory demands boxed them into a no-win situation. I wish I'd read the Scollons' book *before* I did that work.

///

This business of how speech acts start and stop and how turns get organized came out of sociology, of all places. Sociologists paper the world with survey forms and then put the numbers that result through statistical hoops. That's their popular image. But not all of them are like that. In fact, some of them worry about the distance between survey numbers and real life as much as the rest of us.

Harold Garfinkel worried back in the late fifties. He worried because he thought the raw material of sociology should be what the folks were doing on the ground, how it was that they woke up in the morning and started to make things happen. That was where sociology should be located, he argued, not in some number that was the result of a hidden social moment that we outsiders didn't know anything about.

Since he wanted to know how the *folks* actually structured everyday life, since he was after the *methods* they used to get things done, he called his version of sociology *ethnomethodology*.

The similarity between this clunky word and the cognitive anthropologists' words like *ethnobotany* and *ethnozoology* isn't an accident. Garfinkel worked with some of the early cognitive anthropologists at the beginning of his career, and he took the famous *ethno-* prefix from them.

In fact, it's easy to get carried away. You can "ethno" almost anything—ethnopoetics, ethnopornography, ethnopolitics. *Ethno* is a prefix that throws a switch, an important one, that changes the point of view. Ethno-*X* means that you're interested in *X* from the point of view of some group, not from the point of view of the anointed experts in *X*.

Garfinkel invented a way to check ethnomethods. One way to make them explicit was to ignore them. If you acted in opposition to some ethnomethod buried in the unconscious, you'd get a reaction from the people around you. In other words, you make a mistake on purpose. If you think you've figured out an expectation in some frame that structures discourse, then you don't do it. You create a rich point and see if people have the "say what?" reaction that they should.

This trick is now called, appropriately enough, *Garfinkeling*. There are plenty of stories about Garfinkeling, and they aren't always methods of social research. Once I was making a person-to-person collect call. The operator and I were running through the drill according to our shared frames. Then she asked me for my name and I told her.

"Oh, are you Mary's brother?"

"Huh? Mary? Yes, I am."

"God, we went to school together. Far out. How is she? I haven't seen her in years."

It took me awhile to recover from my blown frames. I had to shift from dealing with a long-distance operator to chatting with an old friend of my sister's. I'd been Garfinkeled, pleasantly enough, but Garfinkeled all the same. Long-distance operators had no business turning into old friends of my sister's.

Margaret Mead was another famous telephone Garfinkeler. She never answered the phone right. Usually you pick up the phone, say "hello," and the person identifies herself or, if it's someone you'd better recognize or else, just returns the greeting.

This little telephone opener always involves two parts. When you greet somebody, you expect them to greet you in return, on the telephone or anywhere else. The ethnomethodologists call this bit of structure an *adjacency pair*. There are lots of them—question and answer is another famous example. Adjacency pairs are pieces of structure that litter our world. We expect people to play their parts.

You know the old joke about the guy who, when you ask him how he's doing, actually tells you? The guy doesn't play his part. He's supposed to say "fine" or "lousy," not take the question as an actual request for him to deliver an existential monologue. If you don't think adjacency pairs are real, try not filling in the second part of the pair sometime and see what kind of peculiar look you get. Go ahead and Garfinkel a little.

Margaret Mead didn't ever fill in her second part when she made a telephone call. As soon as the answerer said "hello," she launched off into whatever was on her mind. When you're famous you get to break the rules more. But then Mead was a master Garfinkeler. She Garfinkeled the whole American culture, starting with *Coming of Age in Samoa*.

Garfinkeling is about moments in discourse when the frames don't work. It's about languaculture, about making a rich point happen to prove that a frame is real.

///

Some of the ethnomethodologists who followed Garfinkel turned their attention to language, to how people talked when they had conversations out there in the ordinary world. Though they started out with conversations, and continue to obsess over them by and large, the bits of structure they came up with turn out to apply to numerous speech acts, just as the Scollons showed in their work.

One of the interesting things about conversations, they noticed, is that they don't have the same rigid rules that a classroom or a job interview does. Conversations are wide open at the beginning. No one sits in an official role, no one person has the right to run the show. In conversations, at least in principle, everyone is created equal.

So, some serious organizational problems have to get solved every time a conversation is held. One problem is, what will be talked about? A *topic* has to be established, and everybody has to agree it's a good idea to talk about it. And when that topic peters out, or when someone has something else they want to talk about, a new topic has to be introduced and the group has to accept or reject it and, if they accept, *shift* the *topic*.

A second problem: Since there's no Robert's Rules of Order for conversations, the group has to figure out who gets to talk when and for how long. One person has to get and hold the floor while he or she talks, then a transition is made to another person, and so on. In a refreshing burst of ordinary language, this problem is called *turn-taking*.

The conversational analysts also deal with openings and closings and many other problems that I won't go into here. But *topic shift* and *turn-taking* are two of the classics, two proposed similarities to carry forth into the languacultural world. The way these problems get solved are important methods by which folks build conversations, two of the most important *ethnomethods*.

Different groups solve the problems in different ways, so when a member of one group encounters another, rich points appear. The Scollons showed us that the Athabaskans and the Anglos had different ethnomethods for turns and topics. The differences resulted in two musicians playing different tunes and created a dissonant mess.

But there are differences even among the Anglos. Deborah Tannen wrote a book about a Thanksgiving dinner she held in her apartment in Berkeley. She invited some friends from New York City and some Berserklians. I especially like this study because I'm a northern Californian who lived in New York for a couple of years and in Washington, D.C., for more years than I can remember.

New Yorkers speak more quickly and shift topics more rapidly. We all know that. But the way it's done is fascinating. At least it fascinated me when I first moved to New York. Someone has the floor and talks. As soon as I know what they're going to say, I can jump in, finish the sentence to show I understand, and take off into my own turn.

The northern California I know isn't like that. Someone talks, and I lie back and listen and let them roll for a while. When they're done, there'll be a pause that will flash like a green light to announce that someone else can have the floor.

So guess what happened at the Thanksgiving dinner? Right. The New Yorkers steamrollered the Californians, not with any bad intentions, but just because their *conversational style* was different.

I still get in trouble when I go back to California until I readjust. After years in Washington, my normal style is pretty East Coast, more like New York than California. But I'll go out to California, to Nevada City where my kinfolks live, and sometimes I pack up a project, like this book, and stay out there a month so I can concentrate free of telephone calls and memos.

The first few days are hell.

Last time I ran into a woman who used to work on my father's newspaper. She was standing around talking with a bunch of people, most of them vaguely old-hippie-looking. She was talking about how she met her new boyfriend, who lived in New York, how she just ran into him in the lobby of a hotel in Chicago. I picked up at "in the lobby" and overlapped and made a wisecrack.

"Yeah, that's a service a lot of hotels provide now."

She and one guy laughed, but the other four people looked at me, horrified that I'd interrupt and say such a thing. I'd broken local ethnomethods for turn and topic at the same time. My California side flipped over on top and I explained that I didn't mean anything bad by it, it was just a joke, that among my friends in D.C. we joked with each other like that all the time.

The guy who'd laughed, bearded, in a flannel shirt and old jeans, looked down at the ground and shook his head.

"Yeah, I grew up in Brooklyn. I miss it."

///

Turns and topics have to be managed so that a conversation, or any other speech act for that matter, can happen. The way they are managed changes from group to group. Even within the group, the way people act is different. Some people shove topics down your throat and jump into a turn with karate kicks; others oil their topics and slide them in; still others introduce them like a shy newcomer at the garden party.

That's one of the reasons the sociologists were so fascinated. They wonder about social relationships, about power differences, about status and authority, about how those abstractions cook down to a group of people actually making a moment in the social world happen. Turns and topics are where you can see those differences come to life.

I wish I had a nickel for every time I've heard this story. An authority figure, a boss or a parent, sits down with his subordinates, employees or kids, and says he wants to have a talk, an open, honest talk. You know, "forget I'm the boss" or "forget I'm your father or mother."

That last line's a little off. A kid whose parent said "forget I'm your father or mother" would be one messed-up kid.

The employees or the kids usually aren't that comfortable, because they can smell what's coming. What's coming is that the usual frames for conversation are supposed to operate, but the boss or the parent won't let them. If the employee or kid tries to introduce a topic, the boss or parent just picks it up and tosses it away. If the boss or parent has something to say, they jump in, maybe while the other is in mid-sentence, and grab the floor.

It makes employees and kids crazy, this announcement that turns and topics are up for grabs, conversation-style, followed by behavior that makes it clear that the old system still operates, that the boss or parent is in control. Bosses and parents don't even notice; employees and kids do. When you pay attention to topics and turns, the verbal texture of the local political game becomes clear.

Topics and turns are also two concepts on which those who study the differences between men and women often hang their analysis. Men are more competitive, women more cooperative, according to one hypothesis. In the details of the conversation, men impose their topics and refuse to recognize it when others try to bring something else up. Men will grab a turn, hang on to it, and fight intruders off, while women will cooperate more to involve other participants.

Those are the default values in the frame, and we've all been in conversations that support them. But some conversations show the opposite, with women who compete with their turns and topics and men who hang on to the flying conversation by their fingernails. Things can also be more mixed up than either extreme would suggest.

There's a problem here that I've ignored and will continue to ignore until the chapter after next. All Anglo-Americans aren't the same, since conversation structure can be a rich point between New Yorkers and northern Californians. But then Anglo New Yorkers aren't the same, since it can be a rich point between men and women. But then men aren't all the same, since some of them include others when they talk.

Just to complicate things more, some people struggle against how they're supposed to structure speech acts because they're creative, or rebels, or Garfinkelers working on a dissertation in ethnomethodology.

While languaculture, I hope, gets clearer and clearer, the simple way I've attributed it to different social identities gets more and more complicated. How can I claim that Mexicans, Californians, or junkies *all* have such and such a languaculture? Are the social facts really so crisp and clear?

No. Later in the book, the problem of social identity needs dusting off. And the dust will obscure the clean edges of the social facts and blur the view of languacultural boundaries.

///

Whenever you talk, whenever you listen, you're in the middle of a *speech act,* whether you like it or not. The grammar and dictionary are just part of something larger, some frames that go well beyond them, frames that tell you whether the discourse *structure* is right or not. Speech-act structure can be a rich point just as much as words and grammatical constructions can. What *you* think of as a conversation and a lie might not have much to do with what *they* think conversations and lies are.

And conversations and lies are just samples. Academics *present papers.* Ethnographers *interview* and *take notes.* Businesspeople *negotiate.* Folks at dinner *tell stories.* People who disagree *argue.* Students *learn.* Job applicants *interview.* People who want expert advice *consult*. Customers in a clothing store *make a purchase*. Patients *go to doctors* and lawyers *consult their clients*.

Those are just a few of a long, long list of speech acts. And they aren't so neatly separated, either. Several speech acts dance around a particular moment of talk. The point isn't to work all this out, not in this book. The point is that speech acts break the circle around language, finally and for all time.

Speech acts add new depth to languaculture. Now rich points aren't triggered only by words and sentences. There might be no problems at that level. Sentences might be easily understood, one by one, as they flow by. Instead, the rich point is inspired by discourse, because of broken expectations in the speech-act frame, the frame that people are using to guide what it is they're doing with those words and sentences.

You can't assume that *your* version of the speech act is what everyone else is operating with. If there's a problem, it might have nothing to do with words and grammar, but rather with the unconscious frames that are laying out a different speech-act structure. The frames, as usual, have to be hauled up into awareness and changed if you want to communicate.

The experience of culture isn't just inspired by—maybe not even mostly inspired by—words and sentences. The experience also flows out of differences in what those words and sentences are *doing,* in the speech acts that give them their shape.

///

Speech acts have a structure; but they also have *content*. Once you know the new frames for a conversation structure, you're only partway home. You don't just talk structure. You need something to talk *about*. Once you've learned what's a lie and what isn't, you use your new frames to lie or tell the truth about something.

Say I tell you the perfect American lie—I mean to deceive you, I know what I'm saying is false, and I say it. That's the structure. I also lie *about* something. I say, "If you don't buy this book, my wife and kids will starve." Or I say, "If you don't buy this book, a baby seal will die." Or, "If you don't buy this book, I won't be able to get an Uzi."

Those are all lies. By their structure shall you know them. I don't have a wife or kids, I have no intention of taking the royalties from a book and somehow making it available to a baby seal, and I don't want an Uzi. I know these things aren't true, and when I say them, I intend to deceive you.

The structure is the road map to the local territory. It shows the interstate and the location of the on- and off-ramps. But the content is the landscape, the hills and valleys and trees, what you see when you *look out the window.*

A few years ago I talked with a freighter captain in Seattle. He complained about the new crew who climbed onto the bridge and did amazing tricks with computer printouts and digital readouts. Recently, there'd been some accidents due to local problems that could have been avoided if they'd just looked outside instead of at the technology. His new mission in life, he said, was to walk onto the bridge, clear his throat, and shout, "Look out the window."

The content of the lies, what you see when you look out the window, tells you more than that they are false, that I know they're false, and that I intend to deceive you. There's more to the lies than just structure. Each particular lie also has some content that broadcasts all kinds of rich points.

Lie number one, about the wife and kids, rests on an outdated model of nuclear-family life, the working husband/father with the little woman and the rug rats at home waiting for his paycheck. Sort of a *Married with Children* format, if you know that TV show.

Nowadays I use the "wife and kids" cliché as a joke. I'll ask a female colleague how the wife and kids are doing. It's a joke because two-income households are normal now, and many women in the workplace—with and without rug rats—live husband-free. Lie number one dances with an American story about recent changes in family and political economy, and connects further, if I wanted to take the time, with issues of child rearing and child care, all the way over to the fact that latchkey kids are now one of the public libraries' main afternoon clients. The content of lie number one ties into numerous frames of American languaculture.

Different connections appear with lies two and three. "Save a baby seal" is a play on the "save an *X*" cliché that arose in the sixties, plus an association with environmental consciousness by alluding to a famous and horrible hunting practice. "Buy an Uzi" calls up all kinds of associations around how easy it is to get an attack weapon in the United States, together with all the aggressive or defensive reasons people buy them.

Each lie individually associates with how the American world works and the history and politics that explain why it works that way. The content of the lies ties into frames about America, ties the discourse into society. Those ties pull outsiders deeper into the languaculture, make them communicatively competent, turn them into people who hear the echoes and associations in the things Americans say.

But that's not the end of the story. If we compare the three lies, we see a thread running through them. All three lies are about the monetary value of the book. (By the way, I only noticed that after I made them up.) You should buy the book because it produces revenue for the author; then the author can take that money and do something else with it.

I could have thought of other lies. "If you buy this book, you can start your car easier on cold mornings." "If you buy this book, you'll learn how to make a better salsa." But I didn't. The lies I *did* tell all foregrounded the material value of the book. Earlier, I told a story to illustrate that the old stereotype of the materialistic American might have something to it. I just demonstrated that theme again without meaning to.

Once the content of the lies enters the picture, frames arc away from the speech acts into the American story. The analysis begins to resemble the distances traveled into the Austrian story from the simple word *Schmäh*. Richer points would be hard to find.

Content is where the action is; structure is how you get there. When you deal with a grammar, with a vocabulary, with a speech act, you need a structure to approach them. Structure *can* be a rich point, no doubt about that. But structure lets you make sense out of content, what it is that's being said and done inside that particular moment, and content is where most of the languacultural action is. Content is the major source of rich points, the places where the differences are so grand that you put up a fence with construction signs and build new frames.

Content isn't very academic. Academics celebrate structure. It's important work, because without structure you can't get started. Besides, people who dwell only on content deceive themselves; they use some kind of structure and deny it at the same time. Number-one types use a structure all the time. It goes like this: Anything that I don't understand is a deficiency on the part of the other person. That's an example of a structure that is guaranteed to get you no-where.

But content, I'm telling you, content is where the action is. Content is what happened last summer in Mexico City when I saw an example of the new Mexican cinema and realized it had something to do with an article I'd read in a magazine, a recent change announced by the Mexican president, two conversations I'd had that week, and something I'd seen happen in the streets. In Mexico I learned some different structures, but content moved me most deeply into Mexican languaculture.

///

I wish I knew more about music. I'd like to write about jazz in a sophisticated way, but I don't have the musical training to do it. The reason I'd like to write about it is to make some sense out of the blend of structure and content. I know that American jazz structure grew out of a mix of African and European musical traditions. I know that jazz musicians experiment with many other traditions as well—Caribbean, Latin American, and Asian, and plenty of others.

Right now I'm listening to a tape of Jan Garbarek, a Norwegian jazz musician who experiments with influences from ancient Norse music. Last summer in Mexico City I listened to a group—named, ironically enough, Antropólogo—play jazz laced with traditional Mexican musical ideas. In Vienna a few years ago a group took off into a jazz piece after they introduced Strauss waltz themes. In all these cases, there was no doubt that the music was jazz.

I know that classical musicians can do the same thing. Bartók traveled around Hungary and picked up folk music traditions that he used in his compositions. Dvořák composed something new and different when he visited America and heard some local music. Stravinsky was a jazz fan. But there's no doubt that their music is classical.

I know about world music, rock and roll that picks up and uses musical ideas from all over the globe. But it's still rock and roll.

There's something about jazz, classical, and rock and roll that you recognize, something about the way it's put together, its structure. Even the blended styles, like fusion—a mix of jazz notes and rock rhythms—are considered blends because you hear jazz and rock structures at the same time.

Music is a structure, a similarity, something that is part of the human situation wherever you find it. Different musical structures exist. I've just mentioned three Western structures that have gone global—jazz, classical, and rock. But once you've got the structure, think of all the different songs you can play.

Languaculture is the same. When you explore another languaculture, you have to locate and fix the structural rich points. Things *can't* make sense because you don't know how they're organized. Grammar and the structure of speech acts are the front end of some important rich points that you must build frames for.

Just as Boas and Margaret Mead said, structure is something that you have to master to get on with fieldwork. And just as the early linguistic anthropologists said, there are some interesting rich points in those structures, like numeral classifiers, like pronouns, like verb conjugations. And just as the examples of conversations and lies show, rich points lurk in speech-act structures as well.

But structure is just the beginning, the way into content. Content opens up the meaning of the linguistic surfaces. Content lets you start hearing the echoes in those surfaces, echoes of associations to other people, other situations, to history and politics. Content reveals the themes that give you a sense of the major differences between the world that shaped you and the one you've just encountered.

Structure is the path. But content is what you see while you're walking, if you look around you or "out the window," and what you hear when you listen to the song.

///

Turn-taking and topic shift reveal structural paths, important ones that backlight rich points in conversations, between Athabaskans and Anglos, between Mexicans, Austrians, and Americans, between New Yorkers and Californians, and between men and women.

Turn-taking and topic shift unlocked structural differences in those examples. But what about content? Once you understand *how* to talk in a Mexican or Austrian or American conversation, you have to know what people are talking about and have something to say.

Maybe turn-taking and topic shift are like the fundamentals of conversational music, markers of a rhythm that let you look at content anywhere. Michael Moerman wrote a book called *Talking Culture* in which he argued exactly that point.

Moerman worked in Thailand, so first of all he had to ask the structural question: Does the idea of turns and topics, a way that grew out of American conversations, work in Thailand? Or does it actually just mirror a bunch of hidden American frames that don't work anywhere else?

Do turns and topics help see the structure and content of what the Thai are doing? They work pretty well, it turns out. In fact, Moerman talks about conversational analysis as a "metric," a "sort of background graph paper" to lay particular conversations on to get to content. He uses turns and topics as a similarity in terms of which to go after differences.

He doesn't just deal with conversations. He uses the "metric," the similarities that conversational analysis provides, to range across several different kinds of Thai situations. For example, he looks at the courtroom. There's a different structure in this case, compared to what a fan of Judge Wapner would expect. Rich points everywhere. There are no arguments and challenges. The judge writes notes from the questions and answers of lawyers and defendant and then later writes up a summary.

When Moerman lays bare the structure of the courtroom with conversational analysis, the Thai style comes to life. To take just one quick example, a Thai lawyer asks a question, and if the answer doesn't fit, he quickly follows up with another version that tries to force the answer in the direction he needs it to go. When he gets an answer he wants, he pauses to signal to the judge that the time has come to write something down. The strategy doesn't always work, but it's Thai-style courtroom procedure, one that fits into broader Thai themes about avoiding confrontation and conflict when one person talks with another.

Turns and topics are a metric that helps an outsider build frames for a new structure. Now, what about content? Though Moerman uses the structure to get to content in his courtroom studies, I'm going to shift to a more straightforward example from his book that will serve my purposes here.

In the original, Moerman gives us the Thai text, a close translation, and a gloss into English. He lays out detail in terms of pause and intonation and other important aspects of how people talk. I'll just include a couple of things in the English version I'm giving you here—pause and overlap. When two speakers talk at the same time, the overlap is marked by "//" to show where it occurs.

Here's the cast of characters: the district officer is a local government official; Sam and Bob are villagers, though I've given them American names to match the initials Moerman used in the original for ease of reading. Sam's wife, unnamed in the original, participates as well. Ba Naa is the person they are talking about.

DISTRICT OFFICER: Where was the singer from (.7-second pause)?
   Someone from this village?
SAM: Um a guy um who stays at the infirmary at Acan B's there.
BOB: What you talking about the singer?
SAM: That's right. That Ba Naa.
SAM'S WIFE: Ba Naa the l//eper
SAM: //he is sort of sick, that guy.
BOB: hmmm
SAM: He usually stays with A//can B
SAM'S WIFE: //Baa Naa the son of methaw Mun of
   Chiengban. uncle.
BOB: Oh.
SAM: That Ba Naa.

The example shows some of the eternal verities of conversational analysis. The district officer opens with a question, and after a long pause, asks the question a different way. He's made the first move in a question/answer adjacency pair, and when no answer comes he waits for it and then tries the question again. Exactly what happens in conversations everywhere. Sam cuts in on his wife while she's talking, just like guys are stereotypically said to do, though she does the same later on. As far as structure goes, similarities connect us to the Thai villagers in a pretty straightforward way.

But then Moerman uses the structure to get at content, to

the critical question, What in the world is going on here? Ba Naa, it turns out, has a serious skin disease. It's not leprosy, as Sam knows, since he works at the clinic. But the disease produced a nickname for Ba Naa, namely, Ba Naa the leper, and some villagers, thinking he really does have leprosy, have been complaining about having him around.

The district officer, the highest government official any villager is ever likely to meet, could cause some trouble here. In the course of talking about music, the district officer slides dangerously close to a problem that Sam wants to keep him distant from.

That's why the district officer doesn't get a quick answer. That's why Sam "ums" around when he takes his turn. That's why Sam cuts off his wife when she uses Ba Naa's nickname "the leper," and that's why she cuts him off later with a full specification to make sure Bob the village elder gets the idea that they want to avoid his nickname. That's why Sam shifts from "infirmary" in one turn to "stays with Acan B" in a later one.

The villagers are protecting Ba Naa from any bright official ideas the district officer might get if he puts two and two together.

The structure of turns and topics works as a bridge from us to the Thai villagers. It lays bare the content, and the content forces us to build frames to deal with the rich points. There are things going on with disease, with villager-government relations, with the role of singers, and with husbands and wives and elders that are different from what we know about.

The content confronts us with the differences that we need to go after to learn about the Thai village life that makes up Thai village languaculture. The *structure* of village conversation renders those *content* differences visible to us, the American outsiders.

///

At the beginning of my senior year in college, I received a letter from some official office, blinking red, with flames shooting off the side of it, urgent. I was supposed to graduate in a year and I hadn't taken several requirements—P.E., for example. You were supposed to have six one-credit courses in P.E., unless you were married or a member of the ROTC. Really, that was the rule.

Another of my missing requirements was a humanities course.

So I signed up for an introduction to art history class, art appreciation, that sort of thing. For the first time in years I was grateful I'd gone to Catholic school. I knew who all those saints were. I was way ahead of the Protestants and Jews in terms of content.

But I didn't know anything about structure. During the class the prof talked about line and shadow, color and texture, composition and perspective. He was an old pro at the course—made teaching look easy, which I now know only reflected how hard he worked at it. The prof taught me how to *see* a painting, how to look at its structure.

Toward the end of the class, he sent us all to the university museum to look at a painting, any painting, and write a description of it. Going in I wondered how I was going to fill a page. I can't remember what painting I picked, but I think it had a lot of overweight angels in it. I looked for a couple of minutes, saw things I'd never noticed before, and wrote and wrote. What he'd taught me about structure led me into deeper views of content.

That's what *this* book is, a language appreciation course, a use of structure to get at content. That's why I've complained so often about language inside the circle, because the structure it offers doesn't let you see the right content to get at languaculture. That's why communicative competence requires the experience of culture, because you can't flip from one structure to another without realizing, first, that there *is* a structure, and second, that it isn't written in stone; others are possible, and those others lead you to see different content.

Once you learn to see in terms of structure, content appears richer, more dramatic, more intricate and complicated and revealing.

///

Structure lets you see rich points in your own language as well. What follows is a fragment of transcript from an interview I did with an independent trucker named Ted Brooks. I spent a year trying to find out how independent trucking looked from the trucker's point of view. One kind of raw material for my work was a career history interview, a fancy name for asking people how they got into trucking and then sitting back and listening to their story.

I went on a trip with Ted from Baltimore to Oregon with several thousand pounds of sheet plastic in the trailer. The trip took place during one of the most miserable winters of the eighties, and I proved Whorf right by learning four hundred different words for *cold.*

As we rambled along the well-kept interstate in Minnesota, slicing through the cold clear air in "Phredd," the name of Ted's truck, I suggested we do "the interview." Ted, bored by the lack of disasters that he usually had to deal with, agreed that the time was right.

Interviews aren't as full of turns as conversations are. They're full of long passages where one person speaks and tells his story. That's one of the reasons ethnographic interviews are so easy to get people to agree to. How many times in life do you have the opportunity to talk at great length about how you think the world works to a person who is genuinely fascinated by what you're saying?

The more normal case is what Fran Lebowitz described in her book *Social Studies:* "The opposite of talking isn't listening; the opposite of talking is waiting."

When I got home and transcribed Ted's interview, I decided to take some *structural* ideas from discourse analysis and see how they would help me with the *content.* The example contains some new symbols I have to tell you about first.

There are *pause* symbols: Long pauses are shown with a number in parentheses, like (2.4), that tells you the actual length in seconds. A + means a pause longer than what you'd expect, but less than a second. An = means a run-on—the speaker continued without the normal pause that he uses.

Punctuation marks are similar to what you're used to, but they follow the intonation of the speaker. A . or period means a falling intonation, the "I'm done with this chunk of talk" signal. A , or comma means a rising "more to come" intonation. "So you know, I went to the store and I picked up ten jars of peanut butter because they were on sale." Listen to the intonation you make when you say that sentence as you say "know," "store," and "butter." You're signaling the listener that you're not done yet, probably with a rising tone. Compare these with the "I'm done" falling tone as you say "sale." A ? or question mark, just as it suggests, signals a rising intonation that marks a question.

Words that are *emphasized* in some way, by stress or volume or pitch, are italicized. A : or colon after a sound means it's stretched out. An "a:h," for example, would be a drawn-out "aaaah," the sound you make after the first swig of cold beer on a hot day.

All these symbols, stolen from the ethnomethodologists, put people off at first. The only person who ever appreciated them right away was an ethnomusicologist, a jazz musician, who took a grad seminar with me. I still remember the look in his eyes when he glanced up from a transcript I'd handed out and said, "You mean, you could actually *score* a conversation?"

But the symbols do have a purpose. Here's a selection from the transcript of the interview with Ted. He's talking about going in for a job interview early in his trucking career.

> heh + so I went home got all sharped up.=put a suit on. and I get a heh + went down and finally found ABC Freight Line steel division office which is a (1.6) little white *bungalow,* (1.2) a very *sma:ll* bungalow, a (1.4) actually a one room *sha:ck* (1.4) on a *dirt parkin lot* down at Sparrow's Point, a:nd I walked in=here's all + half a dozen guys sittin around in *work clothes.*

Ted is a poet and doesn't know it. The details, the structure of the conversational music, make the poetry explicit.

It's like putting your hand under an ultraviolet light so that the mark shows. It's like putting an engine block under a Magnaflux to show if there are any hidden cracks. It's like injecting someone with thalium so that the X ray can trace blood flow to the heart. It's the same strategy Moerman used with Thai conversations. He used turns and topics so we could see patterns of pause and overlap, and then those patterns led into frames about the world that the villagers talked inside of.

What the pauses and punctuation and emphases in Ted's transcript show are patterns of *foregrounding* and *backgrounding,* of *rhythm* and *timing,* of *poetry.*

The first clue is in the *coreference*—how does Ted refer to the same thing as he talks, how does the reference change so that the speaker creates an image of something or someone?

Look at the pattern of coreference for the office. It changes from a "bungalow" to a "shack." And how it changes. Look at the pauses and the emphases.

(1.6) little white *bungalow,*

(1.2) a very *sm:all* bungalow, a

(1.4) actually a one room *sha:ck* (1.4) on a *dirt parkin lot* down at
Sparrow's Point,

The pauses show how Ted got into a rhythm as the coreference changed, a rhythm with pauses longer than usual that set off each phrase. The emphasis, shown with italics and stretched vowels, runs from *bungalow* to *small* to *shack.* The trucking company office goes from elegant to funky in three graceful moves.

This is poetry. The transcript shows how the surface features of the language, the pattern of sounds, shape the meanings, and that's what poetry is all about. The poetry appears at the beginning and end of the example as well. It begins with "suit," added on as an afterthought, and ends with an emphasized "*work clothes.*"

From *suit and bungalow* to *shack and work clothes.*

The structure makes the poetry explicit. But why this poetry, why this poem, why bungalow to shack, why this *content*? The answer, as usual, calls for new frames. And the frames, as usual, aren't lying in the transcript waiting to be lifted out.

Ted, it turns out, didn't go into trucking until fairly late in life, in his mid-thirties. He graduated from college and worked for some years as a white-collar salesman. As he traveled from place to place in his car, he'd look at the trucks rolling along the road. He eventually had a "take this job and shove it" attack, went out and bought a truck, and decided to become an independent trucker.

The transcript passage is a little piece of poetry that represents this contradiction between his white-collar past and his blue-collar present. During the time I did the research, Ted was *still* living the contradiction. When I took the trip with him, he was a trucker, as comfortable sitting around the horseshoe at the truck stop and talking shop as anyone else. When I'd go to a hearing on Capitol Hill, Ted would appear as an expert witness, clad in elegant suit, speaking articulately about the nature of the trucking industry and the role of independent truckers within it.

Both his biography and his current life make Ted a white-collar and blue-collar man at the same time. When the contradiction surfaced in his story, it pushed out poetry. I don't have any elegant theory, no well-worked-out similarity, to account for why this happened, but I think that truth and beauty do run in tandem, that when people "get on a roll," as the popular phrase puts it, they're rolling because of some powerful and coherent truth inside them that drives their words.

The structure of pause and emphasis helps us see what we hear. The transcript makes the poetry explicit. And the poetry serves as a rich point that calls for frames about the speaker, his biography, and the world he currently works in. Structure leads to a rich appreciation of the content it packages.

///

Readers of this book are people interested in life in a culturally complicated world. They're not professional analysts of languaculture. Chances are they'll never do a transcript in their lives. Can't you figure out how to talk in a conversation without a tape recorder and a transcript? Of course you can. People do it all the time.

But transcripts are snapshots, pictures of discourse that you can stare at, wonder about, fine-comb the details of. Transcripts are where you look for the little clues that answer the big questions of where the rich points are and what frames to build.

The passage from Ted's interview stands out; the details show why—it's a compact piece of poetry—and then the details lead into what the poem is about. Same with the Thai transcript. It freezes a moment of discourse so that we can dive into its details. And once we stumble over the overlaps and pauses—the trees—we can back away and start to build frames to understand the forest. For professionals, transcripts are the tools of the trade.

You, the reader, may never transcribe, though I hope you do. Try it sometime. Toss a cassette recorder on the table during dinner, listen to it a few times, transcribe part of it that strikes you as rich and go over the details. Just that exercise will change the way you listen forever. That's one of the few things left in the world I'm sure of. I've seen it happen over the years to hundreds of undergrad and grad students.

Even if you never do that, think of a newspaper article or a memo as a transcript sometime and read it with a rich-point antenna extended.

The important truth about transcripts is, *they're not automatic and accurate.* Remember Watergate? When Tricky Dick turned out to be pretty tricky after all? When John Dean read prepared testimony that he later turned into a best-seller? When Charles Colson announced he'd been born again? God, those were the days of *real* politicians.

You don't remember? You were only five then?

Watergate was a big day for us discourse types, because, just for a few months there, *everybody* was interested in transcripts. President Nixon had taped conversations in the Oval Office, and when the investigators found out, they transcribed the tapes and put them into the record. You can hear the tapes now, I'm told, at the National Archives. I've never gone. Listening to tapes isn't my idea of what to do on my time off.

The thing was, everybody was amazed at how difficult it was to get an *accurate* transcript. Transcribers tended to leave things out and put other things in. If you listened to the "tone of voice," sometimes something you'd read one way came across in a completely different way when you heard it. And once the arguments over transcripts started, what the lawyers said Nixon *meant* involved a lot more than what he just *said,* a fact that an understanding of languaculture automatically provides—transcripts don't have frames in them.

The public was surprised. From a naive point of view, transcribing should be simple. You listen to the tape and write down what's on it. Transcribers—any of us—know better. We need several passes to get it halfway right. We listen, but we hear what we expect to hear. We fill in things that we think should be there and miss things that our frames don't have room for.

When I transcribe a tape, I do it once, then "proof-listen" a couple of times. Then I listen and read some more when I chop up the transcript for analysis. Even at the end, where I listen to a piece of tape to check a passage I'm going to use in an article or book, I might still pick up something I missed or something I put in that wasn't there.

Transcriptions take a long time—maybe eight hours for a clean hour of tape on the first run-through—and they won't be accurate on that first run-through, either. Worse yet, the methods to transcribe aren't automatic. In the first part of this book, examples of talk were just written in ordinary English. The excerpt from Ted's interview dropped in a little more detail to show how the sound stream flowed. But there's room for much, much more.

You could include phonetic detail, all the way down to the exhalation of air right after the *p* in "pin." You could put in intonation, the rise and fall of pitch that travels with all talk. You could include notation for eye gaze—who is looking at whom for how long. A version of dance notation would let you include body motion. You could videotape the whole thing and get lost in the nonverbal details for the rest of your life.

No transcript is ever complete or correct, just another example of the general principle that no account of a situation can ever be as rich as the situation itself. In principle a transcript can include levels of detail beyond your wildest dreams, to the point where a few minutes of transcription can take days. And even that won't be the whole story.

Sometimes I wish I'd been born before tape recorders were invented. Malinowski and Whorf just used notebooks, and they did all right. Nowadays, I could videotape a moment of talk, approach the tape with sophisticated transcription techniques, and then ponder that transcription with the many cameras, lenses, and filters of discourse analysis. I could spend the rest of my life with thirty seconds of tape.

I'm not sure this is progress.

On the other hand, those snapshots, however imperfect, however partial, however much of a pain they are to produce, do let me show a reader—beginner or pro—a fragment of spoken life, a piece of discourse that someone actually produced.

Those snapshots display the details where the abstractions of rich point and frame and languaculture and identity come to life. And, as Edward T. Hall, one of the founders of the field of intercultural communication, said when he explained this kind of analysis, "God is in the details." No one ever said finding God was easy.

///

Transcripts are the *evidence* that the pros use to make a case for the frames they build. Transcripts are *natural experiments,* partial records of things that occurred "out there" in the world whose rich points you want to account for with frames. Transcripts keep you honest, limit the number and kinds of frames you can invent.

A friend of mine, a psychologist, once told me about her view of experiments. I was brought up to think of experiments as the high point of science, the controlled laboratory where universal truth was hammered down once and for all. But she thought about them differently. She thought of experiments as things you made up, situations you created that show how some abstract concept could be made to come to life.

The difference is, she starts with a general idea, then makes up experiments to show how they work. I look at some experiment that the world just performed for me, and *then* try to figure out what general ideas were in there. Transcripts are frozen moments of talk that you can pin down, small slices of life through which you can show how large ideas actually dress up and make an appearance. My friend tests hypotheses; I set out to learn about something I don't know is there yet. Different methods, different folks.

///

In the languaculture game, transcripts show people that rich points occurred and that new frames make sense. In fact, you can use transcripts to build frames that ascend into a massive understanding of the new society that goes with your new language, as I tried to do in Austria, as I tried to show with the examples of lies.

The structure and content of speech acts, it turns out, can lead you well beyond the speech act into history and the society where the talking occurred, and then back again. That's the power of frames rather than a precise, well-defined framework of similarities. Frames let you go where you need to go to figure out rich points.

With or without transcripts, as you pursue different rich points the frames you build start to link together. Themes that cycle through them point to some fundamental differences between you and them, differences that bubble up over and over in different moments of talk.

You begin to find the *coherence* among the different frames, the weave that pulls them together into ever more elaborate ideas about the new languaculture, ideas that tantalize you with that elusive "feel" for the people you're trying to understand. That "feel," once you've articulated it, teaches you some grand differences between you and them, differences that go by the name of history, of fundamental premises of existence, of politics, of economics. Coherence brings to life all those foggy abstractions. With coherence, you don't just handle rich points; you sense what it's like to lead a different kind of *life,* to see and act with a different *mentality,* to move through a fundamentally different kind of *world.*

Coherence

WHEN I first lived in Austria, when I was a kid in '62, I caught a powerful case of culture, though I didn't know how to diagnose it then. I lived with a family that I'm still close to, a family I've mentioned a couple of times in this book. I went to school and made friends and acquired a new identity as an obnoxious Austrian teenager.

A few years ago I looked at what I'd written in the family "guest book" just before I returned to the United States—"*Ich werde immer zum Teil ein Neumann sein.*" "I'll always be in part a Neumann," Neumann being the family name. I take that place personally. Culture has to do with who you are.

At the time I left for Austria, my high school consciousness wasn't very sophisticated. The main problem we worried about was who had a twenty-one-year-old friend or relative who would buy beer. However, I *did* know that there had been a war, and that the United States had been on one side and Austria on the other. I didn't know much more than that, because World History was an elective in my high school, and I'd taken Electronics instead.

Following my American conversational rules, I never brought up the subject of World War II during the early part of my stay in

Austria. You weren't supposed to talk about sex, politics, or religion. As you'll see in a moment, my American rule actually fit in with an Austrian rule about the topic, a different rule with the same results, silence about World War II.

One evening, a couple of weeks before I left Austria, the family gathered late in the evening, as it often did, for a glass of wine and conversation. (The first sign that I'd like the place came when I arrived and found out I didn't need a twenty-one-year-old friend or relative who'd buy me beer.) My Austrian parents turned to me and said they knew that I was probably curious about the war. I admitted that I was.

I knew my Austrian father had been a prisoner of war in Georgia—in the United States, not in what used to be the Soviet Union. He hardly spoke any English, but we'd been working together in the basement on a Christmas present, and he hit his finger with a hammer. He looked at me, his face in pain, and threw out, without any hesitation at all, "goddamned son of a bitch." Then he grinned and said, "Georgia." That's about all I knew of the Neumanns in World War II.

That evening, over wine, things changed. Mother talked about how she was a member of the Nazi girls' organization and father talked about his life in the German army. They described how bad things were in Germany after World War I, how Hitler made sense when he first appeared, given those circumstances. They talked about how they never knew anything about the concentration camps. They'd heard rumors toward the end, they said, but by then you couldn't do anything that wouldn't endanger your own life.

I listened, fascinated, and noticed that my two Austrian brothers just sat quietly and didn't say a thing.

As the years went by, I returned to visit the family several times. One visit I remember, not so long ago. One of my Austrian brothers had married and had kids. He lived in the lower apartment in the old family house, while the parents lived upstairs. The issue of the war had pushed through the surface, he said. He talked about how the parents were just old Nazis, how they wouldn't discuss anything about World War II. When I'd go upstairs, the parents would say they couldn't talk with the kids anymore about the war, because they just thought they were old Nazis.

When the subject came up at family dinners, the usual lively conversation turned stiff and hostile. The parents said the kids couldn't possibly understand, since they hadn't lived through it. The kids said the parents had to know more than they were letting on. After all, a concentration camp had been located just a few miles away.

I was more of a Neumann than I'd thought, because I was going through the same changes as my Austrian brothers. It started to get under my skin. How could this have happened? How could these good, decent people—my Austrian parents and many others of their generation that I'd met—have gone along with the Hitler regime and all it stood for? *Why wouldn't they talk about it?* The Nazi era lurked under the surface like an evil ghost. It had to be brought out and confronted. It started to drive me crazy, this rich point that consumed me. And I was only a part-timer. For my Austrian brothers and others born after the war, it became an obsession.

///

In 1986, when I went back to Vienna for a semester, I stepped into the historical moment when Austria confronted its past. Dr. Kurt Waldheim, former secretary-general of the United Nations, had been nominated as the conservative party candidate for the presidency. After the first election he and the socialist candidate, as expected, went into the runoff and started campaigning. But then the past hit the fan. The Austrian newsweekly *Profil* published an article that showed Waldheim had lied about his war record. Instead of staying in Vienna after he'd been wounded on the Russian front, as he'd always claimed he'd done, he'd been posted to southern Europe, to areas where the so-called "deportation" of Jews had taken place.

I'm not going to tell the entire Waldheim story here. What I am going to tell you is that Waldheim became the symbol of Austria's hidden past.

The *official* story, from 1945 until Waldheim, was that Austria was "Hitler's first victim," that Austria's Jews had "emigrated," that in 1945 Austria had been "liberated," that the country had been "de-Nazified." The postwar kids, like my Austrian brothers, knew this was, in good part, nonsense. They'd seen the documentary footage of Austrians cheering Hitler's entry into the country in 1938, the packed crowds in Vienna's Heldenplatz when Hitler made his speech. They knew that Austrian Jews had fled or been murdered, that in 1945 Austria lost a war, that the older generation who had controlled Austrian government and industry all had stories to tell, some of them noble, but others, horrible.

But until Waldheim, nobody talked much about World War II, not in public. And conversation around the family table turned hostile and defensive. What Austrians called the "culture of silence" dominated discourse. There were some things you just didn't talk about, and Austria's involvement in World War II was one of them.

But once the "Waldheim affair" started, the talk didn't stop. The pressure of the aging postwar generation, and their children as well, together with the attention of the international press, kept Waldheim on the front burner, and with him, the uncomfortable questions about Austria that he had come to symbolize.

I arrived in Austria in September. The affair had started the preceding May. Conversations, newspapers, TV, anyplace language appeared, Waldheim and the issues he represented had a good chance of showing up as the topic. Waldheim was an *issue,* and the issue was a powerful, magnificent rich point for anybody trying to plunge deeper inside of Austrian languaculture.

I realized then, and believe even more now, that issues are one of the things you take on when you tackle modern languaculture. When I lived in Austria, I lived like a lot of other people. I read a newspaper on the way to work, chatted with my colleagues over coffee, went home and watched the news, and had a social conversation later with friends.

The language I encountered and used of course involved words and sentences and speech acts. But the discourse had a topic, a content, and the topic that surfaced all the time in '86, in personal talk and media reports, was the issue of Austria's past.

Any modern languaculture requires frames to understand the issues that thread topically through speech acts. An issue is a rich point, a topic people talk about, read about, or watch on TV. Issues are about *content,* content that dips down into specific moments of talk, but then sweeps back into history and up into the nature of the society.

Issues are rich points that you need to build frames for, and the frames carry you into a sophisticated appreciation of where you are and who you're talking with that travels well beyond any particular speech act.

The Waldheim affair helped me, as a student of Austrian languaculture, organize several differences between me and them into coherent frames. I've already put some of the pieces in place in the previous section, but I need to remind you, and me, that they weren't so well connected until after I did a lot of work on the details. An example of that work follows in just a minute.

///

Before I start with the details, I need to talk about an important difference between this example and the others I've presented before. In earlier examples—like my own from Austria and Mexico, or borrowed ones from Thailand or Alaska—I've taken the viewpoint of an *outsider looking in,* of a student of a particular languaculture who's got a fair amount of grammar and vocabulary to play with, but who trips and stumbles over rich points, either in grammar and vocabulary or in the speech acts that they accomplish.

But learning a languaculture is a process that never stops. It goes on and on, into ever more details, ever more connections. That's why, in other places in this book, I've used American examples that, I hope, produced as many "aha" reactions among readers as the foreign examples did. Junkies, northern Californians, a seafood restaurant, and a parking ticket on the Maryland campus all popped up in one place or another.

Culture happens to you when differences, rich points, inspire awareness of old frames and construction of new ones. But the differences arise *within* what we usually think of as languacultures—northern Californians and New Yorkers—as well as *between* them—American English and Mexican Spanish. When you approach Mexican Spanish, you expect languaculture to be relevant; when you approach American independent truckers, you don't. But it is relevant because, to some extent, truckers will talk in words and sentences and speech acts that are *different,* and if you want to figure out what they're saying, you're in the languaculture game. The amount of work you have to do might be less inside the same broad languaculture, but the way the work gets done will be the same.

The Waldheim case mixes this up in just the right way to make the point, a point that will be elaborated in the next chapter. With the Waldheim transcript I'm about to show you, I'm taking a position *further inside* Austrian languaculture than the positions I've taken before. I'm noticing details that I wouldn't have noticed unless I'd already done a lot of work.

By the time I got around to Waldheim, I was closer to the point I'm usually at when I work in America. I'm looking at rich points that don't appear until you're *inside*. When I watched a videotape of an interview with Waldheim, my intuitions were that this was a weird situation. The Austrians who saw or read it said the same.

For instance, when Waldheim takes his turn, he starts with a phrase, "My dear Mr. Nagiller." And then he uses Austrian dialect before he shifts back into standard Austrian German. Toward the end of his turn, he switches into "bureaucratese," and then he laughs, of all things. These aspects of Waldheim's language strike one as strange, given Austrian frames for a television interview. But you have to be more than an outsider to have the experience.

When Waldheim says "My dear Mr. Nagiller," the tone is what the Austrians call "uncle-ish," sort of a patronizing pat on the head, "there, there, kid." And dialect is something for friends and family, not for an official occasion like a TV interview. The bureaucratese is out of place at the end, since he's talking to the interviewer and through him, to the public. And the laugh just makes no sense at all. There's nothing funny in what he's saying.

In previous examples, rich points appeared because a frame from my American languaculture didn't work. But now I'm inside Austria, instead of between Austria and America. I've got frames for an Austrian TV interview with politicians, and they work. I can make sense out of Austrian interviews. I can watch them and talk about them with other Austrians.

The reason the Waldheim interview looks weird isn't that my *American* frames don't work; the reason is that my *Austrian* frames aren't working. I've gone from learning a second languaculture from the outside to learning more *about* it from the inside. The game is the same, but the source of the frames has changed.

///

The Waldheim transcript came from a seminar my friend Ruth Wodak ran during my visit. I participated and worked with a student,
Johanna Pelikan, on a transcript of Waldheim answering questions
at a press conference. She transcribed part of that interview, casu-
ally, without the details that you saw in Ted's discussion of his
trucking career. As we worked over it, we found some moments that
helped us see a piece of Austrian history and how it came alive inside
one particular speech act.

I'll just present the English translation here. The interviewer is a
journalist named Nagiller, a well-known Austrian media personality
who is of the postwar generation. Waldheim is the now world-
famous presidential candidate for the conservative party.

NAGILLER: Doctor Waldheim you said in the TV press conference
at the beginning of March that you did your duty as a soldier in
the war just like a hundred thousand other Austrians you said. This
remark started criticisms, not so much because you had this feeling
of duty then, but rather because you because this remark could be
taken to mean that you would also have it today. Uh today with
your knowledge and our our knowledge about this war and about
the criminal commander in chief Adolf Hitler that would then be—
if you should think the same today—doing one's duty in service of
a criminal and that can't be, that is immoral, uh military service
for a criminal can't be doing one's duty. And another thing. If you
had done your duty then uh then your friend Fritz Molden who
supported you, who deserted and went to the resistance, he would
have violated his duty and that is a completely absurd thought.

WALDHEIM: My dear Mr. Nagiller that is the typical erroneous interpretation distortions imputations that I energetically reject. If I
spoke of duty uh then it had to do with the comradely duty of
soldiers. I'll tell you an example. As I was wounded in Russia we
were surrounded, I couldn't for fourteen days be brought to the
hospital. A comrade came, pulled me with him, dragged me with
him on a Panje sled, a Russian sled, fourteen days long in forty
degrees below in a snowstorm. He did his duty toward me and
certainly for many other comrades as well. That was the duty that
I spoke of, not about serving a hateful regime like the the the Hitler

regime. I've said that I was drawn into this war with mixed feelings, so I ask please that this correction be taken into account in case there's should be a misunderstanding here. *(Laughs.)*

Nagiller starts out with classic journalist moves. He hands Waldheim something that he, Waldheim, said. He uses an Austrian key word, "duty," *Pflicht* in German. He uses an impersonal subject— "This remark started criticisms. . . . "

Right out of journalistic frames according to Hoyle. Journalists often use a quotation from the politician they are interviewing, especially a quote that contains a loaded political word. And the question should be impersonal, all business, about issues, not about personalities. The impersonal tone is even more important in Austria, given the Austrian style of politeness.

Nagiller wants to convey that he's not after Waldheim personally: Waldheim said something, and he used a rich languacultural term—*duty*—to say it. Comments about what he said are already out there in public. Regrettable though it may be, the topic is worth some attention in this public forum. It's not Nagiller's fault for bringing the forbidden topic up.

But it doesn't take long for the *personal* to slip in. It's in the details of what from an American point of view is a rather long question. Turns are longer in Austria; one gets more time to talk once one has the floor. It took me a while to learn that. When my turn came in conversation, I'd often say something, and then wonder why everyone was looking at me and not responding. They were waiting for me to continue.

Nagiller's personal attack creeps in early, but you need to dive into the details to see it. Nagiller says, "because you because this remark can be taken to mean . . . " This is a *repair,* another standard concept of conversation analysis. In this case, the repair changes a direct statement, a direct Nagiller-to-Waldheim *you,* to a passive construction—*"this remark could be taken to mean . . . "* The tiny detail, in and of itself, doesn't mean anything. But it is a piece of a pattern that's emerging, the hint of a shift to come, a shift from the proper *impersonal* tone, set up at the beginning of the question, toward a rather *personal* attack.

This active/passive switch, by the way, is one of the most powerful grammatical tricks that languages offer, and they all offer it.

The switch is powerful because it's a piece of grammar that connects with differences in speech acts, differences around the kind of relationship that's appropriate—polite, or personal, or anonymous, or what have you. With an active construction, somebody is actually doing something; with the passive, something is happening, but it's not clear who is responsible. The passive is less personal.

There's a second powerful grammatical switch at work here, the switch from indicative to subjunctive. American English lost this switch some time ago, though its ghost remains here and there, as in "If I *were* to do that . . . " The subjunctive is famous for throwing Americans off when they learn languages like German, French, or Spanish, because they all still have it and use it.

The subjunctive smooths the rough edges of a statement; it dissolves things into a mist of uncertainty or possibility. If a person uses the subjunctive when he makes a statement about another, it softens the blow. "You *might* or *could be* such and such," rather than the more arrogant and direct "You *are* such and such."

Subjunctive/indicative, like active/passive, is a grammatical construction that carries a lot of speech-act freight, an inside-the-circle choice with ties into the social world of the people who use the language.

You can't see it in the English transcript, but it's there in the German. When Nagiller slipped into "you" and repaired it to "this remark . . . ," he used a verb in the indicative. But he'd used a subjunctive form just before that—"you'd had this feeling of duty then"—and then he drops back into the subjunctive right after, as he should in this speech act, with "you would still have it even today."

Throughout the transcript Nagiller slips and slides toward the active and indicative, *direct and personal,* and direct and personal is just exactly what he's *not* supposed to be.

A second repair later in the transcript—"your knowledge and our our knowledge"—clues the listener in to a generational difference. In the stories I told earlier, I mentioned that when the topic of World War II came up, parents would often say, "You can't understand; you weren't there." Nagiller, the younger Austrian, is blocking this typical older-generation escape clause, and the repetition makes it stand out in the transcript.

In Ted's description of his trucking career, repetition and coreference foregrounded content, put it on the front burner so the listener would pay attention. Nagiller uses the same strategy when he says, "the criminal commander in chief Adolf Hitler," and he repeats "criminal" right after that. He doesn't just say the forbidden name; he strings it out in all its ugly glory and repeats one of the ugliest terms later.

I can't tell you how striking this was to an Austrian audience at the time. Nagiller doesn't just mention Hitler; he drags him out of the closet and linguistically hits Waldheim, and the audience, over the head with him.

Other powerful examples of the subjunctive/indicative switch follow. When Nagiller talks about something that *describes* Waldheim's actions in the past, he uses the subjunctive, as he should. This might have happened; this is possibly the case. But then when he comments on what it would mean if those things *did* happen, he switches to the indicative to make a more powerful, direct statement: "That can't be. That is immoral. Military service for a criminal can't be doing one's duty." And: "That is a fully absurd thought." Statements about Waldheim are properly subjunctive, but *if* what Nagiller hints might be the case is true, then—in the indicative—Waldheim is, without doubt, in the wrong.

In the course of this brief transcript, Nagiller changes from the impersonal tone of a journalist to the personal tone of an attack. He completes the change at the end, when he talks about Waldheim's friend. Notice the pattern—"your friend," "is supporting you," "deserted," "resistance," "violated his duty." Waldheim's friend, *friend* mind you, is thrown at him as an example of how everything that Waldheim claims justifies what *he* did makes his noble friend look despicable.

The proper journalist has turned into an unruly kid. Waldheim comes in with the striking line I've already mentioned—"My dear Mr. Nagiller"—and then he does his brief shift into Austrian dialect. And finally, that peculiar bureaucratese and the weird laugh at the end.

Waldheim does more than just this, if you read the transcript—he redefines "duty," emphasizes generational solidarity, and retells his story about being wounded on the Russian front, a powerful symbol in Austria. I don't know the actual data, but you often hear in Vienna that Hitler used Austrians disproportionately in that terrible campaign.

But for now we've done enough. The details in Nagiller's question grew into a pattern, a rich point, rich because the details depart from expectations in frames. And this time the frames came from *within* the languaculture where the speech act took place. The details—repairs, the active/passive and indicative/subjunctive switches, patterns of coreference—backlit the strange nature of this peculiar exchange. According to expectations, according to the run-of-the-mill social facts, the journalist should maintain an impersonal tone and talk about issues. What happens here is that the journalist slides from what's expected into a direct, personal attack.

Now Waldheim's opening line makes sense. He pats the unruly kid on the head and says "there, there," and does it in Austrian dialect, the form used in the home when head-patting gets done.

The weird ending, the bureaucratese and the laugh, is something I don't really know quite what to do with; neither did the Austrians. Waldheim closes with a style that is the opposite of the style he opened with, as though he is now a government official finishing up a memo. Maybe that's why he laughs. An Austrian-American colleague of mine whose family fled when Hitler came to power said the laugh was *Schadenfreude*, pleasure at the pain of others. I'm just not sure.

///

Once I understood the pattern, once I'd run through the details and figured out that all the broken default values in my frames cohered into a pattern, I had one of those mammoth "aha" reactions that link your heart and your mind and throw them into a new dimension. Frames clattered into place like a jigsaw puzzle programmed to solve itself.

I understood that Nagiller and Waldheim weren't just doing an interview. They were reading from a script that I knew very well, one I'd participated in over the years with my exchange-family in Austria, the Neumanns. Nagiller and Waldheim weren't *just* journalist and politician; they were the postwar kids and the veterans of the Nazi era arguing over the family dinner table. Nagiller was the son—"C'mon, what happened, what really happened, I'm fed up with silence and little anecdotes." And Waldheim was the father—"Settle down, kid, we all did our duty and got by the best way we could, and anyway, what do you know, you weren't there."

Nagiller wanted the forbidden topic out in the open; Waldheim wanted to keep it under wraps. The same old story, the one I'd lived through as a family member, the one I'd heard countless times from Austrian age-mates as well.

A friend and colleague in Vienna, about my age, sat down next to me one day when I was puzzling over the transcript. I told him what I thought I was learning. He looked off, out the window at the gray sky, and talked, almost to himself. It was funny, he said, how things went right after the war when he was a young schoolkid. Suddenly they were told they couldn't sing some of their songs anymore. Too German. And they changed the name of the German class to a class in the "language of instruction." Austria scrambled back as fast as it could, away from any identification with Nazi Germany.

Austria, with the support of the four occupying powers, the United States among them, built a myth after the war, one that absolved it of the war crimes of the Nazis. The myth was fragile; the rules of public discourse protected it by sheltering it from view.

With Waldheim, the myth was shattered beyond repair. I felt, in 1986, the same relief that my Austrian brothers and many other friends and acquaintances of our generation felt. It was painful, it was at times horrible to confront, at times inspiring when tales of heroism surfaced, but at last, at long last, the topic was out in the open. At last you could *talk* about it.

But there was more to the lesson than this.

I understood the spot that Nagiller and Waldheim were in more sympathetically. There was, at that moment in history, *no* language in which Austrians could discuss the evils of the Nazi era in public. After the war, Austria hammered some new social facts into place, some new limits on what you could say under what circumstances, and those new social facts said, "Keep your words off World War II, unless they fit the new myth." Neither Nagiller nor Waldheim was personally responsible for that.

But in 1986 the world conspired to force them to talk, in public. The world, in a confusing twist, included Austria—the Austrian newsweekly that started the scandal when it published the documents, and the pressure of the postwar generations, like my Austrian brothers, who wanted to push the topic into public as much as the international press did.

The problem was, how do you talk about something that you're not supposed to talk about, how do you talk about something in public for which there is no language?

What Nagiller and Waldheim did was use the only available discourse for the conversation, namely, the discourse around the family dinner table. The younger generation pushes for information, and the older swats them for their impudence. Austrian languaculture started to move with changing circumstances. And the way it moved, in this example, was by stretching the old languaculture over areas it was never meant to cover. The stretching, the rips and tears that it caused, showed up in the details of the transcript, in the ways that the details deviated from what was expected.

The idea is as old as Freud and as recent as the sociology of Jürgen Habermas. When people depart from the frames that everyone agrees *should* be guiding the speech acts, then some other speech act might be pushing against the surface trying to get out. The differences between what people are *officially* doing and what they *actually* do may teach you something about the cracks in the social facts, cracks that let you glimpse contradictions in current ideas about what the world is and how it works.

A final lesson, one that leads into the next chapter. I started learning Austrian languaculture by working on the differences between me and them. Now the game has shifted. In the Waldheim example, I learned *more* about Austria by working on the differences that appeared *inside* the languaculture, differences between frames I'd built and what people actually did when they talked.

I went from American English into Austrian German by stumbling across rich points and building frames so that I could understand them. But then I traveled further into Austrian German by stumbling across new rich points, points that were rich in terms of frames I'd *already* built for Austrian German, points that were rich for Austrians as well as for me.

Learning a new languaculture isn't just a trip from outside to inside. No sooner do you feel that you've started inside than the process starts all over. An infinite job stretches out in front of you, a job in which there will always be new rich points, new frames, new links between one frame and another.

Learning a languaculture from outside and learning a languaculture from inside are *the same thing*. Learning from outside, the rich points stand out because you aren't communicatively competent. Learning from inside is more subtle, because of a shared myth, the myth that everyone speaks the *same* language, a myth made possible by the inside-the-circle view. The myth is as fragile as the myth that postwar Austria invented to hold its past at arm's length, and just as deserving of destruction.

Here's a twist, though, that calls up, for the second time, the spirit of the next chapter. With the Waldheim analysis I've gone further inside Austria. But some of the frames for Austrian TV interviews with politicians weren't all that different from the frames I brought with me from the United States. My guess is that the international world of broadcast journalism, with its roots in American languaculture, contains similar speech acts wherever you go.

The easy use of labels like "American" and "Austrian," not to mention "Mexican" or "Hopi," continues to lose its edge. The rich points I saw in the Waldheim interview, the things that I didn't understand that made me wonder what was going on are rich points *in terms of Austrian frames*. But the Austrian frames include frames that look like they might go with an occupational role, *journalist,* anywhere in the world. The Austrian frames aren't working, but the frames aren't just Austrian, either.

These neat labels of social identity—Austria, America, Mexico— are going to have to go soon, but that's the business of the next chapter.

Waldheim and Austria's past pulled me into dimensions of the languaculture that I'd first encountered as a teenager, when I was an exchange student, dimensions that I'd felt but never understood. Because of what I went through with my Austrian family, friends, and colleagues in '86, I felt an Austrian identity snap into focus. Not that I thought I'd become Austrian. I grew up American. But something new had been added, something that changed the old identities I carried around as well.

The change was this: Up until the Waldheim experience, I'd worked over the years to learn some new Austrian German *social facts.* I'd built some new frames and learned to work within them. But with Waldheim, I struggled against them, fought the old boundaries and participated in a nationwide effort to tear them down. It was the languacultural equivalent of what happened in Berlin a few years later when Germans from both sides tore down the wall.

Once you learn a new languaculture, you embark on the road to communicative competence. Once you struggle against it in the company of its other participants, you've made it your own. It changes. It's personal. It's not just something you use to communicate; it's a part of what you are.

///

A few years ago I was invited to deliver a keynote lecture to the German anthropology meetings. I was honored, and still am. In fact, it's one of the greatest compliments I've ever received.

I've always had this feeling—I don't know where it came from, but somewhere in the California valley where I grew up—that if you're going to say something about somebody, you should say it to his or her face. I break this rule often, but as I've gotten older and confronted the unpleasant hypocrisies I've practiced, that value is one I still aspire to.

When the Germans invited me, I was working on the Waldheim transcript. I knew that Germany and Austria were different in ways that many Americans don't suspect, but I knew that a talk about problems with the Nazi past would be as relevant there as it was in Austria. If I thought I was right, I should say it to the people it was about. I decided to present a talk on what I was doing with Waldheim.

So I did. I wrote it in German and a German graduate student at the University of Maryland helped me polish it up. After I gave the talk, very much like what you've just read, the moderator called for questions. There weren't any. By then I was an old pro. I knew the talk wasn't bad, but still I felt uncomfortable. Finally, a young, punk-looking woman raised her hand. She made a comment—I didn't understand all of it, I was too nervous—about how the prohibition on talk was still in effect. Why, she asked, didn't people ever talk about the fact that a concentration camp had been located right outside of Cologne, where this meeting was being held? A few older tongues clucked, but otherwise no one responded.

Later, over coffee—a lot of people talked to me over coffee, privately—the woman looked at me and shook her head. I can't remember exactly what she said, but it went something like this: "So you lecture about how certain things can't be talked about and you don't get any questions. What did you expect?"

A while later, *Anthropology Today,* a popular magazine about anthropology published in England, printed a summary of the conference. It reported what my talk was about, but then went on to say that many at the conference considered it to be outside the boundaries of the discipline.

I smiled when I read that. My talk was *about* going outside the boundaries set by the social facts. Apparently the topic had shoved the talk itself outside those same boundaries.

///

I remember, after the German meetings, riding the airplane back home. I remember thinking that what I'd experienced wasn't just about Germany or Austria.

I grew up in the Vietnam era. I'm one of the lucky few who managed to land in a position with the Public Health Service that led to a career instead of to a bunker or a jail cell or a Canadian or Swedish city.

One of the things that happened after America was chased out of Vietnam, bodies dangling from the helicopter skids, was that America didn't want to talk about it. Our World War II good guy image shattered. We'd screwed up but good. Reasons for the screwup varied with experience and political persuasion—we never should have done it or we should have done it right—but the conclusion was the same. We'd screwed up.

America didn't handle that evaluation very well. America put a seal around the topic as tight as the seal Austria had put around the Nazi era. Vietnam was something you didn't talk about. America, it occurred to me on that plane ride, wasn't that different from Austria. Not that Vietnam and the Nazis were the same, not at all. But the walls around talk, the walls built after the fact, *were* the same. Vietnam was a topic you avoided, vets and protesters alike.

In the early seventies, I received a phone call from Bruce Spivey.

He was working in a drug treatment center in Chicago and had read something I'd written about junkies that made sense to him. We met at the anthropology meetings in San Francisco in 1975. Bruce had been a Green Beret in Vietnam.

One day, he told me, he'd gone into an army psychiatrist's office. He told this as a funny story. Combat had started to twist his soul, started to make him wonder what the point was. The psychiatrist, he said, had a picture of Nixon on the wall behind him and flags on either side of his desk.

The psychiatrist asked him what his problem was. Spivey told him about moving into a village and diving into a firefight. He said that it had started to bother him, that it didn't make sense anymore.

"Yes," the psychiatrist said, "but what is your problem?"

His mind snapped, Bruce said. It was the beginning of the end. He felt the ties to who he was and what America was all about unravel. When he returned to Chicago, he enrolled in anthropology courses, the field where questions about your own languaculture are one way to get started.

Over the years we'd meet and talk, passionate talk about our generation, what the world was all about, about the forbidden topic, Vietnam. We were untangling the puzzle of men our age—how did similar people wind up in such different places, and how could they reconnect? America treated Spivey as the psychiatrist had—it wouldn't let him talk. When he brought Vietnam up, everyone got uncomfortable and changed the subject.

In 1985 I ran into a mutual friend, and I asked him how Spivey was doing. "You don't want to know," he said. "Why not?" I asked, the chill creeping from my spine into my hands and feet. "Because," said the friend, "he checked out."

I was so angry at Spivey that I could hardly see straight. I thought, with a selfishness that I'm ashamed of, what right did he have just to give up like that? And then I fell into a dark hole. When I think of him I still do.

Languaculture isn't a lightweight, nickel-and-dime, glass-bead game, not just a crossword puzzle you work to kill time during the train ride. At least it wasn't for Spivey, and it isn't for me. I've used him here to make a point, but I think he would have approved. And now you understand, if you read the preface, why this book is dedicated to the memory of Bruce Spivey, former Green Beret turned anthropologist, who struggled against the languaculture's power to keep him from saying what should be said.

Languaculture is a *social fact*. It sets limits on what you can say and sets up expectations of how you're supposed to talk. But there are people, like Spivey, who *struggle* against the limits. Their experience of culture takes shape *within* their own. Rich points come into consciousness and inspire new frames, frames that make a new kind of discourse possible.

A while back, when Franz Boas entered the picture, I quoted his words about learning to recognize a tradition so that one could free oneself from its shackles. That's what many Austrians and Americans did—are still doing—with the topics of World War II and Vietnam.

Up until now, I've written of entering a new languaculture as a way to become communicatively competent. But now, the new languaculture is something you invent, something you win in a struggle with the old, something that tears down the old social fact walls and lets new discourse in. The new languaculture is a *way to change the world* by changing what it is that can be thought, said, and done.

///

I haven't used the title of this chapter—"Coherence"—much in the writing of it. There's a reason for that. I'd have had to chant it every few lines as all the rich points were laid out and put into place.

Earlier in the book, when I first used Mexico as an example, I said I was a beginner, and the example would show how rich points and frames look in the early stages. It was easier to lay them out and comment then, one by one, because there weren't so many of them. Austria is more toward the other end of the scale. I'd already traveled a ways inside the languaculture over the years, so a vat full of rich points went into the stew.

Consider all the different rich points and frames that were woven together. The subjunctive and the passive, key words and repetitions, politeness and profession, family dinners and TV interviews and conversations and professional meetings, World War II and public discourse, generation and politics, and the way an entire society struggled to change.

That's one hell of a list. You could concentrate on any item in it and go into more details. If you did, you'd find similarities you could use. But the emphasis isn't on developing and filling out frameworks of similarities; instead, it's on finding the connections among different rich points at different levels, in different places at different times with different people. The emphasis is on finding a *story,* the story that pulls the rich points together into an understanding of how they all *cohere,* a story that sketches the broader historical and political moment of which you, the former outsider, are now a part. The loose version of "frame" I've used here lets you do that; narrow theories of similarities, useful as they might be in solving specific problems, don't.

At the same time, one similarity stood out as particularly critical. I obviously already had a bad case of culture by the time I worked on Waldheim, but the case turned more complicated when I realized the tie between Austria and America, World War II and Vietnam. The tie had to do with how it is that a society turns part of itself into an unacceptable topic, a topic to avoid. What are those topics? Why do they do it? How is it done?

Coherence in Austria taught me something about coherence in my home languaculture: the similarity that let me travel between the two illuminated characteristics of both. That's what the *experience* of culture is supposed to do, move you in a new direction that changes who you are, in both the old territory and the new. You turn from passive student into active participant in the new territory, but you also participate differently in the old. Culture has to do *with who you are,* with what you *become* when you take a rainbow of rich points and follow them to a coherent pot of gold, however tarnished that gold might turn out to be.

Variations on a Frame

STORIES of struggle against the languacultural edges, in both Austria and America, bring up a more general problem, one I've been ignoring for most of the book. When people struggle against the edges in their different ways, when local and world histories collide and cause storms, when a journalist speaks German through international frames, when people turn into something you never knew they were before, what happens to the neat social facts?

Saussure's idea of *social fact* was too simple to handle all this. He wrote as if a language—English, say—labeled a clear social fact boundary. It doesn't. In fact, it doesn't less and less as the years go on. Just when you think you've learned a languaculture, discourse and frames can *vary* all over the place.

Once you've built up a coherent piece of languaculture, once you've hooked together the rich points you've encountered and the frames that make them sensible, you don't know how widely they apply. Is what you've learned just good for the people you learned it from and nobody else in the world? Or is it good for anyone who speaks a particular language? Or anyone from a particular country? Or just for men or southerners or jazz fans? Or what?

The culture in languaculture means the frames you build to fill in the differences between you and them. Languaculture isn't some universal, objective, complete truth. Instead, it's a languaculture *of* some social identity. But of *what* social identity? Who else can you use what you've learned with? What's the *scope* of what you've learned?

///

One popular way to say what you've learned is to answer with the traditional name of a language. Do you speak Spanish? Sure, *un poco*. But a few weeks' travel from Spain to Mexico to Argentina will convince you that you've lied, at least in part. You know enough inside-the-circle material to function in all three countries, but there'll be new words, different favored grammatical constructions, new speech-act structure and content, and all those social and historical frames. You'll be able to function at a basic level, but you won't be communicatively competent.

Labels for the language don't work. They especially don't work when you ask about two languages that, from the outside, are treated as almost identical, even though they have separate names. They are treated as the same because of their inside-the-circle similarities.

In American universities you can study "Serbo-Croatian." Try asking a Serb if Croatian is the "same" language that he speaks. You can also study something called "Hindi/Urdu." Ask an Indian Moslem if she speaks the same language as the Hindus. Their answers aren't based on subtle differences in verb tenses; they're based on the wildly different frames that make up those different social identities, differences that, in both cases, led recently to horrible conflicts.

Two languages are classified as the same primarily in terms of the inside-the-circle grammar and dictionary. And it's true, of course, that if you live, say, in Spain and travel to Mexico you've got a tremendous head start over someone who's never learned Spanish before.

But the similarity is a surface illusion, just another heartbreak of inside-the-circle language for the person who wants to *use* the language to communicate. As soon as language is stretched out into languaculture, Spanish in Spain and Spanish in Mexico, Serbian and

Croatian, Hindi and Urdu, American English and British English aren't the same at all. The inside-the-circle linguists try to handle the differences with "dialect" or "variant," but if languaculture is what you're after, the differences go well beyond what those concepts suggest.

At a meeting in Germany I asked a colleague how it was talking with the newly arrived East Germans. This was right after the flood of immigration from the East to the West had started, but before the two Germanies reunited. "At the level of propositional content there is no problem," he said. He was a linguist, so he spoke to me in our common jargon, but all he meant was that from the grammar and the dictionary he could figure out any individual sentence. "But in terms of their attitudes, the beliefs and values behind their language, what they're trying to say, I often don't understand."

From the languaculture point of view, the labels for a language don't tell you much, because they don't tell you anything about the frames, and without the missing frames, you don't know how to do things with language in a particular world with a particular group of speakers and hearers. From the languaculture point of view, the name of the language doesn't tell you enough about the scope of what you've learned.

///

How about labels like "American" and "Mexican" and "Austrian"? Do they define the scope of what you've learned? They define the scope of *some* of what you've learned, but there's a bothersome complication, because such labels might refer to a *nation* or to a *state* or to both.

A *nation* is a group of people who see themselves as having a shared history, a shared language, a common bond that defines many aspects of who they are and what they do. But a *state* is a political unit, something with citizens who live inside of borders and orient to the same authorities and institutions.

The Austro-Hungarian Empire, that great block of central Europe that lasted for centuries up until the First World War, was a magnificent, grand state. But it contained many different nations—Austrians, Italians, Rumanians, Czechs, Slovaks, Magyars, Slovenes, Croats, to name a few. The conflict between state and nations disrupted the state continually. In fact, World War I started when a Serb nationalist shot the Austrian archduke, and after the war the new map of Europe shuffled the nations into smaller states that better approximated national boundaries.

That hasn't worked either, since as I write this the Serbs are at war with the Croats and the Slovenes, and the Czechs and Slovaks are arguing as well. And the current chaos as the former Soviet Union reorganizes itself is another powerful example of how nations and states don't coincide and what the consequences can be.

The difficult history of sub-Saharan Africa is another testament to the clash between nation and state. The European colonizers drew state boundaries without paying much attention to the way they were chopping up traditional African nations. The results have produced terrible conflicts, like the past war between Hausa and Ibo in Nigeria, the current troubles among Kikuyu, Kalenjin, Luo, and Luhya in Kenya, and the difficulties between the African National Congress and the Zulus in the newly emerging politics of South Africa. And those are just three of many examples.

Even in good old America, a country that we'd come to believe was both nation and state, the edges have blurred. The nation-state identity was based on the common denominators of European ancestry, the English language, and the shared plight of people who had left their old lives to start anew in an unknown and rich land with a frontier that never ended. African-Americans and Indians were held off on the periphery.

But then things started to get more complicated. Afro- and Native Americans demanded their rights as citizens and celebrated their common heritage. Waves of immigrants from different Spanish-speaking countries filled the cities. More open immigration policies in the 1980s resulted in new Asian and African populations. The Anglo-European descendants are in the minority in some areas now.

And, in the current era, these new nations—and that's what they are, groups of people who see themselves as bound up in a shared history—aren't buying the old argument that being American means taking on Anglo-European national traditions. They want to be citizens in an American state, but keep their national identity intact.

States and nations are out of sync all over the world. The challenge for the new century is to figure out and resolve this problem. The old solution—one national group in the state takes power and jails or shoots anyone from another national group who complains—is, with any luck at all, acquiring the reputation of brutality and oppression that it deserves. If that trend continues, it would be incredibly good historical news. But even the fall from grace of the old brutal solutions still wouldn't solve the problem.

Nations are languacultures, ways of communicating, discourse together with the frames that enable its use. So why can't they just coexist? Because, as we've seen with the number-one types, all over the world, a personal bond to a languaculture has an unfortunate and frequent side effect—namely, that when you encounter people living inside of another languaculture, the tendency is to characterize them in terms of what they lack.

Rising above that languacultural ceiling calls for the sort of frame building I've talked about in this book. It calls for a sacrifice of the security of the one-dimensional languacultural life in favor of new frames, a new view of things that is different from the one you started with, a new self that is neither what you were nor the way those other people are, but something that can handle both.

That's asking a lot. But that's what has to happen. To solve the problem, people have to forge an identity that isn't just national, yet at the same time, respect and acknowledge and enjoy that same national background. Nations are languacultures, and all of us have a strong identity shaped by them. But people have to turn to culture and stretch beyond those identities in the multinational state, if we are to have multinational states at all. And have them, in one form or another, we must.

///

Nations are languacultures, but—a messy complication—so are states. In Austria, at the Linguistics Institute in 1986, I was a foreign guest. But other foreigners would drop by. I finally noticed that they'd come from Slovenia, from Hungary, from Poland, from Rumania—but not a one from Germany. Then one day an Austrian colleague from another department leaned toward me and told me I shouldn't talk this up too much, but actually he preferred going to conferences in Eastern Europe rather than in Germany.

A couple of days later I happened to read something about an Austrian linguist's concept of the *Sprachbund,* a concept that means

speech or language—*Sprache* means both—and grouping or tie—
Bund comes from *binden,* to tie or connect.

Notice the lack of distinction between language and speech, and
the concept of a tie or connection because of it. People thought
about language differently inside the Austrian languaculture. A lot
of what I'm writing here became clear after I built some new professional frames over there.

The linguist wrote that many speech acts were similar in the old
Austro-Hungarian countries. The styles in Prague and Budapest, say,
would be more comfortable to a Viennese than would the styles of
talking in northern Germany. All those years of empire led to shared
speech acts, together with frames for society and history that were
bound—as in *Bund*—to them. Even though language inside the circle, the grammar and dictionary, were wildly different in Prague and
Budapest and Vienna, many of the frames weren't so far apart. Compared to Germany, they weren't so different at all.

All those different nations had a long shared history as part of
the same *state,* and the state, like the many nations that made it up,
was a languaculture, too. My guess, for what it's worth, is that once
the states that used to be the Soviet Union get over their new independence, some of them are going to find out they've got more in
common than they thought they did and come back closer together.

States are political entities, but they set up a world in which
speech acts and frames are organized. It's not hard to understand
why. When you cross a state boundary, institutions change, institutions that have to do with where and how you work, what the
economy is like, how the schools are run, how health care works,
how the police operate, what shape the media take, and who runs
the place in general.

The world you move through, the world within which you get
things done, changes at the border. Citizens grow up and then function as adults in terms of that institutional world. They communicate within it, and their communication is, as usual, in part the
grammar and the dictionary, and in part the frames that organize
how they use it.

In Mexico I went to open a bank account. I talked with a friendly
manager, and he gave me some forms to fill out. I went through
another visit's worth of forms, and he, friendly as ever, always had
some kind of problem that prohibited me from opening the account.

I started to have the stereotypical gringo feelings of inefficiency and I thought of corruption. Maybe he wanted me to offer him a bribe.

I went back to my hotel and joked with the guys at the reception desk about how impossible it was to open an account in Mexico. The owner of the hotel walked by, stopped, and said he had his account there and could I go with him to the bank the next morning? I did, the owner and the manager greeted each other and chatted for a while, and within a few minutes I had an account. The hotel owner turned to me and smiled and said, "We do things differently here," and the bank manager laughed. I got the point.

On a train from Austria to Zagreb, the capital of Croatia, I walked back to the service compartment and asked for a cup of coffee, in German. The Yugoslav sitting in the compartment didn't even look up from his newspaper. "We don't have any."

I'd heard stories about lousy service and hostile employees in Yugoslavia, but this struck me as pretty ridiculous. I took it as a challenge to see if this guy was wired into his identity or if he was human after all.

I talked about how I was going to Dubrovnik to teach a course, how I was an American, how my friend there had worked in Zagreb for years and spoke fluent Croatian. I tried to distance myself from the Austrian tourist identity he'd put me in and strike up a conversation rather than ask him to provide a service.

He chatted back, offered me a cigarette, and without any comment on the irony of it all, brewed us up two cups of coffee. Turned out to be a nice guy, and we talked for an hour and shook hands when I left the train in Zagreb. The Yugoslavs I told this story to loved it, laughed and considered it typical Yugoslav—*Yugoslav*, not Croatian or Serbian or Slovenian—hostile service by a person who, outside that identity, was a very human and warm guy.

In Mexico I dealt with a bank, and in Yugoslavia with the trains, but in both cases I approached institutions with my American frames and didn't get anywhere. In America, when I go to banks or ride one of the few trains left, I deal with people I expect to represent their institutions, people I expect to "do their job." The job, I suspect, isn't as central to identity in Mexico or what used to be Yugoslavia; other things are, and it's those "other things" that let you get the job done.

Frames for trains and banks are a function of the state. So were

some of the frames I built for the examples I showed you from
Austria. So were the frames that Michael Moerman presented in the
Thai example when he talked about the courtrooms or when the
district officer showed up in the village transcript we looked at in
some detail.

A state is a languaculture, just as a nation is. When you learn to
communicate, some of the frames you build will tie the details of
language into the institutional structures of the state. Some of what
you learn as you build languaculture will have a scope that ranges
across the human territory inside political frontiers.

Some of languaculture will be Mexican or American or Austrian
or Thai just because the frames tie into the institutions of the state
in which the talking and hearing are done. On the other hand, some
of the languaculture will be Mexican or American or Austrian or
Thai just because of a national identity that your conversational
partners belong to, a national tradition that might be dominant in,
or overlap with, or be related to, or be in opposition to, the state
in which you find it.

///

This state and nation business gets pretty complicated. States don't
exist independent of national traditions, and nations always have
their political organizations and agendas. Nation and state languacultures always mix and blend to some extent.

And the blends, as the stories have shown, can vary. At one
extreme, Israel represents a state founded by a nation. Even there,
the people they displaced—Palestinians—have become a nation
within the state who want land and rights, and internal differences,
like the recent one in news stories about immigrants from the former
Soviet Union, show that there are different Jewish nations within
the state as well.

At the other extreme is India, a state with so many nations in it
that it's hard for a Western outsider to understand why it doesn't
just fly apart. In fact, when I look at the map, I sometimes think
the only reason India is a state is because it's a state-sized chunk of
land with water on both sides and a mountain range to the north.

India tries to handle some of its national difference by drawing
internal boundaries that correspond to a language difference. Kar-

nataka, for instance, the state I worked in, includes areas where the majority speak Kannada. From a languacultural point of view, it won't surprise you to hear that there are border disputes all the time, sometimes turning downright violent, and that the Kannada part of the state that used to be under the old Moslem nizam of Hyderabad and the part that was under the Hindu maharajah of Mysore are about as similar as the English languacultures of New Orleans in Louisiana and County Cork in Ireland.

Even in India, though, centuries of history under various emperors and colonial life under the British, not to mention a shared history of independence since 1948, have turned the state into a languaculture. Indian English is enough to make that case, since, try as some might, India can't get rid of it. Indian English started as the language of the elites, though it is used more and more widely as a solution to the need for a state language that puts everybody at an equal advantage.

Over the years Indians took the language of the colonizers, gave its surface their own twists in grammar and dictionary and speech acts, uncoupled it from the frames of the colonial power, and re-wired it into India. Indian English is its own languaculture, with its own speech acts, its own ties to Indian history and society, its own literature and media. Indian English is a sign that, in spite of all the distinct and strong national forces in India, India the state is a languaculture, too.

///

By now the reader is weary of the complications with nation and state. So is the writer. But the twisted ride through the concepts helps correct the mistake we all repeatedly make, and will continue to make, but need to be aware of.

Several sections ago I asked the rhetorical question, once you've learned a new bit of languaculture from some people, can you say that what you've learned goes beyond just that group? If I learn a bit of languaculture from an academic colleague in Vienna, can I call it Austrian German? Does an expression I pick up from my business partner in Mexico City count as Mexican Spanish?

The problem is the *scope* of what one learns, and the key terms are *Austrian* and *Mexican*. Those kinds of national/state labels are used all the time to label the scope of languaculture.

So, step one in the qualification of the use of those labels: Such labels have to do with *both* nation *and* state. *Some* part of what people do, some part of what you learn, will work with other members of a national identity and with other citizens of the state, or maybe with both.

The problem I'm left with, though, is that claiming that something works throughout a national or state languaculture isn't automatic. It isn't guaranteed to work. Nation and state identities can stand in different relationships to different people at different points in time. In the sixties my father suddenly "discovered" he was Irish and started talking about corned beef and cabbage as "soul food." Nation and state identities can overlap or be separate. They can work against each other in open conflict.

Nation and state identities are *candidates* to tag the scope of what you've learned, but use them with care. They are neither automatic nor comprehensive in their coverage. Part of what I learned from my business partners in Mexico I'll bet I can wind up calling "Mexican," because I'll find it works all over the country, though I worry about repeated sayings that the North is a different country, "more like the United States," and that the South is, too—"very Indian" is what they say in Mexico City.

But part of what I've learned, I know, will tie in with other aspects of my partners' social identities. One partner is from a wealthy family of Spanish descent and the other is from a poor mestizo family, a former federal police officer who's worked his way up. The difference, between "Spanish" and "mestizo," has been around since the conquest and it pushes its way into Mexican discourse frequently. Octavio Paz based much of *The Labyrinth of Solitude* on it.

That's the uncomfortable point. National and state identity are the coin of the realm, the vocabulary by which we all organize our discussions of languacultural differences in the modern world. I wish I had a nickel for every time I've seen or heard something that characterizes *the* Japanese, for example.

State and nation are social identities that you can attribute *some of* languaculture to, but you have to check it out with many more people than just the ones you learned it from to make sure.

And state and nation don't define a rulebook, a recipe, a guide to exactly what to do under circumstances X, Y, and Z, either. Languacultures, state and nation or any other, are social facts, limits on what you can do together with expectations of how they might be done. But variation within those limits and expectations is part of the game. Some variation is due to the peculiar twist a particular individual offers the world. But some of it is due to other social identities, more fine-grained than nation or state, and, sometimes, in conflict with them.

These more specific identities vary, on the one hand, because of different social identities *inside* a languaculture. And they vary, on the other hand, because some social identities *cross* languacultural boundaries.

///

The other day I was talking to someone I'd never talked with before. He said he'd invested ten thousand dollars in a lottery and won. I looked at him and he read the question mark in my eyes. I had an image of him walking out of a convenience store with a trunk full of tickets. No, he said, not that kind of lottery. He'd meant a lottery held by the Federal Communications Commission. He'd won the right to ownership of a cellular network in a town in the East. *Lottery* meant something quite different from what I'd thought.

That evening I talked with my girlfriend on the phone. I told her I'd been "counseling" somebody. "Counseling or consoling?" she asked. She asked that because we'd been having conversations about men and women and how differently they talk. One of the recent ideas we'd tossed around was that when women talked about a problem, they wanted to just talk about it. But when men talked about a problem, they wanted to solve it. "Counseling," I answered, since I'd been trying to solve a problem rather than just listen to it. (That *just*, written automatically and not edited out later, shows how there might be a difference. She would never have written *just*.)

Within a few hours I'd tripped over two rich points in my own languaculture, two words that carried different frames for different social identities. The experienced investor taught me what a *lottery* was all about, and my girlfriend taught me that *counseling* tied to *consoling* for her, whereas it tied to *problem-solving* for me.

The same thing happens in other nation-state languacultures as well. One day I was talking to a businessman in Mexico City. He was negotiating with a new U.S. partner now, he said, to represent his products in Mexico, and he waxed enthusiastic about the free trade agreement with the United States and Canada and the changes in Mexico under President Salinas. GDP and foreign reserves were up, inflation was down, Mexico was on an express train to prosperity.

After he left, I talked with a waiter in the restaurant where we'd been sitting. Pretty exciting, all these changes in Mexico, I suggested. The waiter's smile turned downward and he shook his head. No, he said, things are worse. Of course they were, I thought, inflation has outstripped wages by several furlongs in the last few years. As far as the waiter was concerned, national prosperity was purchased at the cost of his real standard of living. "Changes in the Mexican economy" was a rich point that required different frames for the entrepreneur and the worker.

In Vienna one day I was walking into my apartment building and it struck me that a lot of people said, "*Guten Tag,*" "Good day." I'd always used the characteristic Austrian greeting, "*Grüss Gott,*" which means "greet God" or "God's greeting" or something like that.

Why so many German-style *Guten Tag*s in an Austrian apartment building? Finally I asked a neighbor, and he smiled and said, "A lot of us are socialists." The building was a product of Vienna's socialist government, and people who got apartments there had paid their party dues for some time.

Grüss Gott is a Catholic greeting for a Catholic country, where the church and the conservative party, as usual, often ride in tandem. Socialists, needless to say, aren't crazy about this alliance. Besides, they have historical ties to that famous German who wrote that religion is the opiate of the masses. Greeting people with words that haul up frames of Catholic conservatism just doesn't start the day right, as far as many Austrian socialists are concerned, so they use the more standard German greeting, *Guten Tag,* instead.

I told this story to an Austrian friend, a socialist who lived in another city building. Yes, he laughed, he could tell if he'd dialed the right number when he called Vienna city hall, the headquarters of the socialist city government. The operator always said "*Guten Tag,*" not "*Grüss Gott.*"

These stories show that once you're inside a languaculture, rich points don't stop. They demonstrate variation among different social identities—between investors and academics, between men and women, between workers and entrepreneurs, and between socialists and conservatives. And these identities, born of economics, gender, and politics, only top a long, long list.

This sounds so simple that it's embarrassing to point it out. But I guess I have to, since we all forget that it's true. I've conveniently forgotten for most of the book and tossed around categories like "Austrian" and "Mexican" and "American." Saussure forgot when he wrote of "German" and "French," as if those were identical everywhere. Intercultural communication types forget when they talk about how *the* Japanese *are,* and bilingual types forget when they talk about a Spanish-English bilingual. Everybody forgets, all the time.

///

It's not as if nobody ever noticed variation before. In fact, there's a huge literature on social variation, one that features several cameras and lenses and filters to focus on language, a literature that in itself would justify several books, and several have been written. This literature goes by the name of *sociolinguistics.*

Sociolinguists handle variation inside the circle—peculiar combinations of accent, local words and idioms, and unique grammatical twists that change across regions or social class. Variation by region or class is called *dialect.*

Dialect isn't the only kind of variation. Different styles of speaking, different *registers,* also shift with identity. Say a person talks differently, depending on whether he's receiving the Nobel prize, explaining why he joined Earth First! at a family dinner to all his relatives who are in the timber industry, or having a coffee break with his friends. The shift in words and grammar and speech acts is a shift in register.

Variation *inside* the circle is part of languaculture, no question about it, and the sociolinguists have documented it well. But what about all the frames outside the circle?

Here the sociolinguists shine and earn the *socio* in their name. They correlate variation inside the circle with *social identity*. Vari-

ation *means* something about the identity of the speaker, or of the
hearer, or it tells you something about the kind of situation they are
in. Why does that person speak that way? She's from *the South,* an
answer in terms of dialect. Or she's a *professor, teaching a class,* an
answer in terms of register.

Dialect and register are important, as far as they go. The description of details in the Waldheim transcript smuggled in that truth
without announcing it first. Waldheim shifted into Austrian *dialect*
at the start of his turn, and I claimed that it *meant* a shift from TV
studio to the family dinner table, from politician to father. And
Waldheim shifted into a bureaucratic *register* when he laughed, and
I told you that I wasn't sure what that *meant,* though I speculated
some about it. Waldheim shifted in both dialect and register during
his interview, and the shifts meant something about his social identity.

That's how sociolinguistics works. You figure out which surface
features of language signal a shift in dialect or register, then you
look at how people *switch* among them—the famous *code switching*—and then you learn the social meanings that are conveyed when
speakers throw the dialect/register switches.

Important and interesting as this all is, I don't want to launch
off into sociolinguistics right now. I want to stay with languaculture,
and languaculture goes after the frames that vary as much as the
surface forms of language that the sociolinguists look at.

Sociolinguistics is a help, because it shows how important the
neglected topic of variation is. It shows the relation between language variation and social identity. But by and large the sociolinguists don't plunge into the frames that travel with that social
identity. They don't handle langua*culture* variation in all its messy
splendor.

Though they tie variation to social identity, the sociolinguists
usually stop there. They talk about how dialect or register *means*
some social identity, but then they don't develop much of the languaculture *of* that social identity. They don't unearth the frames that
travel with it. They correlate the *langua* half of languaculture with
social identity, but not the *culture* half.

///

One exception is my old teacher John Gumperz, the one who told the joke about how anthropologists never use the word *culture*. John wanted to make sense out of why people of different ethnic backgrounds talked in the "same" language but failed to understand each other. He looked at what happened in job interviews and service encounters in England when Anglo-British and Asian- or West Indian British came into contact. He found out that different surface forms of language—intonation, words, grammatical constructions—told people which frames were the right ones to use.

Since members of different ethnic groups paid attention to different surface forms and used different frames, the encounters could turn a pas de deux into a wrestling match. Remember the Scollons' work with the Athabaskans and the Anglos? They were inspired in part by John's work. The BBC did a show on his work, a show called *Crosstalk* that you can find in university libraries. If you're reading this book, you'd enjoy viewing it.

Gumperz's work on inside-the-circle language and the frames that it signals, together with his efforts to tie all that in to particular social identities, is a way of seeing things that seeped into me over the years, a way I've stolen to build this book. (You're allowed to steal from your teachers; it's called "learning.")

But his way doesn't go quite far enough to handle languaculture. South Asian Brits, for instance, might use similar surface forms when they talk, true enough. But those forms might be hooked up to different frames. Some South Asians, for example, will know and/or use Anglo-British job interview frames better than others. And miscommunication might occur because of other social identities or twists in personal biographies. Success or failure might be due to different frames, which might or might not travel with the languaculture of the identity.

And being South Asian British is more than just being labeled South Asian British. It has to do with centuries of colonial history, who else you think you are, and how connected you are to England. Hanif Kureishi, a Pakistani Briton known for screenplays like *My Beautiful Launderette* and *Sammy and Rosie Get Laid,* recently wrote his first novel, *The Buddha of Suburbia.* Both the films and the novel show the kinds of complications I'm talking about here.

Frames have to handle the culture part of languaculture, but the sociolinguists typically don't include them. They notice variation inside the circle, correlate it to social identity, talk about the results in terms of misread intentions, and stop there. Variation has to handle the frames that make up the *culture* side of languaculture as well as the *langua* side. It has to handle the cases in which the language, in fact, is the same as far as language inside the circle goes, where the variation is all in the frames, not in the surface of language at all.

A journal called *World English* features the different ways people in different countries use English as a world language. Some articles show that just because people are using the same grammar and dictionary, it doesn't mean they're using the same language. That truth is no surprise here. With their different histories, with the different frames that come from the native languacultures of World English speakers, the World English that they speak might be wildly different. There are times when two speakers of World English might not use the same languaculture at all.

John Gumperz's work moved sociolinguistics in this direction. All I'm trying to do is move it a little further. That's what students are supposed to do.

///

Variation exists, period. And people, like me and most everybody who speaks of languacultures, ignore it, period. Something's broken and we need to fix it. Variation *inside* a languaculture belongs in the picture. But another fix is needed as well. Another kind of variation appears because some social identities *cross* languacultures.

When I visited Prague in 1989, my host told me about a meeting of linguists, the kind who deal with discourse. Since the meeting involved what were then East Germans together with Czechs who worked on German, the language of the meeting would be German. I was invited to attend.

I did. It was eerie. Here I was in this very different place, with these very different people in this very different language—different not only from my native language but also from the Austrian German I'd learned. But people presented papers on speech-act structure and content, talked about turns and topics and coreference. True, there were issues in there that I didn't get, rich points that came out of a different intellectual tradition. But on the whole, we shared a professional identity. We'd all read the same books that laid out the new linguistics. I connected and comprehended and commented coherently, right away, in spite of all the other differences.

Earlier in the book I told a story about a friend from India and an Austrian friend. At the time, I was showing how eating was something that varied with culture. But I also parodied all three of us as latter-day culture vultures who liked jazz and Gabriel García Marquez and wore Levis as our uniform.

When it came to meals, languacultural differences mattered. But when it came to other identities, those differences washed out. Some of the time, we communicated with the same languacultural frames, even though the surface form of language was different. My Indian friend spoke with the musical lilt of Indian English, and my Austrian friend spoke with me in Austrian German, but the frames that guided our talk were, sometimes, the same.

Shortly after I moved to Hawaii, I took a scuba course. The club that most of us joined after graduation, the one that our instructor ran, turned out to be one of the most ethnically diverse in Hawaii, with people of haole (Anglo), Hawaiian, Samoan, Japanese, and Chinese descent, together with all the mixes that you find on the island.

One day four of us were sitting on the foredeck of a boat, returning from an offshore dive. I was haole; still am, actually. My dive partner was Japanese, and the two other guys were Chinese and Samoan. We chatted away about how beautiful the dive had been in our different versions of Hawaiian English. A tourist boat cut across our bow and rocked our little dive boat with its wake. "Fucking haoles," said my Japanese partner and the Samoan in stereo. It never occurred to any of us that they meant me. Our common identity of the moment—local Hawaiian divers—overrode other differences among us, though those differences, in other situations, might have made a very great difference indeed.

When I moved from Hawaii to New York City in 1973, a culture shock that rivaled my first move to India, I had just gotten interested in jazz. I became a regular at a local bar called Stryker's two blocks from my apartment. I would often sit at the bar and, during the break, talk with the people on either side of me. It wasn't unusual that the person on one side would be Hispanic and the one on the other Black. The Hispanic would speak with all the surface forms that signaled a Hispanic identity, and the Black would use features of Black English. And I, naturally, spoke a White version of the language, though I'm not sure how to characterize it. Part street, part sixties, part bookish, part cowboy, I guess.

In that situation it just didn't matter; we weren't signaling social identity as much as we were talking in our normal way about a music we all enjoyed. In fact, it would have been strange and made us wonder if one of us spoke in the style of the other. The point of our talk was the jazz, our appreciation of what we'd just heard. The bond of the music, and the frames that went with it, overrode identity differences that might have mattered otherwise.

Another series of stories, another litany of anecdotes that complicates variation by dramatizing social identities that *cross* languacultures. This kind of variation also appeared in the Waldheim material. When I mentioned my frames for an interview with a politician on Austrian TV, I said that some of them weren't all that different from the ones I used in the United States. The reason, I speculated, was that the broadcast journalist role was something that was international, something that probably had its roots in American languaculture in the first place.

The stories I just told make the same point. An identity based on professional linguistics, culture vulture tastes, diving, or jazz, cuts across other languacultural differences. Those differences washed out because the other identities spanned them. Some social identities *cross* what we usually think of as languacultures, increasingly so in our fast-paced world linked by transportation and communication unimagined just a generation ago.

///

Variation within and similarities across nation and state languacultures turn the crisp social facts soggy. Does it make any sense at all to use terms like "America" and "Mexico" and "English" and "German" as labels for a single languaculture? Does a Mexican teenager who's a rock and roll fanatic have more in common with a similarly obsessed American teenager than she does with her parents? Does a Tzeltal Indian in the Mexican state of Chiapas have more in common with a Guatemalan Indian than he does with a corporate manager in Mexico City?

Just how powerful are those labels of nationality and state and language?

Sometimes such labels *conceal differences*. I still remember the first time I visited London, feeling relaxed that when I arrived I could use my native language. But then I'd talk to someone on the phone and realize with a shock that I'd understood every word and sentence, but had no idea what they were talking about. And sometimes such labels *conceal similarities*. I still remember my shock at having a conversation about Faulkner with an Austrian friend that would have been a rare occurrence in the United States.

The question is, is there any way to draw boundaries around, say, *American* languaculture? Does "America" tag a social fact boundary? Do such labels make any sense? Is there anything out there that is common and core and coherent and shared by a group of people you want to communicate with? Or do variation within and similarities across nation-state languacultures mean that the whole thing just slides around like mercury on an inclined plane?

Even the Americans aren't sure what the answer is anymore. As I write this, our national political theater, the 1992 presidential primaries, is live and in color. The news media use the occasion to teach us something about how varied we've become. For example, in the last week two articles in different papers featured Texas and Florida. The point of both drives the variation theme home—neither state is coherent, the way it used to be. Migration, ethnic diversity, links to national and global markets—there just isn't any "Florida vote" or "Texas vote" anymore.

When you learn something about a languaculture, what is the *scope* of its application? With whom can you use it? Does it apply to a nation or a state or a language, or to a more narrow social identity, or only to one person's peculiar biography, or what?

There's an easy out based on the work I've done so far in this book, and after all this work I'm tempted to take it. The easy out is, what difference does it make? Who cares? The point is to communicate. The problems you have are rich points. So you build frames, continue linking them together, encounter new rich points, and just keep on keeping on. The acid test is, as you work along, do you communicate better? The world you live in will give you the answer.

Who cares if you can find the edges to what you've learned? Who cares which parts of what you learned go with which social identities? The easy out might work for a single individual who learns a new languaculture, someone who's only doing it for him or herself.

The easy out *doesn't* work if you want to talk *in general,* if you want to talk *about* languaculture, about what it is and how it works, either to friends in conversation, or to colleagues in some professional format, or to newcomers you're trying to teach. If you want to talk in general, the languaculture has to be anchored with reference to some group, people who actually *use* it. Languaculture has to be linked to some *social identity*.

There are contemporary theories that say "forget it." In what has something to do with "postmodernism," the argument runs that the globe has shrunk due to migration and war and tourism and information flow and media and international everything, that there just aren't any edges around languacultures anymore. We're all a mix of a little of this and a little of that, an idiosyncratic mix that just doesn't match anybody else. There are no coherent social identities; there are no coherent selves. The shared base of "manners and morals," as the writers like to call it, has disappeared. When you communicate with somebody, you presuppose nothing, no shared frames. Everything is up for grabs.

The argument isn't crazy. A person who lives actively in a city anywhere in the world now is connected to multiple languacultures in multiple ways. At the level of the *person,* at the level of the *individual biography,* there's room for all kinds of weird combinations. Blend in all those within and across languacultural variations and who knows who in the hell you're dealing with?

At the same time, remember Saussure's use of the idea of *social fact.* The almighty individual that American languaculture celebrates, the lone cowboy out on the range with nothing but his harmonica and his horse, is a myth. The fact, the social fact, is that you can't just do anything you want and still communicate. Your native languaculture is something you start learning from the adults and kids around you. It continues, with a vengeance, when you go to school, hang around with other kids, and go home and watch TV. It lands on you like a grand piano when you go to work, try to find housing you can afford, and start your own family.

Your native languaculture isn't something you get to make up on your own and use alone in the privacy of your own home. It's something you use in *society,* something you learn and use in concert with others, something that lets you accomplish daily life. You can develop your own individual style, you can play with the edges of what's acceptable, you can dedicate your life to a struggle against them, but if you go too far outside too many of those edges, the social world won't make any sense out of you, won't know who you are or what you're trying to do, and you'll be awarded the labels "criminal" or "crazy."

Life, I think, is more loaded with rich points than it ever has been before, more interesting or more terrifying, depending on how comfortable with culture you are. But languaculture is still a social fact. It has to be or society can't operate. It sets limits on what you can do if you want to participate in the social flow. Languacultures have to have edges, not as clear and crisp as Saussure suggested, but border areas all the same.

When you tinker with a new languaculture, you learn some new social facts. You enter into a flow of experience with others, and you see that expectations aren't met, that disruptions wreck the communication. Then, starting with the default values that aren't met, you haul out the frames that contain them, dust them off, and build new frames that you then install until they become as habitual as the old ones were. Then—and this is the test—you reenter the flow of experience and see if you can participate.

I don't mean you're locked into a process of mindless adaptation, though at first it looks like that. You learn and change in the beginning, like the passive student that you are. But once the frames are built, you can joke, disagree, and struggle against the edges. But now there's a big difference. Now you don't protest the frame by disrupting the flow and making social life impossible; now you protest because you understand the frames, and you do it in a way that makes sense to the others. Now they know you're protesting instead of acting incoherently. What you say is *critical* rather than *nonsense.*

Social facts have lost their sharp edges, if they ever had them. And several sets of them might compete for your attention at the same time. Things are more complicated now, no doubt about it. But there are still social identities, all the way from nation or state down to what you do in your spare time, and when you meet "another one" you can talk about a range of things in a way an outsider won't understand. The way languacultures move and blend with others now, defining the scope of what you've learned, is harder than it's ever been. But languacultures are still out there, all the same.

///

With social identities other than nation or state—the kinds of identities laid out in story after story in this chapter—things get complicated fast. In fact, social identity is a topic for another book or two, because the list of identities that also have a languaculture associated with them goes on forever.

I'll start off by plugging books by a couple of colleagues, written for nonlinguists, not that they need any help. Deborah Tannen wrote a book called *You Just Don't Understand* that looks at the social identities of men and women and ties them to different languacultures. Robin Lakoff wrote *Language and Power,* a book that deals with professional social identities, like lawyer and therapist, and their languacultures. There is also a literature on social identities in the classroom, teacher and student, that if stacked vertically would reach Pluto.

And that's just the beginning. John Gumperz looks at social identities that are usually attributed to ethnicity, though these are what I call *nations* here. And he's not the only one. Literature in the new linguistics treats languacultural differences among ethnic/cultural/racial identities in virtually every place that linguists have worked.

I've told stories about social identities that included junkies, *a deviant group;* independent truckers, *an occupational group;* jazz buffs and scuba divers, *special interest groups;* and I've made wisecracks several times in the book about how younger readers won't understand what I'm talking about, which implies *generational groups* as well.

I used another study by Deborah Tannen and some stories of my own to talk about *regional* identities, New York and California. I referred to hippies and yuppies here and there, and these are social identities of what I might as well call *lifestyles* as well.

Then there's the experience we've all had, the one where someone tells a story and says, "You know the type," and the listener nods knowingly. The two of them are operating with a sense of a social identity tied to languaculture that doesn't even have a name.

The number of social identities tied to languaculture is phenomenal. All I want to do here is establish that fact and then spin out a couple of consequences, so that I don't leave you—or me—with the idea that once nation and state are straight you've solved the problem of defining the scope of what you've learned.

///

Social identities are more or less demanding in terms of just how much of a languaculture they drag along with them. One of the things I said in my book about independent truckers, *Independents Declared,* a suitable gift for birthdays, weddings, or bar mitzvahs, is that independent trucking isn't something you *do;* independent trucker is something that you *are.*

What I meant with this pithy prose is that the social identity, and the languaculture that goes with it, spills into family and social life in a way that, say, typing letters all day on a word processor doesn't. Independent trucking is *high density;* word processing, *low density.*

Same way with junkies. Being a junkie is *high density;* it means that much of your life is organized around junkie ways of talking and junkie frames, or junkie languaculture. Being a scuba diver, even if you start feeling withdrawal after a dive, is much less so; it's *low density,* even though an intense conversation on a dive boat, a pure scuba conversation, would create some problems for a nondiver.

The point is that a social identity might carry a languaculture that is pretty minimal and simple, a few bits of language and pieces of frames. Or the identity might carry a massive dictionary and favored grammatical constructions, together with new frames that would fill a warehouse.

When I was a kid I decided to hustle a few bucks by painting house numbers on curbs. The new occupational identity didn't take a hell of a lot of time to master once I got past the concept of "stencil." As an adult I fell into discourse analysis, and that carries a dictionary and some phrases and frames that if left to their own devices could wrap my mind in lead. In fact, in my identity as discourse analyst, I can only talk at high speed on specialized issues to others with the same languaculture. And, if you remember the story about the meeting in Prague, the high density discourse analysis identity was the reason I could walk into a room full of different people in a different place, people who also had that identity, and talk with them immediately about a large number of things.

What you learn as you enter a new languaculture *may* come from social identities that are more specific than nation or state, either identities available within the languaculture or identities that may span that languaculture and appear in many others as well.

A friend of mine worked among the Bemba in Africa as a missionary. Once he met an older man who spoke English, but the man kept throwing in weird guttural and hissing sounds as he spoke. It turned out that the man had learned much of his English by listening to BBC radio broadcasts on an old radio suspended in a tree in the middle of a village. The cracks and pops and static of the distant broadcast, he assumed, were part of the sound system of English.

The story may be apocryphal—my friend was a Jesuit—and it deals with inside-the-circle material, but it makes the point. When you learn new pieces of a languaculture and then use them among just a few people, be careful how far you go in your aspirations to think in terms of a more general social identity.

///

I've hammered away at the idea that languaculture is a social fact, in two different ways. First of all, it is a social fact in the Whorfian sense—it sets limits around what can be easily thought and said. Second, it is a social fact in a framelike way—its sets you up to expect certain things to happen.

This is an unfashionable view these days. It's unfashionable because of the view of speakers and hearers that it implies. People just avoid the edges and expect things, where the edges and expectations are *conventional,* the product of shared views about what the world is all about that are drummed into the newcomer.

The more fashionable view is that people collaborate in particular circumstances to create the social moment. They don't just follow rules and avoid trouble; they create and play and innovate and manipulate and deceive. Erving Goffman created a sociology based on that premise. There's of course truth to this, though I've known plenty of people in several languacultural worlds who *do* just drone out the languaculture. There's a technical term for them—they're called *boring*.

Perhaps the difference between the creative and the boring was put best by a Mexican friend who ran a boat off Cozumel. He said that there were always some Americans who came down who were fascinating people to talk with—he spoke good English, needless to say, and knew American frames well, and what he meant was that these Americans didn't just do what he'd learned to expect from them. But most tourists—he shook his head. It was like tossing the same cassette into the player, over and over again.

Some people, some of the time, do wonderful things with raw languacultural material. I don't have any argument with that view. I just think it's a later stage in the process of learning a languaculture. You can't create and play and deceive without a languaculture in terms of which to do them. If you try to do them in terms of *your* languaculture in the company of people who live in the context of *another,* it just won't work. The talk doesn't flow. Rich points pop up everywhere. You've got to build some new frames first.

I remember the magic moments toward the end of my year in Vienna in 1989. I'd gotten to the point where I could understand almost everything. I could speak within several systems of new frames. But when I talked, I sounded flat and boring. I couldn't create, couldn't play, couldn't help make the social moment sparkle with my colleagues or friends.

But then, toward the end, my imagination and my intuitions started to find a way through the languaculture into the surface of speech. It made all the difference in the world. I could, once in a while, improvise something that I thought was interesting and my conversational partners would respond; I could, once in a while, make them laugh. I could *participate*, rather than just *observe.*

Languaculture had shifted from a *constraint*, a set of social facts, to a *resource*. Languaculture had changed from how I've talked about it for most of this book to how the more fashionable view presents it. But first things first. You can't make a conversation sparkle until you know what a conversation is, whom you're talking with, and what the conversation is about. To get to that point, you learn the social facts first, then play with them later.

Over the years I've read dozens of interviews with jazz musicians and contemporary artists. Many of them talk about how they mastered the fundamentals of their craft first, then cut loose and took off into their personal improvisational styles. Some say they return to the fundamentals every now and again, just to enrich the base off which they operate.

Languaculture is the same. First you work on the basics, and—postmodernism be damned—there always are some, or else members of nations and states and other social identities couldn't communicate with other members. Once the basics are under control, you can create, improvise, criticize, or struggle against, as you please. For then your creation, improvisation, criticism, and struggle will be understood by those with whom you're creating a moment of drama in the social world.

///

Once you understand a languaculture, you'll find that people have different relationships to it. Some—the bores—will just act it out. The more interesting ones will play and create. Some act in opposition to the languaculture; some will hate it.

I know I don't like it when I'm bagged with a social identity. There are several psychiatric reasons for this that I refuse to tell you about here. I'll save that for my memoirs. But there are other reasons. One of them is cultural—I grew up an American individualist, and whatever else I do and learn that fundamental premise keeps cropping up. Social identities, by this premise, strip away your individuality. It goes against my fifties American cowboy-movie socialization. I'm aware of this in a way I never used to be—I can counter it for a while, but only for a while.

I like to do or say something that goes so far outside of the default values of what people think I am that the social identity they've pinned on me can't carry the contradictions. It liberates me and opens up space for something new to happen.

Maybe it only works in the context of America. When I try to pull this off in another languaculture, it's hard to do. In Austria one evening, at a dinner, a person asked me what I did. I told him I was a *Gastarbeiter,* a guest worker, a term used to refer to working-class immigrants, usually from Yugoslavia or Turkey. The people who knew me looked horrified. One laughed nervously and corrected the situation—"Oh, Herr Professor."

This value is almost a religious one, so it lets me tell a story I've always wanted to write somewhere, namely, how chicken fried steak became a sacrament.

I moved to Houston from New York City in 1975. People assumed I was an intellectual New Yorker, the worst sort of Yankee, and I suspect several thought that I was Jewish. As a Jewish friend at the university used to joke all the time, "Being in the Jewish community in Houston is like being in the left wing of Rotary."

What people I was introduced to didn't know was that I grew up in a California valley, surrounded by country music and pickup trucks and people wearing boots and cowboy hats. One of the things the guys used to do, late at night after they'd taken their dates home or gone out in the country to drink beer, was drive to a place that no longer exists on old Highway 50 called "The Hungry Truck." We'd order chicken fried steak, a piece of breaded steak with white gravy poured over the top. I still order them when I'm someplace where I can get them.

Texas is a place where you can get them. So, after someone had introduced me in Houston—after the talk started around the assumption that I was a New York Yankee intellectual, probably Jewish—I'd ask a simple question: "Where can you get a good chicken fried steak around here?"

The social identity people had put on me and the frames they'd organized around it fell like an old building when the dynamite goes off. They looked at me and wondered, and that gave me a chance to be somebody besides who they'd already decided I was. So important is that to me, so sacred, that I started referring to chicken fried steak as a sacrament.

Imagine trying to pack that story into a grammar and a dictionary. Imagine laying out all the languaculture that goes into that story in terms of identities and regional variations. Imagine taking all the shared background I've assumed on the part of American readers and filling in the gaps in what I've just told you.

All that would have to be laid out for students of our—my and the American reader's—languaculture, before they could get the point. And then, to do something similar themselves, to take all that and play with it in opposition to social identities, they'd need a degree of familiarity and practice and intuitive availability that would take some time to acquire.

A new languaculture comes out of your encounter with rich points and the frames you build; languaculture as a resource for play takes a little longer. I've only tried to tackle the *first* problem in this book. I'm not sure how to tackle the second. I tend to think that's up to the individual after he or she has learned a new languaculture, but then I'm an American who thinks in terms of individuals.

///

A person is a biographical history wrapped in skin. A social identity is a category that carries a languaculture, however dense it may be. The two aren't the same.

When you communicate, you communicate with a person, at least some of the time. I've mentioned persons who just parrot an identity, but I don't recommend you spend a lot of time with them unless you have to. Once you've learned the social identity, you've learned the person. Life is too short.

More interesting are persons who, at any given point in time, are social identities plus their biography. A few years ago my father started into that slow roll where you lose interest in life, get sicker and sicker, and eventually die. It was a sad and powerful and moving thing to go through, and it's one of the reasons I just wrote "Life is too short."

We dealt with several doctors. Most of them were just doctors. A few let their biography seep into a blend of doctor and who they were. My favorite was a man in his mid-fifties, overweight, who dressed in purple pants and a purple silk shirt open midway down his chest and wore gold chains. His nurse yelled at him all the time and told him what to do. He dropped things and asked us questions in ordinary English about all kinds of nonmedical topics.

He said things like, "Well, I can do this, but that'll be a drag and hurt a lot, so why don't we try this easy thing first and see how it goes."

I don't know how good he was, and that of course was frustrating, dealing with a bunch of doctors who disagreed with each other, who were obviously swimming in a sea of frames only a few of which they could master, none of which I knew. I had no way to evaluate what they said and participate in decisions.

But he was the weirdest doctor I ever met. Nothing in any languacultural frames that I could have laid out would have set an outsider up for that encounter. He was pure biography with a low-density medical touch. *But,* the frames I laid out would have led an outsider to the same conclusion I came to. This guy was one strange doctor.

Personal biography affects how speakers use the social identities relevant to a particular discourse. They might take it seriously and overwhelm you with it, keep their distance from it, or make a point of not doing what they're expected to do. As a newcomer to a languaculture, you'll eventually learn to make such evaluations yourself and talk about them with such a person and with others. But first, you have to know the social facts, the languaculture in question, or else you can't know the relationship of that person to it.

///

So much for the consequences of all those social identities. Variation is normal. When you figure out a languaculture, when you encounter rich points and build frames to bridge the differences between you and them, you want to know how widely you can use your newly won knowledge.

You define the *scope* of what you've learned by tying the languaculture to a *social identity.* People do this all the time, usually by using the name of a language, the name of a nation, or the name of a state. That'll work, for some of what you've learned, some of the time.

But then other social identities exist as well, mounds of them, dealing with everything from gender to region to occupation to leisure time pursuits. Some of these are included in the larger social identity of nation and state, and some of them are identities that span nation-state boundaries. Identities like business and rock and roll tie people together and set them up to communicate, to some extent, whatever their national languaculture.

And once you've mastered some new social identities, particular people will vary in their relationship to them. At one extreme, a person might step into a high-density social identity and *be* it. Another might step into the same one and surprise you because they struggle *against* it, or *play it down* in light of their unique bi-ography. A third might *mix* several social identities in a way that few people do.

There's something to language and nation and state, so you can't toss them out as irrelevant. But they're too broad to handle variation in terms of other social identities and personal biography, and too narrow to handle the growing number of identities that cross lan-guacultures in our shrinking world.

I can't resolve the problem here; I just want to point it out. People who learn a languaculture just stumble along, deeper and deeper into it, and start figuring out the variation on their own. Professional students of languaculture formulate research questions and try to systematically locate a languaculture's edge.

I've neglected variation in this book and, for the most part, used the traditional names for languages—Spanish and German—to-gether with traditional names that blur nation and state—Mexico and Austria—without worrying too much about the complications. I think that the aspects of languaculture I've used in this book are likely candidates for those large social identities, but I wouldn't want to bet large sums of money on it until I'd done more work.

Evil as that is, I've been more careful than most people you read and hear. To keep my own guard up, when I'm on my way into a new languaculture, I've got a pet phrase I tag on to everything— "except when they're not." If someone says the Japanese are ori-ented toward social harmony, I think, yes, that's true, except when they're not. If someone tells me Americans are materialistic, I think, yes, that's true, except when they're not. It starts me thinking about the counterexamples, the complications, the variation within that languaculture, about how biographies and other social identities complicate things in a particular moment of communication.

But for my purposes here, in this book, I've downplayed the problem. My purpose here was to shift the reader's view from lan-guage to languaculture, from grammar and dictionary to discourse plus frames, from linguistic competence to communicative compe-tence. My purpose here was to erase the circle around language, to leave readers with a strange new word, *languaculture,* that would remind them of their inseparable bond. I did that work with ex-amples of the language/nation/state sort, with other examples from less dense social identities thrown in along the way.

Variation is a problem, one that grows more interesting and complicated the further you go into a new languaculture, or the further you go into your old one. You try to solve the problem the same way you started out, by learning a new languaculture, less dense than the one linked to nation or state, but a new languaculture all the same.

When you go from one language/nation/state languaculture to another, you encounter rich points and build frames, what people usually think of when they think of "learning a language," if they're thinking in terms of communicative competence. But once you're inside, differences within the languaculture produce rich points that you also have to contend with, rich points that signal the different social identities at work inside. Learning a new languaculture is something that continues, from the initial differences of the complete outsider point of view to the mastery of ever more subtle details as you move further along.

As several examples in the book have shown, you can encounter new social identities *within* your native languaculture and treat them in exactly the same way.

The other day the radiator in my aging car quit working. For eleven years I've taken the car to a mechanic named Corky. I don't know his real name. We're always Corky and Mike. Garages are like that.

Corky figured out a long time ago that I was interested in his social identity as mechanic and the frames that went with it, so every time I go in, he tosses out a rich point, and I go to work with some questions. I don't know whether I can define what I've learned from him as "mechanic social identity" or not. Besides, his personal biography pushes strongly against the edges of mechanic social facts. But I don't really care. Not in this case. The two of us do this just for fun.

Variation might be a problem for languaculture, in theory, but it makes life more interesting, even in your home languaculture territory. Rich points and frames aren't just a way into a "second language"; they're a way into a broader and deeper understanding of your native languaculture as well.

Sailors and Immigrants

IMAGINE a three-step process on the way to culture. Step one is a *mistake*. Something goes wrong. Step two is *awareness* of frames and possible alternatives. Step three is *repair*, tinkering with old frames, now brought to consciousness, and building new ones, until the gaps between you and them are filled in.

Mistake, *Awareness*, and *Repair*. The initials spell MAR, the Spanish word for ocean. It's an appropriate acronym, because culture makes you aware of the ocean in which you've been swimming. A fish, the old saying goes, would be the last one to notice the water.

"Mistake" isn't just any old mistake. Say you keep messing up the verb endings for the imperfect past in Spanish. Sometimes you use them wrong and sometimes you use them right. As time goes on, you get better and better. That's a mistake, but it's an inside-the-circle mistake. That's not the kind of mistake I'm talking about here.

The kind of mistake I'm talking about is *frame based*. Something happens that you don't expect, and what happens can't be fixed by more drills with the imperfect tense. What happens is that people aren't acting right, the situation isn't working the way it's supposed to. Mistakes happen *in* language—the rich points—but their recognition happens *because of* frames. *Mistakes are things that people do that don't match frame expectations.*

Number-one types might recognize a mistake and be aware of it, but then they just note the deficiency in the other. The other is at fault, just because they aren't acting according to the expectations in the number-one type's frames. That kind of awareness isn't enough to make it on the MAR.

A better version runs like this: A mistake happens, you become aware of it, and then you begin to build a *list* of differences between you and them. "Yes, well, you see, I've lived here a long time, and the X aren't like us. The X do things this way." You hear this sort of thing from foreign "old hands" in another country, old hands who aren't really connected, who spend most of their time with other foreigners and use their local country language mostly to shop and order in restaurants.

The *awareness* in MAR means more than this. When a mistake happens, a motor kicks in, a motor that, allowed to accelerate, starts up a program of change that continues forever. *A mistake means that other frames are operating, frames you aren't using, frames you may never have imagined existed.* Awareness means that buried frames are brought to consciousness and changed, maybe with just a little tinkering, maybe with elaborate new additions.

Changing frames is what *repair* is all about. Repair keeps the process under way once it gets started. Repair carries you further and further into a new languaculture, further out to sea. Frames that always seemed like the "natural" way of doing things turn out, on conscious reflection, to have an arbitrary structure. Other ways are possible.

The way those "other people" do things has its own coherence, a different coherence from yours. As you repair your frames, your mind and heart and soul become more complicated, because you have new ways of seeing and doing. You build a bridge between the two ways so you can get back and forth. The bridge keeps changing as you make new repairs. You step *above* the two languacultures, your native one and the new one you're reaching toward, and forge a higher-level identity that contains them both and shows their connections. What you were—a person in an unconscious "natural" languaculture—changes to what you are now becoming—a person who can understand in terms of different frame systems and tack back and forth between them.

Repair stretches consciousness in two directions: sideways, to accommodate new frames for the new languaculture, and upward, to grow a biographical self that includes what you used to be and organizes what you've become. Biography thickens with new identities and stretches to accommodate them.

///

MAR—mistake, awareness, and repair—puts you *out to sea* in the best sense of the word, at home between lands, able to change course and reach any of them. You talk as much with the other sailors as you do with the landlocked denizens of your home port.

Once you set sail on the MAR, you've a lot in common with those other sailors. You're all *from* somewhere, but you've all become something other than just where you're from. And when you do go home, you live in a port city, metaphorically speaking, like New Orleans, San Francisco, or New York. You've all built an identity that stretches beyond the unconscious shapes your home poured into you. You're all used to being at sea and find it a fascinating place. Two people who know the MAR can talk about differences without guarding their own frames like threatened lands that others want to conquer.

I think that sailors on the MAR are about an evolutionary human development, a shift in the human ecology that *selects for* the ability to take growing up in a particular languaculture as a *resource* rather than a *conclusion*. The number-one Americans—or Austrians, or Mexicans, or anyone else—can't make it. They can't stand at MAR. They suffer from terminal seasickness. They build dikes to hold back the MAR, fortress walls to defend their coasts.

The sailors, the ones who live on land *or* at sea, the ones who grow comfortable with languaculture, are the guides into the next century. They're from somewhere, but they can deal with differences anywhere else. Their biography outgrows their home territory and takes them into a region that nobody grew up in, one that the sailors all know, namely, the MAR.

///

When sailors go ashore in a new land and stay awhile, they change their names. They become immigrants.

Some years ago Salman Rushdie wrote an article in a magazine called *American Film*. This was before he was forced into exile because of *The Satanic Verses*. He wrote of films made with directors, cast, and crew from different countries, in a location native to none of them, based on a story by an author from yet another place.

This kind of situation inspired him to write of an "immigrant sensibility," a sensibility based on the fact that no one deals with the simple world that they grew up in anymore. Everyone forges their way through a world of different kinds of people engaged in common tasks, a world rich in multiple perspectives.

I think there's something to Rushdie's immigrant idea on more than just esthetic grounds. When I went to live in Vienna in 1989, I was one tired linguistic anthropologist. I was tired, partly, because the gap between what I knew how to do and my goal of learning Viennese languaculture had grown so great that I couldn't figure out how to get there.

I decided to let go of my ideas about ethnography, about informal interviews and field notes, about file folders full of newspaper clippings. I had plenty of inside-the-circle German language material to work with. I'd already started on several speech acts and their ties to historical and social frames, like the Waldheim work. I had a job to do at the University of Vienna, I had an apartment to set up, people to talk with, movies to see and music to hear.

I decided the hell with the old research identity. I'd just make sure I kept learning things, in whatever way seemed right, and then later figure out what I'd been doing. I wouldn't study some group of people; I'd just try to figure out how to live in Vienna. My "new" way of thinking about things was obvious in retrospect. I was an *immigrant* to Vienna, a new arrival from a foreign land with a job to do and a life to organize.

I landed with my native languaculture and ran into rich points all over the place as I started to try to function in the new one. From the basics of living to the details of my job to what I did for fun, I had to build and rebuild frames and hook them together into a coherent whole. I had to build a self within the new world, master new social identities, and tie my biography to them.

At the end of the year, I had new identities and my biography had changed. I didn't have an *Austrian* identity. I never could, because Austria had shaped Austrians' development from childhood and America had shaped mine. But I'd learned at least part of a new languaculture, new ways of using language, and who I became in that new languaculture was different from who I'd been in the old one.

The strange thing about the two metaphors I've used—the immigrant and the sea—is that people usually go to sea and then land as immigrants. In Austria it reversed; I learned to be an immigrant and the experience put me out to sea, out into the MAR. But there's no doubt in my mind where I came from—it's clearer to me than it's ever been before—and I still know right from wrong.

///

Margaret Mead wrote something about immigrants without a destination back in the sixties.

It's strange. When I started this book, I never would have guessed that I'd mention Margaret Mead so much. I've mentioned her several times, in part, I admit, because she's a known figure to readers I hope to reach; namely, people who have never read an anthropology or linguistics book in their lives.

The irony is, I never learned anything about her in graduate school. I remember when she died, during the anthropology meetings in 1978. I thought the timing was pretty cosmic and wondered why people didn't talk about her much. Later that year, at the meetings of the Society for Applied Anthropology, people sat around in a room and told stories about her, in the tradition of an Irish wake, which appealed to me, since I'm genetically programmed for them.

They talked about her, about how unappreciated she was, about how one American university wanted to give her an honorary Ph.D. and the anthropology department wouldn't sponsor it. I remember that as I sat and listened to the stories, I thought about Gregory Bateson at Hawaii, how one faculty member said he didn't have much to do with the department, how he only had an M.A.

Margaret Mead and Gregory Bateson were married for a while.

They had their own child, the anthropologist Mary Katherine Bateson, but still, I hope I've been possessed by their ancestral spirits.

Anyway, Margaret Mead wrote a book about the sixties called *Culture and Commitment*. The book talked about how the kids of the sixties weren't just rebels. Rebels were easy to understand; rebels just took the languaculture and did things to oppose it. They defined themselves *in terms of* the languaculture.

The kids of the sixties, some of them anyway, of all different colors, protesters and soldiers, didn't just rebel. They called the languaculture into question. They cast off and sailed the MAR. They said, I'm not interested in just acting in opposition to the frames; I'm interested in questioning the frames and imagining new ones that don't yet exist.

Kids of the sixties were like immigrants to a new country. That's the metaphor Mead used. They were in a place where their parents couldn't give them any instructions, because the parents were bound up in a languaculture and the old frames didn't apply anymore.

The problem for the kids of the sixties was different from the usual immigrant story. They weren't just trying to move from the languaculture of the parents to the languaculture of the new land. No one knew what the languaculture of the new land looked like. The job of the kids of the sixties wasn't just to learn a new languaculture; they had to *invent* it. Most of them gave up. They had to. You can't invent a new languaculture from scratch.

Mead and the sixties were a little off the mark. The problem isn't to invent a brand new languaculture; the problem is to live among several of them, all at once, and create an identity that lets you participate in the synthesis. Anyway, the sixties are long gone, though the conditions that gave rise to them aren't.

///

Now I want to return to the example of one coherent nation-state languaculture, like American English, and a second one in which you want to turn communicatively competent, like Austrian German or Mexican Spanish. I want to ignore problems of variation and less dense social identities. In other words, I want to get as close to the old idea of "learning a second language" as I can in languacultural terms.

The thing I wonder about is: What do you learn, what is its relationship to what you already know, and who are you after you've learned it?

There are some differences between languaculture one, LC1 from here on out, and languaculture two, or LC2, that just aren't very interesting. A "fork" is a *Gabel* in German is a *tenedor* in Spanish, and that's about it. Hardly a rich point. A "dog" is a *Hund* is a *perro*, though here it gets richer, since you've got to watch what you're doing if you call a person a dog. "With" is *mit* is *con*, though I'll tell you, prepositions in every language I've visited slide around more than the grammar books let on.

But, on the whole, these points aren't all that rich. You learn new pieces inside the circle, make a few minimum frame changes, and you're ready to communicate. True for *some* of the new languaculture, but not for *all* of it, as you've seen over and over again in this book. Yet this is the idea of how second-language learning works, in general, in much of the popular and professional imagination.

But give this view its due. Part, not all, but part of the trip from LC1 to LC2 is a piece of cake. There's an easy correspondence between the two, because the frames don't change much. Just those last-minute bits of sound do.

But what about the Austrian examples of *Schmäh* and the Waldheim affair, or my first run at the Mexican concepts of "truth" and "lie." These involve more than a last-minute sound switch. They're the rich-point tip of a frame iceberg, one that connects the moment of use to speech acts and frames for history and society that, in turn, connect with other frames and other rich points. When you need to write an article just to *start* translating a term like *Schmäh*, you're dealing with LC1 and LC2 frames that are very different indeed.

In cases like these, going from LC1 and LC2 is a lot of work. The rich points call for heavy frame construction compared to what you arrived with, and communicative competence requires you to move into those new additions and stay there while you talk and listen.

There are several possibilities between simple and difficult, too. Much of the relation between the old LC1 and the new LC2 will be somewhere in between—not a simple surface jump, but not a move into a brand new frame system, either.

I keep trying to visualize this, and I keep coming up with clay. The reason is, sometimes I write fiction, or try to, and I noticed one day in Vienna that fiction writing was easier there. It was easier because I was stumbling ever deeper into Austrian German, and fiction turned into a way to play with my native languaculture, something I missed. I realized that I could stand apart and look at it in a way I hadn't before, as something distant, something that wasn't the same thing as "me." I started to think of it as clay, raw material that I could throw onto the wheel and mold and shape.

So I'm stuck with clay. Say LC1 is represented by a cone-shaped mass of *red* clay, the lower end is the talk, and as you go up, you ascend through speech acts and the frames that represent fundamental premises about life and the nature of society and history.

Say LC2 is a similar chunk of clay, only this time it's *blue.* The easy part of LC2 learning looks like little flecks of blue at the bottom of the red cone. The hardest part of LC2 is flecks of blue at the bottom that connect with new chunks of blue molded into the red cone you brought in with you. Most things you learn in LC2, though, are changes *here and there,* from the bottom of the cone to the top. In fact, as you become communicatively competent in LC2, the red and blue start to blend together, so that some clay will mix red and blue and turn purple.

This isn't a very attractive metaphor, an original single color cone gone lumpy and multicolored through the addition of new clay. But the point of the metaphor isn't an esthetic one. The point is to break away from the idea that LC1 and LC2 are separate entities afloat in some objective dish. The point is to start thinking about what happens *inside* the person who sails the MAR, who has the experience of culture, who turns into an immigrant, who learns a new languaculture and acquires the ability to function in both the old and the new one.

What happens to the immigrant? What happens to the person who blends LC1 and LC2 inside the same mind? If Rushdie's immigrant sensibility is the wave of the future, what kind of creature are we breeding here?

///

The clay, the metaphor I used to describe the blend of LC1 and LC2, describes the immigrant, and immigrants is what we all have become. Even if you never move from the house you were born in, the structure of the world has changed so that different languacultures land at your door.

The first thing that happens to immigrants is they become aware that there is, in fact, clay. The next thing that happens, they start patching on those little flecks of blue at the bottom and noticing differences. Nothing in the red cone changes much. The new pieces of language from inside the circle, the flecks of blue, are patched-over spots for language forms that are already there. The differences they notice are made sense of in terms of frames already in the cone.

Some immigrants stop there. Most popular images of what "language" is all about stop there, too. The immigrant can probably communicate to survive, but that'll be about it. He or she will know, in a particular situation, that this noun means that thing, and this verb means that action, so the two together mean that action on this thing. That's not so different—no surprise—from what inside-the-circle linguistics offers—word meanings in the sense of reference, and sentence meanings in terms of propositional structure.

What the immigrant won't have at this stage is how those words and sentences shimmer with associations, connotations. What he or she won't have is a sense of how to converse, argue, and tell a lie. What he or she won't have is the sense of who they're talking with and how they see them, of how that specific moment ties in with all the others that go into the flow of daily life, of how the talk fits into the society and the currents of history that lie behind it.

What he or she *will* have is *langua* without the *culture*. What he or she will have is an ability to *talk,* but not to *communicate.* To get to that point, the immigrant has to tinker with the original red cone. New clay has to be stuck onto the side and molded into the original, with all those added lumps of blue and new streaks of purple.

The two languacultures, LC1 and LC2, will stand in several different relationships. Sometimes they'll overlap without much trouble, sometimes they'll blend together into something new that handles both, sometimes they'll remain distinct, because they're just so different that they can't be fit together.

Some would argue that the clay metaphor isn't just about LC1 and LC2; it's about modern life, or, more appropriately, postmodern life. The problem of postmodern life, the story would go, is the problem of unconnected languacultures, social identities that have lost their mutual coherence. The problem is to live with all the fragments and find some way of putting them together into a life. I think that's true, and I think it's more and more true the younger you are.

But then that's why the immigrant metaphor feels right. That's why Rushdie wrote of an immigrant sensibility to characterize us all, why Mead talked about the kids of the sixties as immigrants, why I was so taken with the metaphor when I lived in Vienna in 1989.

Immigrants is what we all need to be to roll into the next century. The number-one response is and always will be a possibility. But in a world gone from distant to local through information and transportation, the number-one philosophy will produce conflicts that can't be resolved, ever.

Immigrants may not resolve the conflicts either, but they'll at least be able to recognize them, understand them, and discuss them before the shooting starts. With any luck, recognition, understanding, discussion, and action will make the shooting irrelevant. Without it, the shooting is inevitable.

Immigrants won't solve problems of fundamental economic and political inequities. Languaculture isn't a magic wand that'll make historically rooted distrust and hatred disappear. It won't neutralize basic differences in moral judgments about right action and the nature of the just society. It won't make unjust and just plain wrong behavior disappear.

What it *will* do is cast languacultural differences in a sympathetic light, let the viewer see them as something other than a deficiency, show them in all their rich interconnections with a way of living in a different world.

Languaculture by itself won't eliminate problems. What it *will* do is let people see them for what they are. With all the tragedies in human history bred by powerful reactions to problems defined in number-one terms, a look at the world through the eyes of sailors and immigrants couldn't hurt.

///

The other evening I was talking to my kid brother about this book. Kid brother—he's thirty years old. I call him that to hold off the approaching horizon of time.

At any rate, Tom, the medical technology sales rep and rock and roll drummer, is seriously interested in languaculture. He lives it. He and his French-Canadian wife Helene are bringing up my nephew bilingual and bicultural, bilanguacultural. He's also traveled—and will travel some more as the global markets continue to shrink—to other lands to represent his company.

Tom moves fast, at a business pace to a rock beat. He wants to know if this book will help him out. And it occurs to me that an answer to him is an answer to several readers. Yep, it will help out. He wants to know if it'll give him quick results. Depends on what you mean by "quick."

Earlier I called the book a "language appreciation course." It's a tragic waste, all the conflict and fear around differences in our ever more complicated, multicultural world. What I wanted to do in this book was show that there's nothing mysterious about languacultural differences. They're located out there in the spaces between people. They can be found and handled, in terms of both structure and content, and the benefits to the handlers are magnificent. Dealing with languaculture stretches and extends them, turns daily life more interesting. Languacultural differences are fascinating.

But—here comes the problem with "quick"—the book also shows that languacultures are complicated things. Grammar and the dictionary and speech acts are just the front end. When you start in with a new languaculture, when you start tangling with all those rich points and frames, a life's work unfolds before you.

Let's say Tom is heading for Japan. Would this book help him get ready for the trip?

Sure it would. Remember the trip I took to the art museum after the introduction to art course? After the course, I saw things in paintings I'd never seen before. They were richer, more interesting, and I could articulate why. On his trip to Japan, Tom would notice things and have a way of thinking about them. He'd look for rich points and tinker with frames. He'd talk to people—in English, of course—about those things. He'd return having taken a first step toward Japanese languaculture, or at least one version of it, but the step would be a short one along a path that stretched well beyond the horizon.

That's the good news.

The bad news is that this book would lead him to shake his head in despair at the usual way we think of preparing for an encounter with Japan. An intensive course in Japanese? A week-long workshop in Japanese culture? If you think of it as a slow start on a long journey, fine. If you think of it as all you need to do, forget it. In fact, considering the business of variation, such short-term training could well do more harm than good.

There's no fast-food approach to languaculture, none, zero, null, nada, nichts. Worse yet, a person can use such quick fixes to *think* the languacultural problem is solved when in fact it's intact. This would change one, in the eyes of the world, from genuinely naive to naive and self-deluded. No improvement there.

Languaculture is rich and complicated. But I don't mean to be destructive or arrogant about this. In fact, three specific recommendations come to mind, all consistent with this book, all aimed at smoothing the process of languaculture contact, none of them "quick" fixes, but all of them aimed at quality.

If Tom were heading off to Japan, here's three things he'd think of doing, after he read this book:

1. He'd know that the space between him and the people he was about to encounter made the Grand Canyon look like a hairline crack, and he'd know why. So, if he wanted to handle that space, he wouldn't think in terms of an intensive course or a one-week seminar. He'd look for *a person* to do it for him.

Earlier, I mentioned translators and interpreters, or other bilanguacultural people. I said their pet peeve was the way the mono-languacultural world looked at them as advanced clerks. Tom wouldn't make that mistake. He'd appreciate and respect the extensive life experience and unique abilities they brought to the task.

As I work on revisions to this book, I'm doing a project for people who deal with refugee mental health. They gave me a book to read. One chapter in particular caught my attention. The writer talked about how there are people buried away in the program organizational chart, usually in low-level positions with names that have nothing to do with the important role they play. They are bilanguacultural, among the best educated of the refugee population. What do they do? They do translation and interpretation, community outreach, recruitment, interviews, follow-up, and, more often than not, therapy as well. They are the unsung languacultural heroes who make the program possible at all. People like them are the quality "quick fix," but they need to be recognized and rewarded for their work.

If Tom had read this book, if he needed languacultural help, he'd find someone who knew the spaces between, could navigate the distance from one to another. He'd respect their hard-won abilities, listen to their advice, and pay them for their help. Such a job description is a critical missing ingredient in most organizations, ironically enough, because many organizations already have the people tucked away in some other job. It's a terrible waste to understand a problem, know that there are people who can help fix it, and neglect the obvious next step.

2. Let's say Tom puts a languacultural expert on the team. But still, he's interested in Japan. Maybe he figures he'll take a few more trips. He'd like to start learning something about the place without investing years of study in grammar and dictionary, never mind speech acts, before he gets to content.

From reading this book, he'd think of *languaculture* instead of "language" and "culture." He'd remember, with any luck, the many stories that talked about how, in becoming communicatively competent, the culture half of languaculture, the "frames" part of "rich point plus frames," is as important as, and often more important than, inside-the-circle linguistic detail.

Tom would wonder about accessing some of the frames using his own grammar and dictionary. Though it's an imperfect solution, he could access quite a lot. He could read Japanese novels in translation and watch films with subtitles. He could read books by Americans who have dedicated their lives to Japanese languaculture and made a career of developing framelike bridges between the two worlds. He could have conversations loaded with languacultural topics with English-speaking Japanese colleagues. Though he'd be hemmed in by his own language, he could still encounter some rich points and work to build new frames.

3. Finally, let's say Tom is fascinated with Japanese languaculture, and he decides to take it on on his own. First of all, from this book he'd have a realistic idea of the job ahead of him. He'd know he was setting out on a lifelong project that he'd never finish. Maybe that's part of what would attract him to the idea in the first place.

He'd have a lifetime hobby, one that would organize much of his leisure time, one that would pay off richly in terms of his personal development, his professional work, and maybe even his music.

He'd start in on the Japanese language and keep working away at it. As he got to the point where the signifiers and the signifieds started coming together, where the rich points and the frames could be handled in Japanese, he'd dive into Japanese languaculture. A visit to the Japanese section of Los Angeles would shimmer with adventures and possibilities. Lunch with a Japanese colleague would produce new pieces of consciousness. Business trips to Kyoto would have a depth that would forever silence the TV in his room. Vacations could be organized to fuel his deeper understanding of Japanese languaculture. And, with time, with an ability to live in the space between languacultures, it goes without saying that his professional opportunities would skyrocket.

So, my answer to Tom, and to readers with his question, is that this book offers two quick solutions. The first is he'll appreciate how important and complex languacultural differences are and enjoy exploring them without any unrealistic expectations of what he can accomplish in a short time. The second is that he'll look for a languacultural expert rather than trying a shoddy quick fix.

The less quick solution lets him approach the frames, the *culture* part of languaculture, by working with Japanese material in English. And the lifelong project lays out a plan for a slow, high-quality trip into the new languaculture, one that'll take time, but one that, with patience, will enrich and change him personally and professionally in ways he'd never imagined.

///

Tom's specific question is an important one, one worth answering, one I ask about things myself, but it's very American. The psychologist Jean Piaget talked about what he called "the American question." After he presented his theory of child development, talked about how children go through different stages, a hand always shot up in his U.S. audience.

"Is there any way we can speed that up?"

No, not really, he'd explain. His theory had to do with biological stages, development that had to take its course. Maybe you could push the edges a little, but not much.

Massive languacultural differences, like those between Japan and the United States, can't be quickly bridged. But once you're *inside* a languaculture, your own or a new one you've worked on for a while, the task isn't quite so massive. The American examples I've used in the book, the talk of variation and the density of social identities, make that case.

One thing you can do, if you're caught the languacultural bug, is go to work, right now, within your own world. There are plenty of different social identities out there, differences in gender, in nation/ethnicity, in occupation and special interest, in generation and lifestyle. Any state contains a number of them. And you can access them, right now, because of an overlap in grammar and dictionary and an overlap in frames.

It's easy. Start a conversation. If you have trouble, you've hit your first rich point. Once it starts, talk for a while and listen even harder. Rich points will pop up in no time at all. I guarantee it. Hundreds of students have done it. They leave class confused about the assignment; they return enthusiastic about what they've learned about someone else, about themselves, about the space between them.

Because of your languaculture bent, you'll see the rich points as signals of frame differences that you don't know about yet, differences that'll teach you about frames that you've never been conscious of, as well as new frames you'll build that you'd never imagined existed.

From a selfish point of view, it'll make life a hell of a lot more interesting. From a social point of view, you'll help move the world toward an informed understanding of differences. Languacultural differences are normal now, in everybody's life, but so far we haven't handled them very well. Understanding them won't solve all the problems. But even if you don't like a new languaculture, even if you find it morally reprehensible—even if those things are true, at least you'll understand what it *is,* not what you think it's *not.*

///

I never know how to end a piece of writing. When the problem came up in a fiction workshop run by Mary Lee Settle, she just shrugged her shoulders and said, "You either kill them off or marry them off." I guess my choice would be to marry them off, since this book tries for marriage more than for murder. Maybe it's the Austrian influence, since the popular historical cliché holds that the Habsburgs built their empire through the careful selection of a spouse for their children.

Now that I'm at the end of this book, I remember a film that Lily Tomlin made. She was putting together a show, so she traveled to several cities to try it out, charged minimal admission in return for the audience's comments and tolerance while they tried out different routines. The film documented the story of how the show gradually took the shape that it did.

Right now I'm remembering a scene. She tried a comedy line but didn't like it. Her assistant came out, and they talked for a few minutes about how to make some minute changes, in a single word, in the intonation, things like that. After they finished, Lily Tomlin turned to the audience and smiled.

"You thought we just came out here and *did* this, didn't you?" Writing a book is the same. A book is its own conclusion.

I finished the final run-through when I was in Nevada City, where my kinfolks live, and I knew that my mother and her friend were down at the National Hotel, having a cup of coffee after dinner. So I walked down to say hello.

The friend's son, Chris, took off to wander the world after he graduated from college. He fell in love with Czechoslovakia, stayed and taught English, and has now become a partner in a business there.

"How's Chris doing," I asked. "His Czech must be pretty good by now."

"Well, Slovak, actually," she said. "It's interesting. He says that the cultures are really different, but when he speaks Slovakian to Czechs they don't get upset. They've been depending on each other for too long, had lots of intermarriage over the years. He says their separation will work out okay, not like Yugoslavia."

Her comment struck me as a pretty good conclusion, a story about how deep-seated languacultural differences don't necessarily lead to bloodshed if the connections are there. History and political economics have handed us a global village littered with social identities that are tearing each other apart. Hatred nurtured for generations and economic inequity won't just disappear. But the repairs can't start without connections, without understanding another point of view, without languaculture. Besides, the experience of culture, the experience of seeing your native land in a new way and finding your way into another, is challenging, interesting, even— serious as it might sometimes be—fun.

I walked back up the hill after coffee, and another conclusion came to mind. The program that sent me to Austria when I was a kid goes by the name of the American Field Service, AFS for short. It was founded by some ambulance drivers who served in World War I, men who wanted to prevent such slaughter from ever happening again. They hoped that if students from different lands lived in another country, they'd overcome the number-one mentality and talk over differences rather than shoot at each other.

They gave the organization a motto. We joked about it when we were AFS kids, and it does sound a little corny now, if not naive, given what I read in the papers and see around me every day. But as I finish this book it keeps coming to mind. It goes something like this: "Walk together, talk together, people of the earth, for only then shall you know peace."

In the first chapter of this book, I mentioned an independent trucker and twisted his words a bit to say maybe experience could generate a little hope. I hope the experience of languaculture, the stories I've told in this book, start a few more walks and talks as we guide the planet towards the next century. That's a conclusion we could live with.

Notes

Now it's time for the footnotes. Writing *Language Shock* was a pleasure, most of the time at least, but the thought of footnotes makes me break out in a rash. I grew up in the academic tradition of writing, where footnotes matter for two reasons. First, they locate your work in some intellectual territory for the reader; second, they give credit where credit is due by showing how the work of others helped you out. The job has turned impossible in the current era of the information explosion, but it's still a worthy goal.

But *Language Shock* isn't an academic book. It's meant to convey a way of thinking about languaculture to readers who, on the one hand, haven't spent much time hanging around linguistics and anthropology, but who, on the other hand, know the problems and joys of coexistence with other languacultures from personal experience. The problem is, most paragraphs in this book could be littered with historical references that show where the topic came from and contemporary references to show the complications in what has just been said.

I obsess about this a good deal, because I care about complexity and the work of others, but I also enjoy communication of fundamental and important ideas to a new audience who want a general map of the territory before they plunge into the details. I've tried to do both in this book. But now that I'm at the footnotes, the difference between the collegial and the general reader pushes out of the depths like the Loch Ness monster.

So here's what I'm going to do: The foundation stones of the book involve ancestors who are discussed by name. For each of them, a key example of their work is cited in the notes, and anyone with more interest can type his name into a library computer and generate a reading list for himself. I also use the work of a few of my contemporaries and mention them by name as well, so naturally the work I'm drawing from appears in the notes as well. And I use a few examples of my own work, so truth in advertising dictates that I cite that work so that an interested reader can go and look at the more technical discussion if they so choose. And finally, *Language Shock* sketches different locations in an elaborate academic landscape. So, in the notes, I've tried to suggest some readings that let a reader take the next step for any particular location, let them move from an aerial view into a closer view at the edge of town. So far so good.

But now for the problem that aggravates my rash. I've tried to convey ideas by showing how they came to life in my own experiences. A good story introduces an idea better than an abstract academic essay. The problem is, I've got hundreds of colleagues in dozens of fields who busy themselves, as I do in my academic life, with the ideas that the stories dramatize. If you want to see the problem for yourself, drop into a university library sometime and peruse just the most recent issue of journals like the *Journal of Linguistic Anthropology, Language and Society, Text, Journal of Pragmatics, Multilingua,* and *World English,* just for openers. With reason, colleagues could say, "Who in the hell are you to tell a story and pretend you just identified this aspect of languaculture? Didn't you read the latest special issue of journal X, or Y's recent book?"

Yeah, I probably did, or at least heard about them, but *Language Shock* is a book for people with an interest in a general view of the territory, not in what's underneath every single rock. So I arrogantly—"who the hell are you"—set myself up as a lone individual voice of a city full of people without listing them all by name. I hope my professional colleagues see the results as an invitation into our collective territory to former outsiders rather than as a neglect of their many contributions to that territory.

On the other hand, I have had a chance to try out the core ideas in *Language Shock* in front of academic audiences, a couple of conference lectures, a couple of articles, though I did them with more footnotes. And, I'm happy to report, the general way of looking at languaculture was interesting and useful to many colleagues as well. The pieces of the book were all lying around, but my angle of vision on how they might all fit together got a couple of "aha's" out of the pros. If nothing else, they liked the stories.

Enough agonizing about the notes. Here they are.

CHAPTER 1, *Culture Blends* / Right off the bat stories are told that involve the sensitive issue of what people want to be called. People, both inside and outside different groups, differ in their preferences. The first story in the book has to do with "Black" and "White" Americans, where some say one should write "Afro-American" and "Anglo-American." "Hispanic," says a recent *Washington Post* article, is now objectionable to some Hispanics, since they want to be known as Salvadorans, Mexicans, Cubans, Puerto Ricans, and so on. Before I read that, I already knew some preferred "Latino" or just "Spanish-speaking." Later in the book I tell a story about two middle eastern students, but a colleague argued that the term is objectionable because it is based on an old British colonial frame of reference. A couple of times I refer to "Eskimo," whereas some now say that "Inuit" is preferable. The issue of showing respect to different groups by using a label members of those groups prefer obviously is an important one. It's easy to know that some terms are unacceptable, but not so easy to know which ones everyone will accept, since sometimes there aren't any. I did the best I could.

There's a huge literature on the many varieties of English, in the United States and elsewhere. A few years ago Robert MacNeil produced a television series, *The Story of English,* for PBS, and you might find the videotapes at a library. The show was later summarized in a book by the same name, by Robert McCrum, William Cran, and Robert MacNeil (New York, Viking, 1986). A book that I've used in introductory classes, one that plays well with students, is Nancy F. Conklin and Margaret A. Lourie, *A Host of Tongues: Language Communities in the United States* (New York, The Free Press, 1983). Another book, with chapters showing the history of different language groups in the United States, is edited by Charles Ferguson and Shirley Brice Heath and titled *Language in the U.S.A.* (Cambridge, England, Cambridge University Press, 1981). And if you're interested in how the "number-one" point of view plays out in the current language politics in the United States, see James Crawford's *Hold Your Tongue: Bilingualism and the Politics of "English Only"* (Reading, Mass., Addison-Wesley, 1992).

The studies of the German of immigrant workers is something I learned about from colleagues in Europe. Most of the published work is, naturally enough, in German. However, Wolfgang Klein's translated book, *Second Language Acquisition* (Cambridge, England, Cambridge University Press, 1986) discusses that research.

Readable books that introduce the general issues of life in more than one language, though they tend to lean toward the language rather than the culture side, include François Grosjean's *Life with Two Languages* (Cambridge, Mass., Harvard University Press, 1982), and Kenji Hakuta's *Mirror of Language: The Debate on Bilingualism* (New York, Basic Books, 1986).

In this chapter I talk about how multiple languages and cultures have become an ordinary feature of American life. While I was revising this book, I met an old friend, Troy Duster of the University of California, Berkeley. Troy, along with other colleagues, had just completed a report called *The Diversity Project* (Institute for the Study of Social Change, University of California, Berkeley, 1991). Berkeley, formerly dominated by students of Anglo-European ancestry, has an undergraduate student body, as of 1990, that is 29 percent Asian, 7 percent Afro-American, 14 percent Hispanic, and 42 percent White. Among many other findings, the project team learned that students want an opportunity *both* to explore their own backgrounds in groups of similar students *and* to explore different cultures with different students. The report recommends that the university structure situations to make both those goals possible. The students give me another glimmer of optimism, since their attitude signals a way of looking at things that this book is all about.

I'm not the only one who's discovered the problems with pronouns that fuel stories in this chapter. The classic article that started it all is by Roger Brown and A. Gilman, "The Pronouns of Power and Solidarity." You can find it in an excellent

collection that contains many of the classics, *The Sociology of Language,* edited by
Joshua Fishman (The Hague, Mouton, 1968). Since that pioneering article, there
have been dozens of articles and books that deal with pronouns in different languages, or, more broadly, with different ways to address and talk about people in
general and what those choices mean.

CHAPTER 2, *The Circle* / There are several histories of linguistics around where
the work of Saussure, and others, is summarized. Among them are R. H. Robins's
A Short History of Linguistics (London, Longman, 1967) and G. Sampson's *Schools
of Linguistics: Competition and Evolution* (London, Hutchinson, 1980). Both books
introduce historical linguistics as well. R. de Beaugrande's recent *Linguistic Theory:
The Discourse of Fundamental Works* (London, Longman, 1991) is heavier sled-
ding, but if you really want to take on the major figures of twentieth-century
linguistics, that's one source that will guide you. You can always go directly to the
master, to the book his students put together after his death, F. de Saussure, *Course
in General Linguistics* (Glasgow, Fontana, 1974).

If the brief reference to semiotics interested you, J. Culler's *The Pursuit of Signs:
Semiotics, Literature, Deconstruction* (Ithaca, N.Y., Cornell University Press, 1981)
will take you through the field and land you in more contemporary arguments
around the dreaded, and now dated, deconstruction. R. Barthes's *Elements of Se-
miology* (New York, Hill and Wang, 1967) is a classic by a grand old man of
criticism. And if you're an Umberto Eco fan based on his fiction, like *The Name
of the Rose* and *Foucault's Pendulum,* you can visit the author in his internationally
known semiotic role in *A Theory of Semiotics* (Bloomington, Indiana University
Press, 1976).

Durkheim's notion of the "social fact" is laid out in his *The Rules of the So-
ciological Method* (New York, The Free Press, 1967). I extend his original idea, in
this chapter and chapters to come, so that I can write about how institutions and
societies try to set limits on what can be said. This extension comes from more
recent theories, like those of Michel Foucault. His translator, Alan Sheridan, wrote
a book that introduces Foucault's work, called *Foucault: The Will to Truth* (London, Tavistock Publications, 1980).

For a discussion of the "standard" as it poses problems for education, see M.
Stubbs's *Educational Linguistics* (Oxford, Basil Blackwell, 1986). To say that
there's a literature that deals with education and the standard would be an understatement. One of my favorites, by a linguistic anthropology colleague who looked
at language in the community and language in schools, is Shirley Brice Heath's
Ways with Words: Language, Life, and Work in Communities and Classrooms
(Cambridge, England, Cambridge University Press, 1983).

I should add something for the note-oriented reader about what I'm calling
"inside-the-circle" linguistics in this book. I've slighted Saussure in two ways. First
of all, I've used his work to show the influence he's had in the present, rather than
adhering to the details of some of his original arguments. For instance, there's some
question about what he thought of grammar, whether it was part of language or
part of speech. I'm acting as if his ideas apply to grammar, because that's the way
they've been used.

The second way I've slighted him, and much of linguistics as well: I'm treating language as built of grammar and the dictionary. I've left out a huge piece of linguistics of whatever sort, namely, *phonology,* the sound system of language. Saussure, in fact, spent much time on issues of phonology. Phonology is important, but what I'm after here is the connection between language and culture and identity. Grammar and the dictionary are richer jumping-off points to use for that discussion. Phonology isn't irrelevant, since what we ordinarily call "accent" and "dialect" play a role, something that will come up in later chapters. But, by and large, the phonological system of a language isn't where the cultural action is.

Later, in the chapters to come, you'll see that not all linguists practice inside-the-circle linguistics. Far from it. But the approach is especially strong, in both the popular and professional imaginations, in the United States. In this sense, this is a very American book. Nowhere is this more apparent than in Julie Tetel Andresen's *Linguistics in America: 1769–1924* (New York, Routledge, 1990). She shows that the version of American inside-the-circle linguistics I introduce and modify here, is, in fact, the standard twentieth-century American story, one that ignores some significant ancestors, among them such illustrious figures as Benjamin Franklin, Thomas Jefferson, and Noah Webster. In this book, though, I'm sticking with the usual story, since that's the one we all have to deal with today.

CHAPTER 3, *The Circle and the Field* / I cribbed many of the biographical notes on Boas from the aged but readable *They Studied Man* by Abram Kardiner and Edward Preble (New York, Meridian Books, 1961). One of the master's most famous statements on language is his introduction to *Handbook of American Indian Languages* (BAE-B 40, part I) (Washington, D.C., Smithsonian Institution, 1911). You can find excerpts from Boas and other historical figures in the classic *Language in Culture and Society,* edited by Dell Hymes (New York, Harper and Row, 1964). Margaret Mead talks about linguistics as a fieldwork tool in her article, "More Comprehensive Field Methods," published in the *American Anthropologist,* Vol. 35 (1933), pp. 1–15, 1933. Boas's concern with American Indians continues to the present in American anthropology. A good, readable book on the subject is Jack Weatherford's *Native Roots: How the Indians Enriched America* (New York, Crown, 1991).

The story of the development of cultural evolutionism can be found in the Kardiner and Preble book, especially the chapter on Edward Tylor, the best of the lot, who struggled with the kinds of problems I've written about here. There are other histories of anthropology that cover the territory more elaborately, notably Marvin Harris's *The Rise of Anthropological Theory: A History of Theories of Culture* (New York, Crowell, 1968). Harris wrote a book for a general audience that will give you a different angle of vision on the field, one that tends toward materialist rather than symbolic understandings of culture. It's called *Our Kind: Who We Are, Where We Came From, Where We Are Going* (New York, Harper and Row, 1989).

The kinship example comes from work I did as an undergraduate, under the supervision of Alan Beals, then on the faculty of Stanford University. I'd cut a deal with Alan that I'd work half-time for him in his village for free if he'd teach me this ethnography business the other half of the time. "My" village was called Ash-apur, a small community of people called the Lambardi, supposedly distant relatives of the Gypsies, who spoke the local language of Kannada as well as their own. I wrote a senior thesis based on the work, but except for bits and pieces I've used in other writings, I never published the study.

"Cultural relativity" is a hot topic in contemporary American life, one of the shibboleths of the "political correctness" wars. For my money, as I write in this chapter, it's a *methodological* strategy, not a moral or ethical one. But my colleague Robert Edgerton just published a new book, *Sick Societies* (New York, The Free Press, 1992), that I'm reading even as I do the final revision of these notes. He argues that anthropology does have a tendency to let its subjects get away with murder, metaphorically if not literally. The difference is, I think, that he's talking about a tendency to understand *by* justifying, and I'm talking about the need to understand *before* you justify *or* condemn in moral or ethical terms.

Ethnography, formerly the province of a few eccentric social researchers, has become something of a buzz word in American social research. People in a number of academic disciplines, organizations, and communities are getting tired of statis-tical tables and beginning to wonder what the world of "those people" is like. Books abound that show how ethnography gets done, but I'll plug my own *The Professional Stranger: An Informal Introduction to Ethnography* (New York, Aca-demic, 1980) and the more technical *Speaking of Ethnography* (Newbury Park, Calif., Sage, 1985). In fact, if you get interested, Sage has made something of an industry out of publishing brief volumes on different aspects of ethnography, which you could check by writing and asking for their catalogue on "qualitative meth-ods." There are plenty of other sources, among them a good pair of introductory books by James Spradley called *The Ethnographic Interview* (1979) and *Participant Observation* (1980), both published by Holt, Rinehart and Winston in New York. Charles Briggs wrote a fine book that combines ethnography and the kind of lin-guistics I'm using in this book, called *Learning How to Ask* (Cambridge, England, Cambridge University Press, 1986).

Bloomfield's book, *Language,* is still available (Chicago, University of Chicago Press, 1933), and you can learn more about him in any of the histories mentioned in the notes to Chapter 2. *Language* pretty much lays out inside-the-circle linguistics until Chomsky, and, from my point of view, Chomsky didn't change things that much, since matters of meaning and context were still left out. More on that in the notes to Chapter 9.

I lifted the example of first person plural pronouns from an introductory text by R. H. Robins, *General Linguistics* (London, Longman, 1989). The example of Indonesian numeral classifiers came from an introduction to that language in the "Teach Yourself Books" series by J. B. Kwee, *Indonesian* (Kent, England, Hodder and Staughton, 1965).

CHAPTER 4, *Cultural Signifieds* / The collected essays of B. L. Whorf are pub-lished in a book called *Language, Thought, and Reality,* under his name (Cambridge, Mass.: MIT Press, 1956). John Carrol edited the work and wrote a lengthy introduction, from which the biographical details were taken.

Edward Sapir, Whorf's teacher and then collaborator, is an important figure in American linguistics and anthropology that I've neglected here. De Beaugrande's history, mentioned in the notes to Chapter 2, has a chapter on him. Sapir's own readable book *Language* (New York, Harcourt, 1921) is still available. A recent biography of Sapir is Regna Darnell's *Edward Sapir: Linguist, Anthropologist, Humanist* (Berkeley, University of California Press, 1990).

John Lucy recently published a thorough overview of the linguistic relativity tradition, showing the development of Whorf's thought from that of Boas and Sapir, and describing and critiquing the many lines of research that Whorf's hypothesis generated. The book is called *Language, Diversity, and Thought: A Reformulation of the Linguistic Relativity Hypothesis* (Cambridge, England, Cambridge University Press, 1992).

The color experiments, should you want to look up the originals, can be found in these two sources: R. W. Brown and E. H. Lenneberg, "A Study in Language and Cognition," *Journal of American Social Psychology*, Vol. 49 (1954), pp. 454–462; and, E. H. Lenneberg and J. M. Roberts, "The Language of Experience: A Case Study," *Memoirs of the International Journal of American Linguistics* no. 13, 1956.

The term *languaculture*, a term that brings together the two main threads of this book, comes from Paul Friedrich's term *linguaculture,* described in his article, "Language, Ideology, and Political Economy" in the *American Anthropologist*, Vol. 91 (1989), p. 295. I modified it to "langua" to bring it in line with the more commonly used "language."

CHAPTER 5, *Similarities and Differences* / Berlin and Kay's book is called *Basic Color Terms* (Berkeley, University of California Press, 1969). In this chapter I've featured only *one* of their significant findings, namely, that basic color terms in different languages share a "most typical" example. There are others. For instance, they found out that basic color terms emerged in a logical order; that is, if you knew a language had two or three or four or up to the maximum of eleven basic terms, you pretty much knew what they were. And subsequent work investigates the relation between the color study and the biology of color perception. Since this book is heavily loaded in the synchronic and cultural rather than the diachronic and biological direction, I've neglected that part of their work. An update of that pioneering research is in P. Kay and C. K. McDaniel, "The Linguistic Significance of Basic Color Terms," *Language*, Vol. 54, pp. 610–646, 1978.

If you're interested in the Human Relations Area Files that Murdock set up, chances are you can check them out at a local university library. The code system he used is published in a book under his name, *Outline of Cultural Materials* (New Haven, Yale University Press, 1950).

A collection of work in cognitive anthropology can be found in R. W. Casson's edited book, *Language, Culture, and Cognition* (New York, Macmillan, 1981). His book contains my article on junkie language that I used in this chapter, called

"Talking about Doing: Lexicon and Event." C. Fillmore's linguistic theory, the one I borrowed from to analyze the junkie terms, was first laid out in "The Case for Case," a chapter in *Universals of Linguistic Theory*, in a book edited by E. Bach and R. T. Harms (New York, Holt, Rinehart and Winston, 1968).

One of the founders of cognitive anthropology, Ward Goodenough, wrote the 1957 article that set out the basics of the field. Later he expanded those and other ideas into a readable introduction to his views, *Culture, Language, and Society* (Menlo Park, Calif., Benjamin/Cummings, 1981). A reading of his book shows how much this book is indebted to the tradition of cognitive anthropology, logically enough, since that is the training I received in graduate school in the sixties.

In this chapter I tell a story about Chuck Frake, another of the founders of cognitive anthropology. A collection of his work is available in *Language and Cultural Description* (Stanford, Calif., Stanford University Press, 1980), and it shows the progression from founder of the field to critic of overschematized approaches to ethnography.

I used taxonomy and the color spectrum as examples, as I said in the book, because they were part of my training and my own past work. There are plenty of other examples I might have used, examples of the so-called universalist approach to languaculture, one that emphasizes similarities to organize differences. One good current version is politeness theory, first introduced by P. Brown and S. Levinson in *Politeness: Some Universals in Language Usage* (Cambridge, Mass., Cambridge University Press, 1987). Politeness, they argue, is a similarity; every group deals with it, but the strategies they use and the conditions under which they use them differ. Since their initial work, journals and books have taken the issue up. If you go to a meeting of the new linguistics, you'll find several sessions organized around the topic. Lately, Levinson and many others are tinkering with another similarity, spatial orientation. Other examples exist, but in this book I'm after the general point about the relationships between similarities and differences, not a discussion of all proposed similarities in the literature.

CHAPTER 6, *Situations* / I lifted pieces of Malinowski's biography out of *They Studied Man,* mentioned in the notes to Chapter 3. The master's theory of language is presented in a couple of places: "The Problem of Meaning in Primitive Languages," in *The Meaning of Meaning,* by C. Ogden and I. A. Richards (London, Paul Trench and Trubner, 1923), and "An Ethnographic Theory of Language and Some Practical Corollaries," a supplement to one of his classic ethnographies of the Trobriand islanders called *Coral Gardens and Their Magic* (New York, Dover, 1978). Excerpts from Malinowski can be found in the edited collection by Dell Hymes mentioned in the notes to Chapter 3.

The casual comment in the chapter that Malinowski's ideas flourished in the United Kingdom is—appropriately enough, given the country I'm referring to—a massive understatement. It's not an accident that so many of the books cited in these notes were published in that country. J. R. Firth, and then his student, M.A.K. Halliday, took seriously the idea that language had to be understood as a vehicle to express meanings in a context of situation and built their theory of language on that foundation. A chapter on each of these two key figures can be found in de Beaugrande's overview, mentioned in the notes for Chapter 2. For an introduction to Halliday's views on language, meaning, and context, see the book he wrote with Ruqaiya Hasan, *Language, Context, and Text: Aspects of Language in a Social-Semiotic Perspective* (Oxford, Oxford University Press, 1989).

If I'd grown up studying linguistics in the United Kingdom, this would be a very different book. Likewise, if I'd grown up studying linguistics in Vienna, it would be yet another version. In fact, both of those national traditions lie behind what I'm doing here; they helped me put together the idea of languaculture, but the idea takes shape in the history of American linguistics and anthropology. As I said in an earlier note, this is a very American book, but one formed as a result of encounters with other national traditions, one in which the American base was changed and extended because of those encounters. In this sense, the book is an example of what the book is about.

I used the *Schmäh* example in an article where I tried to figure out what bilingualism and biculturalism were all about, called "The Biculture in Bilingual," in *Language and Society*, Vol. 20 (1991), pp. 167–181.

CHAPTER 7, *Culture* / The book by Gregory Bateson *Steps to an Ecology of Mind* was published by Ballantine in New York in 1972.

Some impressive names go by pretty quickly in this chapter, like those of Noam Chomsky and John Gumperz. They'll be cited in more detail later in the notes.

The definition of "culture" in the book comes from A. L. Kroeber and C. Kluckhohn, *Culture: A Critical Review of Concepts and Definitions* (New York, Vintage Books, 1966). Since the book was based on a report issued in 1952, it's pretty old stuff. It doesn't matter. The model of culture that the definition lays out still serves as a picture of culture, complete with all its contradictions and ambiguities, that most of the world—and, still, some of anthropology—struggles with. It's a little bit of a straw person, but one that still participates in contemporary discussions.

The version of culture I'm working toward in this book is, to the best of my knowledge, the product of my own twisted language-based mind, though it—like the rest of this book—rests firmly on the words and writings of countless historical figures and contemporaries. But I'm hardly the only one tangling with culture with an eye toward what the world has turned into. A few of my favorite allies in the struggle are Ulf Hannerz, *Cultural Complexity: Studies in the Social Organization of Meaning* (New York, Columbia University Press, 1992), William Roseberry, *Anthropologies and Histories* (New Brunswick, N. J., Rutgers University Press, 1991), and Renato Rosaldo, *Culture and Truth: The Remaking of Social Analysis* (Boston, Beacon Press, 1989).

What we all have in common is a sense that the idea of "culture" is built on a form of human life that hardly exists anymore, and a relationship to those forms of life that kept them at a distance. We all look at different situations, appreciate their complexity and diversity, and tinker with culture to see under what conditions it might be useful. Our solutions differ, naturally, since we come out of different traditions and have different problems in mind. But this isn't the time and place to do the academic dance with colleagues that I hope to do later. I wanted to mention these three books, though, for those readers who might want to pursue this culture monster from a couple of different points of view.

My "truck study" that I refer to came out as a book, *Independents Declared: The Dilemmas of Independent Trucking* (Washington, D.C., Smithsonian Press, 1986).

The argument about the "culture of poverty" is discussed in C. A. Valentine's book, *Culture and Poverty: Critique and Counter-proposals* (Chicago, University of Chicago Press, 1968).

With the concept of "frame" I'm dancing around on the top of a huge mountain. Twenty years or so ago something called "cognitive science" got invented, and it hasn't looked back since. I used to work in the area—a lot of cognitive anthropologists migrated there—but then I gave up trying to figure out what people had going on in their heads and started worrying more about what they were doing. A good, readable story of cognitive science is Howard Gardner's *The Mind's New Science: A History of the Cognitive Revolution* (New York, Basic Books, 1985).

"Frame," and ideas like it with other names ("script," "schema," and the list goes on), came out of that field's computer metaphor to let the researchers talk about "knowledge structures" in more interesting and complicated ways than the old stimulus-response or logical-proposition notions would. I learned about frames, and artificial intelligence in general, when I worked with Jerry Hobbs of the Stanford Research International Artificial Intelligence Center for a couple of years back in the early eighties. A technical discussion of the way we used frame—we called it "schema" then—is in a chapter by the two of us, "How to Grow Schemas Out of Interviews," in *Directions in Cognitive Anthropology,* edited by Janet W. D. Dougherty (Urbana, University of Illinois Press, 1985).

There are dozens of books to send you to for more information, and books that introduce the field of artificial intelligence to general readers abound. I'll just mention one reference, the one that started all the fascination with frames among the noncomputer folks, R. C. Schank and R. P. Abelson, *Scripts, Plans, Goals and Understanding.* (Hillsdale, N. J., Lawrence Erlbaum, 1978). Ron Casson, a linguistic anthropologist, wrote an overview of how the concept has been used called "Schemata in Cultural Anthropology," in the *Annual Review of Anthropology,* Vol. 12 (1983), pp. 429–462.

"Frame" is also an idea that the late Erving Goffman uses to make sense out of what we do as we move through the detailed situations of daily life. His use of "frame" is different from, but compatible with, the artificial intelligence concept, at least as I mix the two here, since frame is a lever into what people are doing with language. His version can be found in his book *Frame Analysis* (New York, Harper and Row, 1974). His later book *Forms of Talk* (Philadelphia, University of Pennsylvania, 1981) applies his ideas more specifically to language.

Several discourse-type linguists also use framelike ideas in their analysis. A couple of recent introductions to discourse that use them are G. Brown and G. Yule's *Discourse Analysis* (Cambridge, England, Cambridge University Press, 1983) and A. M. Bulow-Moller's *The Textlinguistic Omnibus: A Survey of Methods for Analysis* (Copenhagen, Handelshojskolens Forlag, 1989). A more advanced introduction is R. de Beaugrande and W. U. Dressler, *Introduction to Text Linguistics* (London, Longman, 1981).

The most well known frame-discourse-type linguist is Teun van Dijk, for example in *Macrostructures* (Hillsdale, N. J., Lawrence Erlbaum, 1980). Or, for a more readable book that shows what his work produces, without the formalism, *Communicating Racism: Ethnic Prejudices in Thought and Talk* (Newbury Park, Calif., Sage, 1987). De Beaugrande's book, mentioned in the notes to Chapter 2, also has a chapter on van Dijk.

CHAPTER 8, *Speech Acts* / The published article on lies by Linda Coleman and Paul Kay is called "Prototype Semantics: The English Word *Lie*," in *Language*, Vol. 57 (1981), pp. 26–44. For another take on culture and lies, Eve Sweeter, "The Definition of 'lie'," in *Cultural Models in Language and Thought*, edited by Dorothy Holland and Naomi Quinn (Cambridge, England, Cambridge University Press, 1987).

Ludwig Wittgenstein, only alluded to here, is one of the most interesting personalities and profound philosophers of the twentieth century, and his work is as alive today, perhaps even more so, than it was before his death. Fortunately, someone recently produced a readable book that does justice to both the person and the ideas—R. Monk's *Ludwig Wittgenstein: The Duty of Genius* (New York, Penguin, 1990). The story about the old woman who asked after Wittgenstein came from W. W. Bartley's book, *Wittgenstein* (La Salle, Ill., Open Court, 1985).

The two classic books on speech-act philosophy are J. L. Austin, *How to Do Things with Words* (New York, Oxford University Press, 1962) and J. R. Searle, *Speech Acts* (Cambridge, England, Cambridge University Press, 1970). Stephen Levinson, *Pragmatics* (Cambridge, England, Cambridge University Press, 1983), does an excellent summary and critique of the philosophical tradition. He also describes the tradition of conversational analysis, which I use in subsequent chapters.

Now I mention Austin and Searle in a couple of lines in this book. As far as most of my colleagues are concerned, this is like giving a talk on American history from 1929 to 1945 and saying, "So the economy had some problems and then there was this war." But the way I want to use "speech act," the way I show it by example, it covers more discourse and includes more framelike material than the philosophers allow for. Their approach is just too narrow for what I'm trying to do here, so they get short shrift.

Dell Hymes, on the other hand, gets more airtime here, as well he should. He, along with John Gumperz, are the two modern giants of linguistic anthropology whose foundational work made it possible for me to write this thing at all. The Hymes quote in the book is taken from a collection of his essays, *Foundations in Sociolinguistics: An Ethnographic Approach* (Philadelphia, University of Pennsylvania Press, 1974). Another fundamental reference, a collection of chapters edited by both the founders, is J. J. Gumperz and D. Hymes, *Directions in Sociolinguistics: The Ethnography of Communication* (New York, Holt, Rinehart and Winston,

1972). A good introduction to the perspective is M. Saville-Troike, *The Ethnography of Communication: An Introduction* (Oxford, Basil Blackwell, 1989).

Noam Chomsky also gets short shrift here, because the linguistics he so brilliantly invented—and continues inventing—doesn't do the kind of work I'm trying to do. The quote in this chapter comes from his classic *Aspects of the Theory of Syntax* (Cambridge, Mass., MIT Press, 1965), though his theory has mutated several times since then into the current "government and binding" theory.

In his own recent work, Chomsky distinguishes between externalized language (E-language) and internalized language (I-language). I-language is what he does, language and mind. E-language is what I'm doing in this book, language as a "social phenomenon." I've taken this from a good introduction to modern Chomsky by V. J. Cook, *Chomsky's Universal Grammar* (Oxford, Basil Blackwell, 1988). Cook writes that "the opposition between these two approaches in linguistics has been long and acrimonious; neither side concedes the other's reality." It's not *that* bad, but the two approaches sure are different, and no one's figured how to hook them up yet, except in a piecemeal way. Frederick J. Newmeyer, in his *Politics of Linguistics* (Chicago, University of Chicago Press, 1986), traces the history and relationships of the two kinds of linguistics as well.

The quotes from John Condon's work on Mexican-American intercultural communication comes from his book *Good Neighbors: Communicating with the Mexicans* (Yarmouth, Me., Intercultural Press, 1985).

The efforts to popularize discourse analysis that I mention in the book involve a video produced by the BBC called *Crosstalk*, featuring John Gumperz. Sometimes you can find it in university libraries. Some citations to Gumperz's work are in the notes to Chapter 11. And Deborah Tannen's *You Just Don't Understand* (New York, Ballantine, 1990) is a widely read book on communication between men and women that rests on a discourse-analysis base.

CHAPTER 9, *Speech Act Lumber and Paint* / The material on Athabaskan-Anglo communication is taken from the Scollons's book, *Narrative, Literacy and Face in Interethnic Communication* (Norwood, N.J., Ablex, 1981). Another fascinating, well-written book that deals with Native American views of Anglos and the way they use those views in their own world is *Portraits of the Whiteman* by Keith Basso (Cambridge, England, Cambridge University Press, 1979).

Garfinkel's classic book, the one that invented the field in sociology, is *Studies in Ethnomethodology* (New York, Prentice-Hall, 1967). He's difficult to read. An introduction to conversational analysis, the language-oriented version that I'm drawing on here, is in Steve Levinson's book, the one I mentioned in the notes to Chapter 8.

Deborah Tannen's book on the New York–California Thanksgiving dinner is called *Conversational Style* (Norwood, N.J., Ablex, 1984). In that book, she looks at several aspects of the way conversation worked and didn't work, but I've just used one of the results here, namely that New Yorkers show involvement with a turn-taking strategy that allows overlap between speakers.

Michael Moerman's book, the source of the Thai example, is called *Talking*

Culture: Ethnography and Conversational Analysis (Philadelphia, University of Pennsylvania Press, 1988). He takes the conversational-analysis tradition that grew out of ethnomethodology and applies it to an ethnographic study.

The analysis of Ted the trucker's interview was originally published in the proceedings of the Transportation Research Forum meetings, but later I redid the article for a different audience in a more accessible place. It's called "Transcript Handling: An Ethnographic Strategy," published in *Oral History Review,* Vol. 15 (1987), pp. 209–219.

The line from Edward T. Hall came from his book, *The Dance of Life: The Other Dimension of Time* (Garden City, N.Y., Anchor Press, 1983). Hall recently published his autobiography, *An Anthropology of Everyday Life* (New York, Anchor Books, 1992). It's a fascinating and well-written story of a life filled with encounters with numerous different languacultures. In fact, if someone told me they liked this book and wanted to read another, that's the first one I'd recommend.

CHAPTER 10, *Coherence* / The analysis of the Waldheim transcript was published as "Language Scenes and Political Schemas," *Journal of Pragmatics,* Vol. 14 (1990), pp. 25–38. For the full Waldheim story, see Richard Mitten's *The Politics of Antisemitic Prejudice: The Waldheim Phenomenon in Austria* (Boulder, Colo., Westview Press, 1992). I mention the German sociologist J. Habermas in a line in the chapter. He's a major figure in modern sociology, one that I like particularly because he suggests ways to connect the details of discourse with the nation and the political economy in which the talk occurs. His translator, T. A. McCarthy, wrote a book about his work a few years ago that is a good overview, *The Critical Theory of Jürgen Habermas* (Cambridge, Mass., MIT Press, 1978).

The general approach to discourse analysis that looks for the ideology implicit in everyday language is called critical linguistics, with its roots in the work of M.A.K. Halliday, cited in the notes to Chapter 6. A good introduction to the perspective, written for a general audience, is Norman Fairclough, *Language and Power* (London, Longman, 1989). An academic collection, one that will introduce the way a group of my contemporary colleagues in linguistic anthropology look at such problems, is a special issue of *Pragmatics,* edited by Paul Kroskrity, Bambi Schieffelin, and Kathryn Woolard (Vol. 2, No. 3, 1992).

CHAPTER 11, *Variations on a Frame* / Sociolinguistics is a huge field that's been around for a while, and, like many of the other fields discussed in this book, it's floated selectively in and partially merged with the new linguistics of discourse analysis. Saville-Troike's book, mentioned in the notes to Chapter 8, is one introduction, but there are several others. A couple of good ones, both published by Basil Blackwell in Oxford, are Ralph Fasold's *The Sociolinguistics of Society* (1984) and *The Sociolinguistics of Language* (1990).

John Gumperz—the older I get the more I realize I've learned from him—is one of the founders of sociolinguistics, who more recently developed ideas about discourse and frames that are a basic idea of this book. His own book, *Discourse Strategies* (Cambridge, England, Cambridge University Press, 1982), does a nice job of tracing this history and showing how his current theory works in several different cultural settings. Another book that he edited, *Language and Social Identity* (Cambridge, England, Cambridge University Press, 1982), collects chapters from several of his students that show several applications to several different identities.

Deborah Tannen's *You Just Don't Understand* (New York, Ballantine, 1990) and Robin Lakoff's *Talking Power: The Politics of Language* (New York, Basic Books, 1990) are two examples of discourse linguists writing for a general audience who deal with differences in language attributable to different social identities.

I recently came across a good overview of issues in identity and society that develops the political consequences of the issues introduced here. It does so in a way that also shows how the same "culture" can travel with different "languages." The book is called *Language, Society, and Identity*, by John Edwards (Oxford, Basil Blackwell, 1985.

CHAPTER 12, *Sailors and Immigrants* / The book by Margaret Mead that develops the view of sixties kids as immigrants is called *Culture and Commitment: The New Relationships Between the Generations in the 1970s* (Garden City, N.Y., Anchor Press, 1978). The "clay" metaphor I use in this chapter was inspired by Hakuta's book on bilingualism, cited in the notes to Chapter 1, and developed in my own article in *Language and Society,* cited in the notes to Chapter 6. The story about refugee-mental-health programs comes from Eric Egli's chapter, "Bilingual Workers," in *Mental Health Services for Refugees* (DHHS Pub. No. [ADM] 91-1824, Rockville, Md., National Institute of Mental Health, 1991).

Index

A

Aaronson, Karen, 143
active/passive switch, 199–200
acts:
　sequence of, 152, 153
　see also speech acts
adjacency pairs, 170, 181
Africa, sub-Saharan, 214
Agar, Tom, 252–255
agreement:
　of articles, 43–44
　subject-verb, 43
alcohol problems, of American Indians,
　167–168
American English, 36
　double negatives in, 36–37
　money metaphors of, 120–121
　as second language, 17–18, 44
　standard vs. dialects of, 37
American Field Service (AFS), 258
American Film, 245
American Indians:
　conversational style of, 164–167, 171
　Eskimo culture, 49–50
　languages of, 54, 56, 63–64, 67, 69,
　120
　see also specific groups

"American question, the," 255–256
Americans, 21–26
　Anglo-Europeans vs., 26
　being liked and, 24
　change and, 25, 26
　conversations of, 141, 142
　lying of, 146–148, 150, 159, 175–
　177
　naïveté of, 24
　number-one, 22–24
　stereotypes about, 21–23, 29, 141
　subjunctive and, 200
anecdotes:
　conversational style of, 164–167,
　171–172, 174
　Schmäh and, 102–103
　situations and, 98
anthropology:
　jobs in, 112
　see also cognitive anthropology;
　cultural anthropology
Anthropology Today, 207
Antropólogo, 178
Antwerp, linguistics meeting in, 115
art appreciation, 183, 252
articles:
　in English, 43
　in German, 43–44

articles (*continued*)
in Spanish, 43
aspect, 120
perfect *vs.* imperfect, 64–65
Aspects of the Theory of Syntax
(Chomsky), 150–151
Athabaskan Indians, conversations of,
164–167, 171
Austin, John, 150
Australian aborigines, 123
Austria, 192–206
bills and banks in, 133
businessmen of, 24
dinner conversation in, 141, 193–
194
eating style in, 125, 126
electricity bill in, 133–134
Nazism in, 58–59, 193–204
paying restaurant checks in, 141
Waldheim scandal in, 58, 194–206
Wittgenstein in, 149
Austrian German, 44, 94, 96–106
Du vs. *Sie* in, 18–19, 20, 98, 99
Guten Tag vs. *Grüss Gott* in, 222
participation *vs.* observation in, 235
Schmäh in, 99–106, 120, 126, 129,
140, 248
Austro-Hungarian Empire, 213, 216
availability, as measurement, 69–70
awareness, in MAR, 242, 243

B

baap, 52
banks:
Austrian, 133
Mexican, 216–217
Bartók, Béla, 178
Bateson, Gregory, 112–114, 246–247
Bateson, Mary Catherine, 247
Being *vs.* Becoming, 28
Berlin, Brent, 74–76
bilingualism, 67, 68, 70
bills, paying of, in Austria, 133–134
biography, 244, 246
social identity plus, 238–239, 240
Blacks:
culture of, 20
language differences and, 13–14, 16
Bloomfield, Leonard, 55–56, 59, 61,
66, 71
Boas, Franz, 49–57, 59–63, 108, 179,
209
background of, 50, 91

linguistics and, 54–57, 59–60
reaction to cultural evolution of, 50–
54, 77
Whorf compared with, 65, 69, 71,
77
boot, as junkie term, 83, 85
boring *vs.* creative people, 235, 236
bottom-up mode, frames and, 135
Brooks, Ted, 183–189
Brown, Roger, 69–70
Bulgaria, cultural differences in, 29
bullfights, 127, 128
business:
Americans *vs.* foreigners in, 24
in Mexico, 124, 126–130, 142, 156,
222

C

Californians, conversational style of,
171–172, 174
Campbell, Joseph, 113
capotear, 127, 128
cartoon, ostrich, 94
Chambers, Erve, 140
change:
Americans and, 25, 26
culture and, 24–25
chauvinism, 126
chessboard, language compared with,
34, 42
chicken fried steak, 237
child development, Piaget's theory of,
255–256
Chomsky, Noam, 114, 150–151
classical music, 178, 179
clay metaphor, 249–251
codability, as measurement, 69, 70
code switching, 224
cognitive anthropology (ethnographic
semantics; new ethnography), 79–
87
criticism of, 82
heroin addicts and, 82–86
part-whole relationship and, 85–86
stage-process and, 85
taxonomy and, 80–82
use of term, 80
coherence, 190–210, 243
differences and, 128–130, 158
frames and, 204–206
speech acts and, 157, 158, 159
Waldheim analysis and, 194–206
Coleman, Linda, 146–148, 150, 159

Cologne, anthropology meeting in,
    206–207
color studies, 74–76
    Sapir-Whorf hypothesis and, 70, 72
communication, 34
    culture and, 23–24, 29–30
    grammar vs., 15–17, 20, 22, 29–30
    language instruction vs., 15–16
    problems in, 23, 31
    talking vs., 163, 250
communicative competence, 151–152
comparison:
    in cultural anthropology, 109–116,
        132, 137
    frames and, 132, 158
    in linguistics, 32, 33
competence:
    Chomsky's view of, 151
    communicative, 151–152
Condon, John, 155–157
consciousness:
    culture and, 20, 49–50, 79, 108
    language and, 67, 68, 71–72
    number-one types and, 22
    repair and, 244
content, of Brooks's interview, 183–
    187
context, situational, 93
conversations:
    of Anglos vs. Athabaskans, 164–
        167, 171
    closing of, 166
    ethnomethodology and, 170–174
    frames and, 141–144, 156, 157,
        173
    interviews compared with, 184
    of men vs. women, 173–174
    music of, 185–187
    of New Yorkers vs. Californians,
        171–172, 174
    in Thailand, 180–182
    topics in, 165, 171, 172–173, 179–
        180
    turn-taking in, 166, 171, 172–173,
        179–180
cook, as junkie term, 85
counseling vs. consoling, 221
Course in General Linguistics, 34
Cozumel, scuba diving in, 44–45
creative vs. boring people, 235, 236
Crosstalk (TV show), 225
cues, conversational, 165
cultural anthropology:
    Boas's founding of, 49–57, 59–60

comparative perspective, fieldwork
        and holism in, 109–116, 132, 137
    ethnocentrism and, 52–53
    Mandelbaum's view of, 109–112,
        115, 116, 132, 137
cultural evolution, 50–54, 57, 77
cultural relativity, 57–59, 77
cultural signifieds, 61–72
culture, 13–30
    Americans' problem with, 21–23
    Boas's view of, 49–57, 59–60, 108
    change and, 24–25
    changes in concept of, 27–28, 122–
        125
    as coherent connection of
        differences, 128–130
    communication and, 23–24, 29–30
    as conceptual system, 78–79
    consciousness and, 20, 49–50, 79,
        108
    frames and, 130–139
    identity and, 25–26, 126
    importance of, 28–29
    meaning and, 21, 23, 28
    negative side of, 25–26
    patterns and, 115, 118–120
    personal experience and, 108–109
    positive side of, 24–25
    of poverty, 124–125
    problems in definition of, 115–118
    as threat, 24
    traditional view of, 122–123
    use of word, 20–21, 108, 115
Culture and Commitment (Mead), 247
culture shock, 73
cut-lows, *Schmäh* compared with, 103,
    105
cybernetics, 113
Czech, 257
Czechoslovakia, 257

D

Darwin, Charles, 50
data, bad, 51–52, 53, 56–57
date, 17–18, 20
deception, intention and, 146–148,
    175–176
default values, 134–135, 173
deficit theory of differences, 23, 37,
    162
    bad data and, 51–52, 56–57
    kinship and, 51–53
descriptive linguistics, 35–37

descriptive-structural linguistics, 55–56
diachronic linguistics, 35
dialects, 31, 213, 223–224
    nonstandard, 36, 37
dictionary, 47, 55, 212, 216
    communication vs., 15–16 20, 29–
        30
differences:
    coherent connection of, 128–130,
        158
    culture as explanation of, 124–125
    deficit theory of, 23, 37, 51–53, 56–
        57, 162
    as opportunity, 29
    see also differences, languacultural;
        language differences
differences, languacultural, 73–88, 252
    color spectrum and, 74–76
    concealment of, 229
    culture shock and, 73
    taxonomy and, 79–84, 87
    see also similarities, languacultural
discourse, 95–106, 115, 145
    defined, 95
    frames and, 131–132, 139
    Malinowski's view of, 95–96, 140,
        144
    paying restaurant checks and, 140–
        141
    Schmäh and, 99–106
    speech acts and, 144–145, 148, 150,
        157–158, 160
discourse analysis, 96, 160–161
do, in German *vs.* English, 97–98, 99
doctors, 238–239
double negatives, 36–37
draw, as junkie term, 85
drug problems, of American Indians,
    167–168
Durkheim, Émile, 38
Du vs. *Sie,* 18–19, 20, 98, 99
Dvořák, Antonin, 178

E

East Germans, 213
eating styles, 125–126
electricity bills, 133–134
elephant jokes, 116
emphasis, of words, 184–187
ends, speech acts and, 152, 153
English, 33
    articles in, 43
    grammar *vs.* vocabulary of, 44

Indian, 219
    as second language, 17–18, 44, 234
    time and, 63
    verbs in, 63, 65, 97–98, 99
    we in, 56
    World, 226
    see also American English
Eskimos, culture of, 49–50
ethnic groups, language differences
    and, 15–16
ethnocentrism, 52, 53, 126, 162
ethnographic semantics, *see* cognitive
    anthropology
ethnography, 54–57
    Human Relations Area Files and, 78
    Malinowski and, 91–96
    new, *see* cognitive anthropology
    participant observation and, 92–93,
        106–107
    of speaking, 150–154
ethnomethodology, 169–174
    conversations and, 170–174
    Garfinkeling and, 169–170
evolution, cultural, 50–54, 57, 77
expectations:
    frames and, 158, 166, 168
    mistakes and, 243

F

family, Mexican, 159–160
"Far Side, The" (cartoon), 94
fashion, as Saussurian system, 46
fieldwork, 158
    in cultural anthropology, 109–116,
        132, 137
    culture and, 128
    frames and, 132
Fijian, *we* in, 56
Fillmore, Charles, 84, 161
Finnegans Wake (Joyce), 39
first language, 23
    language differences within, 13–15,
        27
    learning about, 15
Firth, J. R., 96
formal models, 109–110
fotía, 41
Frake, Chuck, 86–87
frames, 130–139, 141–145
    active, 158
    in Austria, 133–134
    bottom-up mode and, 135
    coherence and, 204–206

conversations and, 141–144, 156, 157, 173
default values and, 134–135, 173
defined, 130
dynamic, 158
expectations and, 158, 166, 168
Garfinkeling and, 169–170
holistic, 158
issues and, 195–196
language circle and, 225
language labels and, 212–213
MAR and, 242–244
as metaphor, 138–139
national labels and, 213–215
number-one types and, 162–163
paying bills and, 133–134
restaurants and, 131–132, 136, 140
robots and, 130–132
social identity and, 212, 219–223
sociolinguistics and, 223–226
speech acts and, 148, 150, 152–159, 162–163, 166–170, 173, 189–190, 204
states and, 215–223
top-down mode and, 134, 135
transcripts and, 189–190
variations on, 211–241
French, 33, 36
Friedrich, Paul, 60
fusion, 179

G

Gans, Herbert, 122
Garbarek, Jan, 178
Garfinkel, Harold, 168–170
Garfinkeling, 169–170
Gastarbeiter, 236–237
genre, speech acts and, 152, 153
German, 33
  articles in, 43–44
  Du vs. *Sie* in, 18–19, 20, 98, 99
  immigrants' use of, 16–17
  subject-verb agreement in, 43
  see also Austrian German
Germany:
  East Germans in, 213
  intercultural communication conference in, 29
  Nazism in, 206–207
  reunification of, 111–112
get off, as junkie term, 84, 85
Goffman, Erving, 234–235
González, Felipe, 24

Good Neighbors (Condon), 155–157
Göttingen, applied linguistic meetings in, 116–117
grammar, 47, 144, 212, 216
  active/passive switch in, 199–200
  communication *vs.*, 15–17, 20, 22, 29–30
  of demotic Greek, 64–65
  English, 44
  ethnography and, 55, 56–57
  Fillmore's view of, 84–85
  Hopi, 63–64
  numeral classifiers, 56–57
  syntagmatic and paradigmatic relationships and, 43–44
  see also pronouns; verbs
Greek:
  classical, 32
  demotic, 64–65, 120
greetings, *Guten Tag* vs. *Grüss Gott*, 222
group therapy, American Indians and, 167–168
Gruber, Helmut, 97, 98
Grüss Gott, 222
Gumperz, John, 115, 117, 225, 226, 232
Guten Tag, 222

H

Hall, Edward T., 189
Halliday, M.A.K., 96
Hartford Fire Insurance Company, 61, 62
Hawaii, 227
  Bateson in, 112–114
heroin addicts, 122
  languaculture of, 82–86, 90–91
high density social identity, 233, 239–240
Hindi, 36, 212
Hispanics:
  culture of, 20
  language differences and, 15, 16
historical linguistics, 31–35
  as diachronic, 35
hit, as junkie term, 85
Hitler, Adolf, 58–59, 193, 194–195, 198–199, 201
Hoffman, Abbie, 26
holism, 158
  in cultural anthropology, 109–112, 115, 116, 132, 137
  frames and, 132

Hopi Indians, language of, 63–64, 67, 69, 120
How to Do Things with Words (Austin), 150
Human Relations Area Files (HRAF), 78
humor, *Schmäh* and, 102–103, 104
Hymes, Dell, 150–154, 161

I

iconic signs, 41
identity:
    culture and, 25–26, 126
    difference with, 126–128
    national and state, 219–221
    see also social identity
immigrants:
    in Germany, 16–17
    as guest workers, 236–237
    kids of the sixties as, 247
    as metaphor, 243–247, 249–251
    sensibility of, 245, 249, 251
imperfect aspect, 64, 65
Independents Declared (Agar), 233
indexical signs, 41
India, 110
    eating style in, 125, 126
    kinship in, 52–53
    nation-state languaculture blend in, 218–219
Indian English, 219
Indo-European language, 33
Indonesian, numeral classifiers in, 56
instrumentalities, speech acts and, 152, 153
intention:
    lying and, 146–148, 175–176
    speech acts and, 159
International Encyclopedia of the Social Sciences, 109, 111–112, 132
interviews, 184–187
    Nagiller-Waldheim, 197–204
Introduction to Descriptive Linguistics (Gleason), 74
Israel, nation-state languaculture blend in, 218
issues, languaculture and, 195–196

J

Japanese languaculture, 252–254
jargon, 35

jazz, 178, 179, 236
Jews, 237
    Austrian, 58, 194
jokes, 115, 156, 237
    elephant, 116
    linguistics, 21, 31
    Schmäh and, 102, 103
Jones, Sir William, 31–33
Joyce, James, 39
junkies, 122
    languaculture of, 83–86, 89–91, 118, 120, 128–129

K

kaaka, 52–53
Kannada, 219
Karnataka, 218–219
Kay, Paul, 74–76, 146–148, 150, 159
key, speech acts and, 152, 153
kinship:
    deficit theory and, 51–53
    in South India, 52–53
Kluckhohn, Clyde, 116, 118, 120
Kroeber, Alfred, 116, 118, 119–120
Kureishi, Hanif, 225

L

labels:
    differences concealed by, 229
    language, 212–213
    national and state, 213–223, 228
    similarities concealed by, 229
Lakoff, Robin, 232
languaculture, 60, 122
    as constraint *vs.* resource, 235
    culture in, 96, 109, 128, 138, 211–212, 226
    differences within, 196–197, 204
    frames and, 132, 135–138, 225–226; *see also* frames
    issues and, 195–196
    of junkies, 82–85, 89–91, 118, 120, 128–129
    language labels and, 212–213
    langua in, 96, 144, 224, 226
    nations and, 213–215, 219–223
    one (LC,), 248–250
    rich points in, 100–107, 221–223, 231
    second language learning and, 247–249

as social fact, 209, 221, 229–232, 234
social identity and, 212, 223–232
social variations within, 223–226
states and, 215–223
two (LC₂), 248–251
Whorf and, 61–72
see also differences, languacultural; similarities, languacultural; speech acts
language:
chessboard compared with, 34, 42
dialects *vs.*, 31
labels for, 212–213
Malinowski's theory of, 92–93, 98–99
need for change in concept of, 27, 28
perception and, 70-71
perfect, 32
as social fact, 38–39
speech *vs.*, 37–38, 44, 216
as symbolic system, 34, 36, 38–44, 47
see also first language; second language; *specific languages*
Language (Bloomfield), 55–56
Language and Power (Lakoff), 232
language circle, 16, 20, 27, 29–49, 212–213
Boas and, 49, 59–60
Chomsky and, 151
Gumperz and, 225
language *vs.* speech and, 37–38, 44
Malinowski and, 94–96
Saussure and, 34–45, 47–48
situations and, 89
language differences:
importance of, 28–29
within languages, 13–15, 27, 28
as problem, 15
we, 56
worldview and, 64–67
see also differences, languacultural
language games, 149, 150
language instruction, limitations of, 15–16
Larson, Gary, 94
Latin, 32
Lebowitz, Fran, 184
Lenneberg, Eric, 69–70
Lewis, Oscar, 125
Lexington, Kentucky, heroin addicts in, 82–85

linguistic determination, 67, 72
linguistic relativity, 57–59
Sapir-Whorf hypothesis and, 68–72
linguistics:
Boas and, 54–57, 59–60
Chomsky's view of, 114
comparison in, 32, 33
context-of-situation, 93
descriptive, 35–37
descriptive-structural, 55–56
diachronic, 35
discourse analysis, 96
historical, 31–35
jokes and, 21, 31
Mead's view of, 55, 114
modern, founding of, 30–31, 34–44, 47–48
new, 114–115
prescriptive, 35–37, 42
semantics and, 56
synchronic, 35
lottery, 221
low density social identity, 233
lying:
of Americans, 146–148, 150, 159, 175–177
Coleman-Kay research on, 146–148, 150, 159
in Mexico, 154–160, 162
as speech act, 145–148, 150, 154–160, 162, 175–176

M

Malinowski, Bronislaw, 91–96, 101, 108, 115, 122, 151, 189
background of, 91–92
discourse and, 95–96, 140, 144
language theory of, 92–93, 98–99
Wittgenstein compared with, 149–150
Mandelbaum, David, 109–112, 115, 116, 120, 132, 137
Marie Antoinette, queen of France, 103
Maryland, University of, parking rules at, 152–154
masi, 52–53
Mead, Margaret, 54, 55, 114, 170, 179, 246–247
meaning:
culture and, 21, 23, 28
importance of, 16
languaculture and, 96

meaning (*continued*)
 situations and, 96
 study of, *see* semantics
men:
 conversational style of, 173–174
 problem solving of, 221
menus, ordering from, as Saussurian
  system, 45–46
metaphors:
 clay, 249–251
 frames as, 138–139
 immigrant, 245–247, 249–251
 money, 120–121
Mexico, 220
 banks in, 216–217
 business in, 124, 126–130, 142,
  156, 222
 conversation in, 142, 156, 157
 envidia in, 129
 family in, 159–160
 lying in, 154–160, 162
 negotiations in, 126–128
 paying restaurant checks in, 140–141
 slow pace in, 126–127, 128, 142
 U.S. free trade agreement with, 222
Mistake, Awareness, and Repair
  (MAR), 242–244, 246, 249
Moerman, Michael, 180–182, 185, 218
money metaphors, 120–121
moral relativity, 57–59
motobaap, 52–53
Mount Pleasant neighborhood, police-
  Hispanic conflict in, 15, 16
multiculturalism, 23, 26, 29
 culture and, 21
 global concern with, 27
Murdock, George Peter, 78
music:
 conversational, 185–187
 structure of, 178–179

N

Nagiller, Mr., Waldheim interviewed
  by, 197–204
nation, nationality:
 defined, 213
 languaculture and, 213–223, 229
National Indian Board on Alcohol and
  Drug Abuse, 167–168
nature, traditional peoples and, 80, 81
Nazism:
 in Austria, 58–59, 193–204
 in Germany, 206–207

negative concord, 37
negatives, double, 36–37
new ethnography, *see* cognitive
  anthropology
New Yorkers:
 conversational style of, 171–172,
  174
 Texan views of, 237
Nixon, Richard M., 188, 208
nonstandard dialects, 36, 37
norms, speech acts and, 152, 153
Nosbers, Peter, 102
nouns, animate *vs.* inanimate, 43
number-one types, 22–26, 76, 126,
  154, 215
 bad data and, 51–52
 conversation and, 143
 fears of, 163
 frames and, 162–163
 MAR and, 244
 negative side of culture and, 25–26
 speech acts and, 162–163, 167
 top-down mode and, 135
numeral classifiers, 56–57, 120

O

Oceanic Institute, 113
Ojibwa, *we* in, 56
onomatopoeia, 41
ostrich cartoon, 94

P

Paine, Tom, 29
paradigmatic relationship, 42–46, 129
 fashion and, 46
 menus and, 45
 scuba diving and, 44
 speech acts and, 152–154
parking tickets, speech acts and, 152–
  154
participant observation, 92–93, 106–
  107
participants, speech acts and, 152, 153
part-whole relationship, 85–86
pasar un buen momento, 156
patterns:
 culture and, 115, 118–120
 defined, 119
pauses:
 in conversation, 165–166
 in interviews, 184–187
Paz, Octavio, 220

Pelikan, Johanna, 198
perception:
 color, 70, 72, 74–76
 language and, 70–71
perfect aspect, 64, 65
Philosophical Investigations
 (Wittgenstein), 149
Piaget, Jean, 255–256
pivo, 40
poetry, in conversation, 185–187
postmodern life, problem of, 251
poverty, culture of, 124–125
Prague, linguistic meeting in, 226–227
prescriptive linguistics, 35–37, 42
problem solving:
 culture concept and, 124–125
 of men, 221
Profil, 194
pronouns:
 Du vs. *Sie,* 18–19, 20, 98, 99
 we, 56
punctuation marks, 184

R

racism, 126
radical Whorf, 67, 72, 76
Reagan, Ronald, 23
reality, language differences and, 64–
 67
red, perception of, 75
registers, social identity and, 223, 224
relationships:
 conversational style and, 141, 142,
 165
 servicing of, 141, 142
repair:
 in conversations, 199
 in MAR, 242, 243–244
restaurant menus, ordering from, as
 Saussurian system, 45–46
restaurants:
 frames and, 131–132, 136, 140
 paying the check in, 140–141
rich points, 256
 conversation as, 142–144
 culture and, 124, 128–130, 133,
 136, 137, 139
 issues as, 195–196
 in languaculture, 100–107, 221–223,
 231
 second language learning and, 248
 speech acts and, 148, 153–157, 161–
 162

Right Stuff, The (Wolfe), 161
Roberts, Jack, 70
robots, frames and, 130–132, 140
rock and roll, 178–179
room frame, 131, 132, 140
Rushdie, Salman, 245, 251

S

sailors, 28
 MAR and, 244, 246
Sanskrit, 32
Sapir, Edward, 62–63
Sapir-Whorf hypothesis, 63, 66–72, 99
 Brown-Lenneberg test of, 69–70
 linguistic relativity version of, 68–71
 radical, 67, 72, 76
Saussure, Ferdinand de, 31, 34–45,
 47–48, 71, 79, 223, 231
 Boas and, 54, 59
 descriptive linguistics and, 35–37
 on paradigmatic relationships, 42–43
 on sign, signifier, and signified, 39–
 40
 on social facts, 38–39, 211, 230
 on speech *vs.* language, 37–38, 44
 on syntagmatic relationship, 43
Saussurian systems, 39–47
 fashion as, 46
 language as, 34, 36, 39–44, 47
 ordering from menus and, 45–46
 scuba diving as, 44–45
Schmäh, 99–106, 120, 126, 140, 248
 coherence of differences and, 129
 cut-lows compared with, 103, 105
 as deception, 103–104
 humor and, 102–103, 104
Scollon, Ron, 164–168, 225
Scollon, Suzanne, 164–168, 225
scuba diving, 227
 as Saussurian system, 44–45
Searle, John, 150
second language, 28, 94
 Americans' problem with, 21–22
 culture and, 20
 grammar *vs.* communication, 15–17,
 27
 languaculture and, 247–249
 studying of, 15, 27
semantics:
 Bloomfield's view of, 56
 ethnographic, *see* cognitive
 anthropology
 Whorf's view of, 71

semiotics, 47–48
sensibility, immigrant, 245, 249, 251
sentences, 94–95, 96
Serbo-Croatian, 212
setting, speech acts and, 152, 153
Settle, Mary Lee, 257
sexism, 126
shirts, style differences of, 40
shoot, as junkie term, 85
Sie vs. *Du,* 18–19, 20, 98, 99
signifieds, 39–41, 44, 79
  cultural, 61–72
signifiers, 39–41, 44
  words as, 79
signs, 39–43, 47
  iconic, 41
  indexical, 41
  symbols, 41–42
similarities, languacultural, 73–88
  color spectrum and, 74–76
  concealment of, 229
  content and, 86
  heroin addicts and, 82–86
  number-one types and, 76
  taxonomy and, 82
situations, 89–107
  anecdotes and, 98
  context of, 93
  discourse and, 95–106
  junkie terms and, 83, 89–91, 120
  Malinowski and, 91–96, 98–99
  Schmäh and, 99–106
sixties, kids of, 247
Slovak, 257
social facts:
  coherence and, 205–207, 209
  languaculture as, 209, 221, 229–
    232, 234
  Saussure's idea of, 38–39, 211, 230
social identity, 162, 163, 212–241
  plus biography, 238–239, 240
  high vs. low density, 233
  across languacultures, 226–232
  national and state, 205, 213–223,
    231
  sociolinguistics and, 223–226
social lie, 145
Social Studies (Lebowitz), 184
social variation, 221, 223–226, 239–
  241
  dialects, 223, 224
  registers and, 223, 224
  sociolinguistics and, 223–226

society, Durkheim's view of, 38
Society for Applied Anthropology,
  246
sociolinguistics, 223–226
sociology, 234–235
  speech acts and, 168–174
South Asian British, 225
Soviet Union, former, 214
Spanish, 33, 36, 212, 242
  articles in, 43
  studying of, 15
speaking:
  as acronym, 152
  ethnography of, 150–154
speech, language *vs.,* 37–38, 44, 216
speech acts, 140–191
  content of, 163, 175–190
  discourse and, 144–145, 148, 150,
    157–158, 160
  frames and, 148, 150, 152–159,
    162–163, 166–170, 173, 189–190,
    204
  Hymes's view of, 150–154
  lying as, 145–148, 150, 154–160,
    162, 175–176
  sociology and, 168–174
  states and, 216
  structure of, 163, 166–178, 180–
    183, 190
  transcripts and, 184–190
  Wittgenstein and, 149–150
Speech Acts (Searle), 150
Spencer, Herbert, 50
Spivey, Bruce, 207–209
Sprachbund, 215–216
stage-process relationship, 85
standard, the, 35–36, 37
states:
  languaculture and, 213–223, 229
  nations *vs.,* 213–216
Stephens, Dick, 167
Steps to an Ecology of Mind (Bateson),
  113–114
stereotypes:
  about Americans, 21–23, 29, 141
  about Austrians, 141
  about Mexicans, 154
Stravinsky, Igor, 178
structure:
  musical, 178–179
  in speech acts, 163, 166–178, 180–
    183, 190
subject-verb agreement, 43

subjunctive/indicative switch, 200–202
Sweden, conversation in, 143
symbolic system:
    language as, 34, 36, 39–44, 47
    signs as, 41–42
synchronic linguistics, 35, 55
syntagmatic relationships, 43–46, 129
    fashion and, 46
    menus and, 45–46
    scuba diving and, 44–45

T

Tannen, Deborah, 171, 232
taxonomy, 79–84, 87
    junkie terms and, 83, 84
    SPEAKING compared with, 152,
        153
Texas, chicken fried steak in, 237
Thailand, conversation in, 180–182
tie, as junkie term, 83, 85
time, Hopi and, 63–64, 120
Tomlin, Lily, 257
top-down mode, frames and, 134,
    135
topics, of conversations, 165, 171,
    172–173, 179–180
traditional peoples:
    culture of, 121–123
    nature and, 80, 81
trains, in Yugoslavia, 217
transcripts, 184–190
    of Brooks's interview, 184–189
    Thai, 181–182, 187
    Waldheim, 194–206, 224
    Watergate and, 188
translation, 67, 68, 93, 253–254
Trobriand Islands, Malinowski's work
    in, 92–94
truckers, study of, 110, 118–119, 183–
    187, 233
truth, Mexican view of, 155–157,
    159
turn-taking, in conversations, 166,
    171, 172–173, 179–180
Twain, Mark, 16

U

United States:
    Mexico's free trade agreement with,
        222
    nation-state identity of, 214

Vietnam War and, 207, 208
    see also Americans
universals, 74
Urban Villagers, The (Gans), 122

V

Valentine, Betty Lou, 125
Valentine, Charles, 125
vehicles, taxonomies of, 79–80, 81
verbs:
    English, 63, 65, 97–98, 99
    Fillmore's view of, 84
    German, 16–17, 43
    Hopi, 63–64, 69
    perfect *vs.* imperfect aspect of, 64–
        65
    subject's agreement with, 43
    subjunctive/indicative switch and,
        200–202
Vienna, author as immigrant in, 245–
    246
Vienna, University of, Linguistics
    Institute of, 96–97, 100, 215
Vietnam War, 207, 208
vocabulary, 144
    English, 44
    situations and, 89

W

Waldheim, Kurt, 58, 194–206, 224
wari, era wari, warikni, warikngwe,
    64
Washington Post, The, 15
Watergate, 188
we, 56
Webster, Noah, 36
Whorf, Benjamin Lee, 61–72, 77–79,
    87, 101 108, 120, 122, 151, 189
    background of, 61–62
    Boas compared with, 65, 69, 71, 77
    cognitive anthropologists compared
        with, 81
    Malinowski compared with, 93, 94
    see also Sapir-Whorf hypothesis
Wittgenstein, Ludwig, 149–150
Wodak, Ruth, 19, 198
Wolfe, Tom, 161
women:
    conversational style of, 173–174
    culture of, 20
    language differences and, 14, 16

women (*continued*)
    paying restaurant checks and, 141
    problems and, 221
words, 79, 94–95, 96
    emphasized, 184–187
works, as junkie term, 83, 90
World English, 226
World War I, 214
World War II, 58, 192–194, 198–
    204

Y

You Just Don't Understand (Tannen),
    232
Yugoslavia, trains in, 217

Z

Zuni Indians, Brown-Lenneberg test
    and, 70

ABOUT THE AUTHOR

Michael Agar was born in 1945 and grew up in the Chicago and the San Francisco Bay area. Author of *The Professional Stranger*, *Speaking of Ethnography*, and *Independents Declared*, he has written, lectured, and run workshops on language and culture in several countries. He teaches in the Anthropology Department at the University of Maryland in College Park and consults with Ethknoworks in Takoma Park, Maryland.